W9-ACJ-187

WITHDRAWN

Communities of the Heart

Liverpool Science Fiction Texts and Studies

General Editor DAVID SEED

Series Advisers
I. F. Clarke, Edward James, Patrick Parrinder and Brian Stableford

Communities of the Heart

The Rhetoric of Myth
in the Fiction of
Ursula K. Le Guin

WARREN G. ROCHELLE

LIVERPOOL UNIVERSITY PRESS

First published 2001 by
LIVERPOOL UNIVERSITY PRESS
4 Cambridge Street
Liverpool
L69 7ZU

British Library Cataloguing-in-Publication Data
A British Library CIP record is available.

ISBN 0 85323 876 6 cased
ISBN 0 85323 886 3 paperback

Typeset in Meridien by
Koinonia, Bury, Lancashire
Printed and bound in the European Union by
Bell and Bain Ltd, Glasgow

Dedicated to: Hephzibah Roskelly, for her support, advice, encouragement, teaching, patience and friendship.

Love has a right to be spoken. And you have a right to know that somebody loves you. That somebody has loved you, could love you. We all need to know that. Maybe it's what we need most.
 Ursula K. Le Guin, 'Another Story' or 'A Fisherman of the Inland Sea'

Contents

Acknowledgements

I want to thank my UNC Greensboro dissertation committee for their support, advice, encouragement, teaching and patience: Hephzibah Roskelly, chair; Denise Baker, Fred Chappell, Elizabeth Chiseri-Strater and Kelley Griffith – especially Hepsie and Elizabeth for being my teachers, advisers, friends and colleagues, above and beyond the call of duty: *mil gracias*.

I also want to thank Carter Shelley, one of my very best friends, and the best study and reading partner anyone could ask for: a one-woman support team who is wise and kind and good; Jim Clark, a great boss, friend and neighbour, for his unfailing support and interest, a raconteur extraordinaire; Barry Rochelle, computer wizard, great friend, and brother, for laughing at me when I needed it, for helping me keep everything in perspective, and for making the original version of this book look the way the UNCG Graduate School wanted it to look, and for never doubting; Charles and Louise Rochelle, my parents, my older brother David, and my youngest, Greg: I couldn't have done it without your constant support; and Ellen McQueen and Michael Brown, my two oldest friends, for everything, and especially Michael, for the cover illustration that graces this book.

My thanks also to the PhD gang: Al, Anita, Anne, Bob, Carolyn, Cindy, Laurel, Marsha, Janet, Jennifer, Ted, Judy and Sean; my colleagues at Limestone College and Mary Washington College; and the editors at Liverpool University Press, in particular Robin Bloxsidge, Frances Hackeson and Carol Fellingham Webb.

Part of the section 'Language as Story' in Chapter One first appeared in a slightly different form in my essay 'Story, Plato, and Le Guin', in *Extrapolation*, Winter 1996. Some parts of Chapter Four first appeared in my essay 'Community Triumphant: American Romantic/Pragmatic Rhetoric in John Barnes's *Orbital Resonance*', in *Extrapolation*, Spring 1999.

Preface

We live in a society that believes itself to be rational – scientific and quantifiable. Yet, at the same time, we live in a culture that is saturated with the mythic. We speak of life as a journey; we are all heroes on our own quests. We seek the fantastic, the princess in the castle, the wizard peering into a crystal bowl. We tell fantastic stories of our technological age – of space ships, other worlds, aliens. And we tell the same stories – in myth, in fantasy, in science fiction. Or do we? Ursula K. Le Guin would answer yes and no. We do tell the same stories, to better and more fully understand what it means to be human, and yet we reinterpret, reimagine these stories, so that they reflect our contemporary world. It is this reimagining that is examined here and how this reimagining becomes rhetorical. Le Guin, through her revisioning and reshaping of myth in the stories she is telling, subverts myth – in particular the Myth of the Hero and the Quest, and the myth of utopia – as a way of making her argument for the importance of feminist and Native American solutions to our ways of making meaning.

Her rhetoric, when placed in historical and sociocultural context, becomes the rhetoric of Emerson, Thoreau, Peirce and Dewey: American romantic/pragmatic rhetoric – a rhetoric that argues for value to be given to the subjective, the personal and private, the small, and the feminine. The works of Le Guin examined are the *Earthsea* cycle, *The Dispossessed, The Left Hand of Darkness, Always Coming Home, Four Ways to Forgiveness, Another Story* or *A Fisherman of the Inland Sea*; two recent novellas, *Dragonfly* and *Old Music and the Slave Women*; and selected short stories. Among the theorists of language and culture and myth examined are Susanne Langer, Kenneth Burke, Lev Vygotsky, and Walter Fisher. In addition, Carl Jung's and Joseph's Campbell's definitions and functions of myth are also examined, as theirs are the closest to Le Guin's own definitions.

Through story, through myth, through science fiction and fantasy, Le Guin takes us into her communities of the heart, communities that are truly human.

Warren G. Rochelle
Fredericksburg, Virginia
October 2000

CHAPTER ONE

The Making and Remaking of Meaning: Language, Story and Myth

> I'll make my report as if I told a story, for I was taught as a child on my homeworld that Truth is a matter of the imagination. The soundest fact may fail or prevail in the style of its telling: like that singular organic jewel of our seas, which grows brighter as one woman wears it and, worn by another, dulls and goes to dust. Facts are no more solid, coherent, sound, and real than pearls are. But both are sensitive.[1]

Truth changes its shape and colour in the manner in which it is delivered, in the way it is presented, and by the form of its narrative. Truth ultimately becomes a question of language, an issue of story. The teller of the story, the speaker and his or her audience affect the truth of the story and how this truth is perceived and understood. As Ursula K. Le Guin recognizes, relating the truth is not a simple matter of the solidity or coherency of the facts that it comprises. The language used, the style of language, its form and the presentation all affect truth. The intent is also important – the why of the narrative: is this truth, this information, this story being related to inform the audience? Is it being told to allow the storyteller to meditate and reflect? Is the story being told to persuade, to advance an argument, either explicitly or implicitly? What difference does the subject of the story make to the speaker, to the audience? Or in other words, since I have just described the elements of the Aristotelian triad, in what ways is the story rhetorical?

Ursula K. Le Guin argues, and here she echoes Kenneth Burke, that 'all fiction has ethical, political, and social weight'. Fiction, or story, then, becomes argument, and thus is rhetorical. Rhetoric, to use Aristotle's definition, is the art of persuasion. More precisely, rhetoric is the 'instrumental use of language': it is language with intent, with purpose.[2] According to Kenneth Burke, this purpose is to form attitudes and influence action, and in his all-encompassing definition, literature is symbolic action, and a form of 'persuasive discourse'.[3] Telling a story thus becomes a rhetorical act. It is in story as rhetoric, in particular fiction – and in Le Guin's case, primarily science fiction and fantasy – that I am interested here. Specifically, I am interested in how myth, a particular 'charged' kind of story, serves as rhetoric when retold and reinterpreted in Le Guin's fiction. I contend that the essential truth of the core myth remains the same, even as the story is adapted by the author to a new audience in a new context. I will consider what happens to the implicit argument of the original myth as it is retold, how much the argument changes and adapts to its new audience, and what Le Guin does with the mythic truths – or, as she says, what these truths do to her stories.

That fiction can be read as argument is underscored by its use in teaching composition in the American classroom. This is, however, still a controversial practice. The amount of imaginative literature (short stories and poems) used in composition texts is greatly outweighed by the traditional essays and such literature is often relegated to the end of chapters, almost as an afterthought. Many composition teachers feel that it is non-fiction which provides students with the necessary models for the essays they are to write, and the use of fiction would require literary analysis, which is not in their purview. Literary analysis, so the argument goes, belongs in a literature, not a composition class. Literature and rhetoric, it would seem, are in opposition.

But to place these two in opposition in effect negates the idea that literature, like rhetoric, has a purpose, that it *is* language with intent. Le Guin would argue that literature and rhetoric are *connected*. According to Le Guin, 'the use of imaginative literature is to deepen your understanding of your world and your fellow men, and your own feelings, and your destiny'.[4] Imaginative literature becomes, then, a way to argue for this deepening of understanding of the world and other and self, and for what the reader and the author believe is true. Imaginative literature is thus rhetorical.

For Le Guin, science fiction becomes a particular way of making the connection between literature and rhetoric. The term itself literally makes the connection, as science and fiction are often thought to be at odds, the former rational, the latter irrational. Le Guin sees the mediation, science fiction, as a source of truth: 'One of the essential functions of science fiction, I think, is precisely this kind of question-asking: reversals of a habitual way of thinking, metaphors for which our language has no words for [*sic*] as yet, experiments in imagination.'[5] Science fiction becomes, for Le Guin, a tool, like any story, for human understanding:

> Science fiction, properly conceived, like all serious fiction, however funny, is a way of trying to describe what in fact is going on, what people actually do and feel, how people relate to everything else in this vast sack, this belly of the universe, this womb of things to be and tomb of things that were, this unending story.[6]

Le Guin uses these metaphorical tools, these connections in the 'belly of the universe', both the new and the old found in myth and archetype, as a part of her fiction, and thus a part of how she is using imaginative literature rhetorically. It is this rhetorical use of myth in Le Guin's science fiction and fantasy that I am going to examine.

But before considering the rhetoric of myth in Le Guin's fiction, and the argument she is making, some ground work is necessary to establish how myth and story function as rhetoric, ways of interpreting and making meaning out of the human experience. As myth and story are acts of language, the foundation must be in language itself, as language is, according to Edward Sapir, a 'heuristic ... in that its forms predetermine for us certain modes of observation and interpretation'.[7]

Sign

What is language that makes it a heuristic and how can it be defined? The dictionary definition of language begins with the words themselves, and the sounds articulated by the vocal cords, and from there moves to a 'systematic means of communicating ideas or feelings by the use of conventionalized signs, sounds, gestures, or marks having understood meanings', and ends with 'a form or manner of verbal expression ... profanity ... the study of language ...'.[8] What all of these definitions have in common is that in some shape or form or fashion, language is *symbolic of meaning*. Using Howard Gardner's definition of symbol as 'any entity (material or abstract) that can denote or refer to any other entity',[9] even a sound or gesture[10] is symbolic: it represents meaning. The sound or the hand movement, as in sign language, is not the idea or thought itself. The word 'language' as I write here, and the sound I make when I say 'language' out loud, the gesture I would make if I knew sign language, is not language – rather they are signs that symbolize a whole host of ideas and concepts. That I can also say 'lengua' or 'langue' and mean almost the same thing underscores this – the idea remains, even though I have changed the symbol. Plato speaks of this idea about language in the Myth of the Cave in The *Republic,* in which the only true reality is the Forms, the things themselves, the Good, Truth, Beauty. Everything that the men in the cave perceive is but a representation or symbol of the Forms: the warmth of the fire, the shadows on the wall and the artefacts carried by the people on the wall. Plato is speaking of the search for Truth here and not language, but he uses story, a product of language, to represent this search. Language is employed, as Socrates says in the *Phaedrus,* as a tool for understanding, a tool used to describe and make meaning of the world.[11] Language is, as Ernst Cassirer says in his essay 'Art', a process by which 'we ascertain and determine the concepts of the world'.[12]

Theorists from psychology, philosophy and linguistics echo the same perceptions of language as sign. James Britton amplifies this idea in *Language and Learning,* where he defines language as 'a means of organizing a representation of the world ... [and] the representation so created constitutes the world we operate in, the basis of all predictions by which we set the course of our lives'.[13] Susanne Langer, in *Philosophy in a New Key,* emphasizes the representational or symbolic aspects of language when she defines it as 'essentially an organic, functioning system of which the primary elements as well as the constructed products are symbols'.[14] Language is, she adds, 'a highly organized, systematic means of representing experience, and as such, it assists us to organize all other ways of representing'.[15] Representing and interpreting experience, is, according to Edward Sapir, the 'essence of language ... the assigning of conventional, voluntarily articulated sounds, or their equivalents, to the diverse elements of experience'.[16]

To use language to interpret experience symbolically is, according to Britton, what makes us human: 'we are symbol-makers' – or as Ernst Cassirer says, 'animal symbolicum'.[17] As symbol-makers, we use language to 'symbolize what is in the universe'.[18] Kenneth Burke expands this definition when he says that to be human is be a 'symbol-using, symbol-making, and symbol-misusing animal' for whom an 'overwhelming' amount of 'what we mean by reality has been built up for us through nothing but our symbol systems'.[19] Gardner says symbol use is inherently human, and 'participation in the symbolic process is part of the human condition. Humans are as prepared to engage in symbolic processes (from language to dreams) as squirrels are prepared to bury nuts.'[20] Symbol-making, then, through language, is a quintessential human activity – one in which we engage from the very beginning of our attempts to communicate. The baby's cry for food is not hunger itself. The baby's cry is a sign of what the infant needs and wants; it is hunger expressed in symbolic form.

These symbols used, made and misused by humans – or rather a 'stream of [such] symbols,' according to Susanne Langer – 'constitute the human mind'.[21] Using these symbols to create reality is the 'primary task of speech'.[22] The question arises about the connection between language and thought. Ferdinand de Saussure argues that, without language to shape it and give it form, thought is 'a shapeless and indistinct mass'. Without language, thought is 'a vague, uncharted nebula' and contains no 'pre-existing ideas'. Until language appears, nothing is distinct. Language becomes the link between thought and sound (or gesture).[23]

Once language acquisition begins in infancy, the connection between thought and language begins. According to Lev Vygotsky, a Russian psychologist and language theorist, 'thought and speech have different genetic roots', and initially 'develop along different lines and independently of each other'.[24] He notes that 'in the speech development of the child we can with certainty establish a preintellectual phase, and in his thought development, a pre-linguistic stage'.[25] Vygotsky cites William Stern who says that at around two the child 'makes the greatest discovery of his life ... that each thing has its name'.[26] 'Thought becomes verbal and speech becomes rational.'[27]

When the child discovers that everything has a name, his or her world expands and multiplies. Where there was only barking and a big moving shape, there is now a dog. As Howard Rheingold notes in *They Have a Word for It*, there are now dimensions to the child's environment that before he or she couldn't see: 'Finding a name for something is a way of conjuring its existence, of making it possible for people to see a pattern where they didn't see anything before.'[28] This is the mystery of language that is crucial to human development: 'everything has a name and each name gives birth to a new thought'.[29] Language becomes, for adults, as Britton says, what we 'use to represent and communicate any and almost all aspects of experience'.[30] For everything, there is a word, a symbol, a meaning, and 'symbol and meaning make man's world'.[31] This is how we think: 'with symbols – not about them'.[32]

The world is no longer chaos; it has order that humans can understand, an order that humans make by naming. The first task of Adam in the biblical story was to name the animals in the Garden of Eden. Alfred and Theodora Kroeber, Ursula Le Guin's parents, studied this use of naming to order reality in the Yurok and other California Indians. For these Native Americans, to know the name of someone was to have power over them. Each individual had a use-name and a private, true name, revealed, if at all, only to a trusted few. Le Guin echoes this idea of the importance of naming and language in her *Earthsea* cycle where knowing the name of everything in True Speech is the art-magic of the wizards.

In *The Making of Meaning*, Ann Berthoff speaks of this use of language as making meaning out of a chaos of 'images, half-truths, remembrances, syntactic fragments, from the mysterious and the unformed' – the world without language to name it, to 'generate sources of meaning'.[33] Reality now has a form, a shape, a name. As Britton says, we can use language to represent experience. Language allows us to name, to categorize, to classify and to organize our world.[34] We talk to each other, construct our experiences in verbal symbols through language, name our world, and thus make meaning from the human experience. Vygotsky argues that 'word meaning' is 'an elementary cell that cannot be further analyzed' – a word without a thought is 'empty sound', a thought without a word is inexpressible[35] – indeed, it lacks reality. Thought 'does not merely find expression in speech; it finds its reality and form'.[36] He sets this up as a series of connections: 'from the motive that engenders a thought to the shaping of the thought, first in inner speech, then in meanings of words, and finally in words'.[37] The word, language, crowns the deed, creation, an action engendered by thought. Humans as conscious animals, aware of themselves, are thinking, language-using animals. Vygotsky argues that the nature of language and human consciousness is such that:

> The word is a direct expression of the historical nature of human consciousness ... Consciousness is reflected in a word as the sun in a drop of water. A word relates to consciousness as a living cell relates to a whole organism, as

an atom relates to the universe. A word is a microcosm of human consciousness.[38]

Language, then, is a product of human consciousness and – according to Vygotsky – engenders human consciousness or rational, self-aware thought. With consciousness there is an active, thinking mind, and there is learning, from action, from experience. Language allows the individual man or woman to represent experience to him- or herself, and to others. Sound or gesture acquires meaning, as it becomes associated with a thing. In this way the world can be named. That a sound or gesture is used in place of the actual thing makes language inherently symbolic, and a product of the human mind, as well as shaper of the mind.

One aspect of language as symbol is its use in classification. Ernst Cassirer emphasizes that 'classification is one of the most fundamental features of human speech ... To give a name to an object or an action is to subsume [it] under a certain class [or] concept.'[39] To name a thing as flower and then to name flowers as roses or petunias or marigolds is to further use language as a heuristic: to go from a general to a particular concept (key, Vygotsky says, to the development and growth of the human mind).[40] To name one flower rose and another petunia is also to establish a symbolic system, a method of categorizing and organizing what is known. In addition to identity, Cassirer notes that the function of a name is 'to emphasize a particular aspect of a thing', which can restrict or limit a name as, at the same time, it allows for connections to be made. All things with a particular aspect can be grouped together and assumptions, hypotheses and ideas about the group can be explored.

In addition to its naming function, language also functions to connect thoughts and give them meaning in context. As Vygotsky says, a word without a thought is empty: it can't stand alone as sound. The word has to have meaning, association, resonance. Saussure argues that without a system to make connections, there is no meaning.[41] This is similar to I. A. Richards' idea of 'inter-animation' – that a word also acquires meaning in context, in its immediate verbal environment. There is a 'mutual dependence of words', Richards says in *The Philosophy of Rhetoric,* and their meanings depend 'upon the other word before and after them in the sentence' and their meanings depend upon 'words which are not actually uttered and are only in the background'.[42] Words bring to their immediate sentence a context of associations that cling to a word 'through experience'.

That words can have different connotations in different contexts and thus have different symbolic value suggests the powerful role of the language-user. A speaker or writer can use a word one way in one context and differently in another. Different intentions of the speakers and their different audiences suggest the rhetorical nature of language. As humans, we use language to name the world, to relate and interpret our experiences, to make our reality; we are also using it to persuade and to suggest that our perceptions are true. Britton thinks this language function grows from what he calls the expressive use of language, which he defines as 'language close to the self, language that is not called upon to go very far away from the speaker'.[43] Expressive language is the language in which 'most of the important things that there are in the world were probably first discussed'.[44] Expressive language then is the language we use to name, to create identity. As language-use develops, it becomes more specific. According to Britton, there are two basic aims: transactional and poetic. Transactional language is that which is used when the speaker becomes a participant: he or she is trying to get 'something done in the world', and is using language to 'interact with the world and things and make the world go round'. The poetic function of language comes into play when the speaker becomes a spectator, and language is used to 'contemplate what has happened to us, or what might happen'. This is language for the sake of using language, language for play.

Both kinds of language are used, Britton says, to 'construct a representation of the world as we experience it'.[45] Language lets us order these experiences and connect them through cause-and-effect, through which came first and which came last. The succession of experience, as it is related and interpreted and explained, becomes then a narrative or story: *first this happened, because … then this, because … and the result was …* Story, the organizing of experience into narrative, becomes a particular use of language to make meaning.

Language as Story

Story or narrative is the orderly arrangement of experience in an attempt to make meaning out of the experience. I define story in three different ways, depending on the context in which the story is told. Story 1, or logos, is probably the simplest: the true account of a sequence of events. We tell Story 1 stories every day of our lives: *This weekend I went to Chapel Hill ... I stayed home and worked all weekend on my dissertation ... I saw a film ... I cut the grass ...* Story 1 is reporting just what happened; you are telling the truth to an audience – even if the audience is yourself. Joe Friday's laconic introduction to 'Dragnet' is Story 1 at its best. (Joe Friday, the main character in this detective programme, was noted for always asking for 'Just the facts, ma'am'. He was a man of few words.) Another example of Story 1, less mundane than the narrative of last weekend and with more colour than Joe Friday, would be: *the king died, and then the queen died.* Newspapers and the television news are both, ideally, filled with one Story 1 after another.[46]

Story 2 begins with Story 1, but it is no longer a strict factual account. An actual event may be the subject of Story 2, but the reporting includes more than 'just the facts'. The storyteller is evaluating the experience and reinterpreting and elaborating it for his or her audience. The teller is trying to create an impression for the audience or is expressing an opinion about the event: *You will not believe just how bad my weekend was ... That was the worst film I have ever seen, don't waste your money ...* and so on. Another example would be: *the king died, and then the queen died of grief.* Story 2 makes storytelling a triadic relationship: the experience of the event or the action, the storyteller's memory of the experience, and the storyteller's interpretation of the experience through the retelling to the listener. That there is a retelling and an interpretation, an attempt to make meaning, suggests that the truth is no longer a verbatim mirror of reality. The translation of the experience through memory by language adds a fictional element. Autobiography is a particularly good example of this. The retelling of an experience as it is remembered is an interpretation of the experience – not an actual account of what happened years ago.

Story 3 is probably the idea of story which most people would think of first: story as a narrative fiction of certain imagined events, told in a certain order for a certain effect. This is an essentially Aristotelian definition of story or mythos as plot, 'which has beginning, middle, and end', which combine together to make a whole, a unity. 'The story, an imitation of action, must represent one action, a complete whole, with its several incidents so closely connected that the transposing or withdrawal of any one of them would disjoin and dislocate the whole.'[47]

Aristotle is not after verbatim truth either. As he sees it, the poet's or storyteller's job, even though he or she may be using a 'subject from actual history', is to describe 'a kind of thing that might happen, i.e., what is possible as being probable or necessary'. This, for Aristotle, makes poetry (story) 'more philosophic and of graver import than history, since its statements are of the nature rather of universals'.[48] Tim O'Brien, a modern author who uses his Vietnam experiences to make fiction, seems to be echoing Aristotle when he defines story as an objectification of experience, or a way to separate experience from yourself and find its truth. 'You pin down certain truths,' he says. 'You make up others. You start sometimes with an incident that truly happened … and you carry it forward by inventing incidents that did not in fact occur that nonetheless help to clarify and explain.'[49]

As in Stories 1 and 2, and explicit in Aristotle and implicit in O'Brien, Story 3 is being told to an audience. The story is intended to have some effect on the audience – for Aristotle, either pity or fear; for the modern storyteller, a clarifying insight, a sudden understanding, an illumination. Storytelling becomes a way to identify problems and solve them. Storytelling also becomes a way to teach a moral or a lesson or how things are done, as it is instructional, as it helps us, according to Michael Curtis, senior editor of *The Atlantic Monthly*, to 'distinguish the real from the fraudulent' and make 'bearable the otherwise dismaying range of our disappointments and frustrations'.[50]

These ideas from O'Brien or Curtis are not new. Sir Philip Sidney is only one example of the longevity of the notion that fiction or story can instruct and teach and reveal truth. In 'An Apology for Poetry', first published in 1595, Sidney argues that poetry is the 'first light-giver to ignorance, and first nurse, whose milk by little and little enabled them to feed afterwards of tougher knowledge'.[51] Sidney further contends, according to Kaplan and Anderson, that 'neither philosophy nor history can do what poetry does, since poetry combines the precepts of one with the examples of the other, and in addition uses all the pleasurable devices of art to make instruction palatable'.[52]

Seeing story as instructional, and particularly as revealing truth through fiction, is what Robert Coles is speaking of in *The Call of Stories: Teaching and the Moral Imagination*. As a psychiatrist, he tells of people bringing him stories, bringing him *their* stories: 'They hope they tell them well enough so that we understand the truth of their lives.'[53] He is speaking of Story 2 – the use of Story 1 to make meaning, as a matter of identity: 'Few would deny that we all have stories in us which are a compelling part of our psychological and ideological make-up.'[54] We tell stories, in other words, to make sense of ourselves to ourselves – and we all do this, Coles insists, because narrative is a 'universal gift'.[55]

This 'universal gift', Coles says, is not just of use in mental health. He sees it as being very powerful in the classroom. Books and stories – Story 3 – again become tools of understanding: 'Novels lend themselves to such purposes; their plots offer a psychological or moral journey with impasses and breakthroughs, with decisions made and destinations achieved.'[56] It is not enough to tell stories ourselves; our role as listener or reader, our role as audience, is also part of the making of meaning with narrative. Reading the stories of other people, if the connection can be made, allows the novel's story to become the reader's story. The writer Flannery O'Connor's purpose, according to Coles, was 'to tell a good story in a persuasive manner, but also to reach some moral and spiritual side of the reader'.[57] Stories allow us vicarious experiences and they validate our experiences: if this happened, if he or she felt this way when it did, then what I feel now is true.

Storytelling, then, is a vital tool for human understanding and communication. Story 1 permits the speaker to inform his or her audience: *the king died.* Story 2 calls for more interpretation, more opinion: how do we know the queen died of grief? Why was that the worst film you have ever seen? Story 2 allows for the imagination to become active in the story and 'The soundest fact may fail or prevail in the style of its telling.'[58] Story 2 is the making of meaning. With Story 3, narrative fiction, we not only learn that the queen died of grief, but discover the depth of her grief, the abyss left in her heart by the death of the king. Human experience becomes instructive: see, this is grief, this is death – and you may be there now or have been or might be. As Augusta Baker and Ellin Greene say in *Storytelling: Art and Technique,* storytelling is a 'shared experience … a common experience'.[59] And again meaning is made. With the use of metaphor, Story 3 acquires layers of cumulative meaning. As Langer says, certain symbols and metaphors are charged with meaning. Her example is the cross: intersection, turning point, choosing the direction of one's life, x marks the spot, treasure, martyrdom, sacrifice. Metaphor does not preclude truth by any means; rather it shapes it and allows for the speaker and the reader/listener to go beyond the 'truth of fact' to the more general common truths we all share by being human.[60]

The audience becomes as important a part of the story as the storyteller. As Diane Wolkstein says in 'Twenty-five Years of Story-Telling: The Spirit of the Art', the audience's reaction can, in effect, create a new story: 'But once the story begins, and I am standing before the audience, I let the ingredients do their own mixing so I can participate in the alchemical heat which flows back and forth from teller to listener, creating the spirit of a new story.'[61] The story is created not just by the teller; rather it is 'mutual creation'.[62] As Wolfgang Iser says in *The Act of Reading: A Theory of Aesthetic Response*, the reading process (and, I would argue, also the listening process) creates a dynamic, an interaction between the text and the reader, so that the author and the reader share a 'game of imagination'.[63] What Iser calls the reader's 'unfolding multiplicity of perspective' creates a 'network of personal connections', unique to a particular reader.[64] This becomes a reinterpretation of the story or, in other words, the reader is making meaning from the story, by connecting the story to his or her own experiences and the particular metaphors of these experiences. The story of Little Red Riding Hood will have a different meaning, depending on whether the reader is a woodcutter or an animal rights activist or a grandmother. The essential meaning remains, although now it is overlaid with other meaning. This essential meaning cannot be ignored because it is virtual, almost emerging in interaction. As Louise Rosenblatt says in *The Reader, the Text, the Poem: The Transactional Theory of the Literary Work*, 'meaning will emerge from a network of relationships' – the reader's, the text's and the storyteller's.[65] If one uses the charged symbol of the cross, neither the reader nor the writer can ignore the multiple meanings associated with it – not if the story is to make sense. Meaning does not exist in a vacuum. But even so, the reader may think: crucifix, redemption, sacrifice, while the writer may have meant crossroads or turning point: 'What a poem [or story] means is as much what it means to others as what it means to the author.'[66]

Audience means more than an assembly of listeners: it is also the mental image the storyteller has of whom he or she is writing for, or telling the story to. Rosenblatt argues that 'the author must, more or less, consciously create the image of the reader he is addressing'.[67] As Fr Walter Ong points out in 'The Writer's Audience is Always a Fiction', the person to whom 'the writer addresses himself normally is not present at all'.[68] The audience becomes, in effect, another work of fiction in the author's imagination – an audience of 'entertainment seekers, reflective sharers of experience' and so forth.[69] Ong uses as an example Hemingway's *A Farewell to Arms*, where the reader is 'cast as close companion to the writer', and where there is no need for extraneous details: 'description as such would bore a boon companion'.[70] The audience, then, becomes part of the story as they make meaning from the story.

Story has such a powerful effect through its potent symbolic and metaphoric language because it is a part of how we make sense of our world. It is no wonder, then, with this much power in the communicative potential of the story, that story is also said to be the 'basic mode of representing human experience'. According to Walter Fisher in *Human Communication as Narration: Toward a Philosophy of Reason, Value, and Action* this makes humankind *Homo narrans*. Fisher defines *Homo narrans* as a master metaphor, like *Homo faber* or *Homo economicus*, to 'represent the essential nature of human beings'. This metaphor, Fisher argues, 'subsumes' the others, which become 'conceptions that inform various ways of recounting and accounting for human choice and action'. Whether in history, biography, argument, poetry or fiction, 'recounting and accounting for constitute stories we tell ourselves and each other to establish a meaningful life-world'. *Homo narrans* is an 'incorporation and extension of Burke's definition of "man" as the symbol-using animal'.[71] Telling stories is thus how we communicate and make sense of life. Telling stories is what makes us human.

Fisher argues for what he calls the narrative paradigm, which begins with the following assumption: 'all forms of human communication can be seen fundamentally as stories, as interpretations of aspects of the world in time and shaped by history, culture, and character'. Discourse and narrative, Fisher argues, should be considered as 'good reasons', or what he calls 'value-laden warrants for believing or acting in certain ways'.[72] These 'good reasons' – how they are determined and practised – are 'ruled by matters of history, biography, culture, character'. People have an 'inherent awareness' of 'narrative probability: what constitutes a coherent story'. Coupled with this awareness is the 'constant habit of testing' stories with a sense of 'narrative fidelity: whether or not the stories they experience ring true with the stories they know to be true in their lives'.[73] Mary Lee Coe echoes Fisher in her essay 'The Irresistible Loop of Story', when she argues that story-making is 'an urge so basic that it seems to function on a preconscious level before we are even aware we're doing it'. Stories become the way humans explain reality to themselves: 'the more and better our stories ... the better our intelligence'.[74]

Given all this, Fisher sees the world as a 'set of stories which must be chosen among for us to live life in a process of continual re-creation'.[75] In Fisher's narrative paradigm, people are 'story-tellers, authors and co-authors' who 'creatively read and evaluate the texts of life and literature'.[76] According to Fisher, *Homo narrans* combines logos with mythos, logic and rationality with story, to discover and validate 'truth, knowledge, and reality'.[77] The stories told and heard inform each other and accumulate to create the world, much as Britton says language in its different modes, expressive, trans-actional and poetic, represents and interprets experience.

To understand story as Britton and Fisher do is to understand story as rhetorical: it is language with intent, with purpose. Telling a story – interpreting and recounting human experience in an effort to make meaning out of it – becomes a way to persuade the audience of a particular truth. As Coles says, the story also teaches the audience that 'a storyteller's moral imagination, vigorously at work, can enable any of us to learn by example, to take to heart what is, really a gift of grace'.[78] The story, in effect, becomes a symbol for the truth, for the entire experience which is being recounted. That this truth changes and becomes local, as the story is told and retold, as the audience changes, makes it no less true and no less important.

Story, it seems, thus becomes a way of expressing truth which can be expressed in no other way. A prime example of this use of story to express the inexpressible can be found in the Platonic dialogues. I want here to glance briefly at Plato's use of myth[79] before taking a somewhat deeper look at myth in the next section of this chapter.

Plato uses myth or story to express a truth which can be expressed only through the symbolic and metaphoric power of language. Robert Scott Stewart, in his article 'The Epistemological Function of Platonic Myth', takes this a step further, arguing that 'myth is allowed to speak of those things which cannot be dealt with directly ... it is through myth alone that Plato is able to write about that which he is the most serious' – in this case, the Form of the Good and the Beautiful, the first principles of Platonic philosophy. Plato, according to Stewart, *only* discusses the good in symbolic language: using analogy, with the Sun as the Good; through the image of the Line; in the allegorical Myth of the Cave, a story.[80] As Stewart points out, all these allegorical stories come at crucial moments in the dialogue, when Socrates is trying to impress upon his companions an ultimate truth. Straight conversation, or Stories 1 and 2, will not do it, but allegorical story will.

While examples of this allegorical use of story can be found throughout the dialogues, one in particular, the Myth of the Charioteer in the *Phaedrus*, demonstrates how Plato uses symbol and metaphor in story to explicate his philosophy. Plato uses Stories 1, 2 and 3 throughout the dialogues (which are, after all, fiction) in what I argue is a progression, as he moves from logos to Story 3 and beyond, because it is only in the symbolic and metaphoric language of story that Plato can find what he needs to explicate his philosophy. And while he never quite uses myth in any religious sense, he does use it as a way to express in language the inexpressible. Truths, such as the nature of the soul, Plato admits implicitly in the *Phaedrus*, can only be expressed in story. As Walter Hamilton explains in his introduction to the *Phaedrus*, citing Hackforth's earlier commentary: 'what soul is like, however, and the nature of its existence can be described only in symbols or what Plato terms myth'.[81] The power of story is used to transcend plot and express philosophic truth.

The Myth of the Charioteer in the *Phaedrus* is an apt expression of this power. Fiction, in form and content, is used overtly and deliberately here, as Socrates melds 'argument with poetry' and his 'deepest philosophic insights' are portrayed in poetic language and imagery.[82] In this myth, the charioteer, the black horse and the white horse are allegories for the tripartite Platonic soul. Just prior to this allegorical story, Socrates has explained the soul's immortality to Phaedrus, in straight exposition. But to describe the soul's nature that way, Socrates says, 'would require a long exposition of which only a god is capable'. It is better to 'compare the soul to a winged charioteer and his horses acting together'.[83] The good, well-behaved white horse is the rational, and the 'crooked, lumbering, ill-made, stiff-necked, short-throated snub-nosed'[84] black horse is the emotional, the irrational. The charioteer, the Soul, must have both to reach the beloved, the object of desire, or the truth.

Story, myth, can be a way to a philosophic truth. The Myth of the Charioteer, a Platonic story, is a way to the truth of the human psyche as being rational and irrational. Story is a way to find knowledge through the imagination, through symbol and metaphor. Imagination is a way to truth, through the medium of language, in story. That Plato uses myth and allegory – the black horse as the irrational, the imaginative – suggests that story is necessary to reach the truth. Myth, a particular kind of story, opens the way to express what can only be expressed in metaphor and symbol.

Language as Myth

The word 'myth' comes from the Greek *mythos* which means 'story'. Like most stories, myths are an attempt to make meaning out of human experience. According to John Bierhorst in *The Mythology of North America,* true myths owe their existence to storytelling.[85] As David Leeming says in *The World of Myth,* 'human beings have traditionally used stories to describe or explain things they could not otherwise'.[86] To look at myth this way makes myth more than just a story of what happened, or a story told to amuse or to entertain. Leeming goes on to say that 'ancient myths were stories by means of which our forebears were able to assimilate the mysteries that occurred around them'.[87] As such, mythic stories were treated with respect: the children of the Tlingit, a Native American people of the Pacific Northwest, tied the feet of fidgeting children together so as not to disturb the storyteller.[88] Such respect is deserved, as myths are seen as 'narrative patterns that give significance to our existence'.[89] These patterns are very old, and 'are woven into the terrain over the course of thousands of years'. Such mythological patterns offer cohesive patterns of meaning to a people, enough cohesion to hold them together and make them a people.[90]

If a story can hold a people together, give them a cultural identity – and become an 'eternal mirror in which [they] see themselves' – then the story must be more than the ordinary. These extraordinary stories are described again and again as making available in words the inexpressible. J. F. Bierlein in *Parallel Myths* argues that no 'single definition is adequate'. He describes myth in four ways: (1) as the 'first fumbling attempts to explore how things happen' – the beginnings of science; (2) as attempts to explain why things happen – religion and philosophy; (3) as history – the history of prehistory; and (4) as literature, as imaginary stories.[91] It is Bierlein's second and fourth ways, the religious/philosophical and the fictional, that are most commonly associated with explanations of myth.

The religious definitions are perhaps the most basic. Myths are stories of the gods, tales of the divine, that are communications of the sacred: the numinous made visible. Thus myth instructs and guides, and provides models for human society, offering wisdom and knowledge about why things are as they are.[92] Myth thus becomes a 'unique use of language that describes the realities beyond our five senses ... Myth uses objective words depicting concrete things to describe concepts that transcend [these senses], things beyond our comprehension.'[93] No amount of science, for example, has yet been able to fully explain such mysteries as death or the soul's reality.

To define myth as language that takes us beyond what our senses tell us of the world is to do more than define myth in religious terms. It is also a psychological definition – as Bierlein adds that myth 'fills the gap between the images of the unconscious and the language of conscious logic'.[94] It is in the interplay between the two that I think we can find Jung's understanding of myth and Campbell's, which grows out of the Jungian. I want to give attention to these two perspectives over such others as the anthropological, the linguistic and the sociological, because it is the Jungian, primarily, to which Le Guin can be compared. I include Campbell because, even though Le Guin does not mention him in her essays on myth and language, I find her using such key ideas of Campbell's as the monomyth of the Hero and the Quest.

Carl Jung describes the 'human personality as consisting of two things: first of consciousness and whatever this covers, and second, of an indefinitely large hinterland of unconscious psyche'.[95] Each human has a personal unconscious and by the commonality of human experience – birth, sex, death, loss, hunger and so forth – is connected to the universal collective unconscious, the Jungian 'repository of man's experience'. June Singer, in *Boundaries of the Soul: The Practice of Jung's Psychology*, offers what I consider to be a fairly clear definition:

> The collective unconscious is better conceived as an exten-
> sion of the personal unconscious to its wider and broader
> base, encompassing contents which are held in common by

the family, by the social group, by tribe and nation, by race and eventually by all of humanity. Each succeeding level of the unconscious may be thought of as going deeper and becoming more collective in its nature. The wonder of the collective unconscious is that it is all there, all the legend and history of the human race, with its unexorcised demons and its gentle saints, its mysteries and its wisdom, all within each one of us – a microcosm within the microcosm.[96]

This collective unconscious, Jung contends, is an image of the world, 'which has taken aeons to form'.[97] The collective unconscious is, in Le Guin's words, 'a vast common ground on which we can meet, not only rationally, but aesthetically, intuitively, emotionally'.[98]

Within this common ground, 'this common darkness' – what Singer says is 'all there' – are what Jung calls motives and symbols of universal human history and experience, or archetypes. These 'archaic remnants' of 'primordial images' are an 'unrepresentable element of the instinctual structure of the human psyche'.[99] Or as Jung explains in *Memories, Dreams, Reflections:*

> The archetypes, which are pre-existent to consciousness ... appear in the part they actually play in reality: as a priori structural forms of the stuff of consciousness. They do not in any sense represent things as they are in themselves, but rather the forms in which things can be perceived and conceived. Naturally, it is not merely the archetypes that govern the particular nature of perceptions. They account only for the collective components of a perception. As an attribute of instinct they partake of its dynamic nature, and consequently possess a specific energy which causes or compels definite modes of behavior or impulses; that is, they may under certain circumstances have a possessive or obsessive force (numinosity!).[100]

There is a single archetype for each human situation: the child, the mother and the father, the hero, the trickster, the self, the helpful divine being:[101]

> [They are] repeated in all mythologies, fairy tales, religions, traditions, and mysteries. What else is the myth of the night sea voyage, of the wandering hero, or of the sea monster than our timeless knowledge transformed into a picture of the sun's setting and rebirth ... Prometheus, the stealing of

fire, Hercules, the slayer of dragons, the numerous myths of creation ... and many other myths and tales portray psychic processes in symbolic imaginary form.[102]

Myths are, by Jung's definition, the 'narrative elaboration of archetypal images'. The mind becomes aware of the archetypal image and becomes engaged in mythmaking[103] – myth, being, 'the natural and indispensable intermediate stage between unconscious and conscious cognition'. Every myth then has the 'potential for revealing indirectly some unforeseen or neglected aspects of the human psyche,' and a mythology becomes a 'mirror of the collective unconscious'.[104] The need for myths, according to Jung, 'is satisfied when we frame a view of the world which adequately explains the meaning of human existence in the cosmos, a view which springs from our graphic psychic wholeness, from the co-operation between conscious and unconscious'.[105]

To summarize, according to Jung, myths are our expressions of the archetypes inherent in all of us, as our heritage and part in the collective unconscious, that common realm of darkness where the numinous is made visible. Indeed, in the Jungian sense, that is the primary function of myth: to reveal the existence of the unconscious, to provide guidance in dealing with the unconscious, and to open the individual up to the unconscious and its wisdom.[106] Myth thus expresses truths of the human condition in metaphoric and symbolic language, and it is only in this language, in the narrative of the myth, that these truths can be understood. They open the door through story, through language, to the 'latent potentialities of the human psyche – an enormous, inexhaustible store of ancient knowledge concerning the profound relations between God, man, and the cosmos'.[107] Myths are both personal and universal: they must speak to the individual and to the people. 'These symbols from the unconscious, whether they make their appearance in dreams, visions, or fantasies, represent a kind of individual mythology that has its closest analogies in the typical figures of mythology, sagas, and fairy tales.'[108] Universal knowledge must become local knowledge and, for Jung, this occurs through myth.

Even though he professed not to be a Jungian, Joseph Campbell defines myth in ways that are parallel to Jung, if not echoes of him. Campbell himself says Jung was the closest to understanding the true meaning of myth. He cites Jung when he describes myth: 'myths are telling us in picture language of powers of the psyche to

be recognized and integrated in our lives ... Thus they have not
been, and can never be, displaced by the findings of science, which
relate rather to the outside world than to the depths we enter in
sleep.'[109]

For Campbell, myth is found in Jungian territory: 'The material
of myth is the material of our life, the material of our body and the
material of our environment, and a living vital mythology deals
with these in terms that are appropriate to the nature of knowledge
of the time.'[110] Campbell's archetypes and his collective unconscious are Jungian, and his universal knowledge is also made local:

> the human psyche is essentially the same all over the world.
> The psyche is the inward experience of the human body,
> which is essentially the same in all human beings, with the
> same organs, the same instincts, the same impulses, the
> same conflicts, the same fears. Out of this common ground
> have come what Jung has called the archetypes which are
> the common ideas of myth ... [These] archetypes of the
> unconscious are manifestations of the organs of the body
> and their powers [and] are biologically grounded ... All over
> the world and at different times of human history, these
> archetypes or elementary ideas, have appeared in different
> costumes. The differences in the costumes are the results of
> environmental and historical conditions.[111]

Given these commonalities of terminology and definition, where
do Campbell and Jung, the former basically a mythologist, and the
latter a psychologist, differ? Robert Segal notes these differences in
Joseph Campbell: An Introduction. Myth, for Campbell, does not 'just
refer to the archetypes, but actually manifests them', as it 'reveals
the existence of a severed, deeper part of both [man] and the
cosmos'.[112]

Campbell assigns myth four basic functions:

> to instill and maintain a sense of awe and mystery before the
> world ... to explain the world; [as] a mythology is a system
> of effect symbols, signs evoking and directing a psychic
> response; ... to maintain the social order by giving divine
> justification to social practices and institutions; [and] most of
> all, to harmonize the individual with society , the cosmos,
> himself, [by linking] him with everything both outside and
> within.[113]

Campbell, like Jung, sees myth as a tool for the understanding of human psychology, and as an expression of man's relationship with the numinous, the divine, the inexpressible, that which is beyond words. Unlike Jung, Campbell is interested in myth from a socio-logical and anthropological point of view: myth explains, justifies and maintains society as it is. For Campbell, myth is indispensable: no human can survive without it. Indeed, modern man's indiffer-ence to it, according to Campbell, is a key reason for the contem-porary malaise of meaninglessness and disconnection.[114] Jung, however, values the function of myth, as a key to understanding and using the wisdom of the unconscious, far more than myth itself. For the individual a Jungian interpretation of myth would open him or her up to only part of their self; for Campbell, 'to accept myth is to accept it wholly ... [it is] to identify oneself in myth'.[115]

To so wholly identify one's self with the mythic becomes, then, for Campbell, all that is 'necessary and sufficient to deepest human fulfillment'. There is no need for therapy. Segal argues that this is abandonment to myth, something which Jung would never do. To begin with the archetypes, use them and reflect on the myths would be Jungian. For Campbell, 'all the wisdom man needs' is found in myth and mythic archetypes.[116] Myth becomes for Camp-bell something far larger and more encompassing than Jung would have argued for:

> Mythology [is] the study of man's greatest story ... that we have come forth from the one ground of being as mani-festations in the field of time. This field of time is a kind of shadow play over a timeless ground ... The great story is our search to find our place in the dream. To be in accord with the grand symphony that this world is, to put the harmony of our own body in accord with that harmony.[117]

Mythology must, Campbell adds in *The Inner Reaches of Outer Space: Metaphor as Myth and Religion*, first and foremost '[open] the mind and heart to the utter wonder of all being'. Second, mythology must 'represent the universe and [the] whole spectrum of nature' as an epiphany, as a way to recognize divinity.[118] The hero-myth is the perfect example of this universality as its 'ultimate meaning' is 'all is one': there is only hero, with no doubt more than a thousand faces, the supernatural and the everyday are the same, as are the psychological and the metaphysical. 'Every individual hero symbolizes all mankind ...'[119]

While Ursula Le Guin does use Campbell's heroic pattern, the monomyth of the Hero and the Quest in her fantasy and science fiction, her understanding of myth can also be said to parallel the Jungian.[120] In her essay 'The Child and the Shadow' Le Guin says that 'the psychologist whose ideas on art are the most meaningful to most artists [is] Carl Gustav Jung'.[121] Art here means not just the visual, but music and, especially for Le Guin, literature, the story. It is in the story, particularly 'the great fantasies, myths and tales', that Le Guin finds access to the Jungian collective unconscious: 'they speak *from* the unconscious *to* the conscious, in the *language* of the unconscious – symbol and archetype. Though they use words, they work the way music does: they short-circuit verbal reasoning and go straight to the thoughts that lie too deep to utter.'[122] Myth, for Le Guin, thus becomes a way in which humans make meaning: 'Myth is an expression of one of the several ways the human being, body/psyche, perceives, understands, and relates to the world. Like science, it is a basic human mode of comprehension.'[123] As with Jung, myth serves as a connection between the thinking self and the feeling self – it connects 'the idea with value, sensation with intuition, cortex with cerebellum'.[124] And true myth only arises, Le Guin argues, in the process of connecting this rational conscious and 'the unconscious realms'.[125] And as I have already noted, for Le Guin again, this 'unconscious realm' is akin to the Jungian in being both collective and communal: 'we all have the same kind of dragons in our psyche ... [which] is similar in all of us, just as all our bodies are basically similar'.[126] There Le Guin finds archetypes, the stuff of her stories, the agents of the myth that, she says, use her: 'dragons, heroes, quests, objects of power, voyages at night, and under sea'.[127]

Le Guin's understanding of myth clearly parallels Jungian thought. Even so, Le Guin's approach to myth is filtered through feminism, which takes both Jung and Campbell to task. This is especially true in the monomyth of the Hero and the Quest. As Daniel C. Noel explains in his essay 'Revisioning the Hero', the Jungian Hero is a 'deeply problematic model of the Self ... The Hero is inevitably male, unfortunately macho.' As Noel notes, psychologist Carol Gilligan and educational theorist Mary Belenky and others have demonstrated that 'women have other ways of growing and knowing than accounted for in the Hero model'.[128] Gilligan sees feminine morality as one 'organized around notions of responsibility and care', not the masculine morality of right as described by Piaget. What is moral, what is right or wrong, must be seen in context, not in 'blind impartiality'. The hero cannot just whack off the enemy's head without some understanding of the enemy.[129] For Belenky, in *Women's Ways of Knowing: The Development of the Self, Voice, and Mind*, a woman's way of knowing is one that values 'connection over separation, understanding and acceptance over assessment, and collaboration over debate'.[130] Such ways of knowing value the personal, the subjective, interdependence and community. The traditional Hero model, in contrast, is of a person alone and separate, who must be objectively tested to prepare for *his* Quest, a quest which is a public act, with a public grail.

Michel Zimmerman does give Jung credit for a 'critique of the lopsidedness of patriarchal culture', yet even so he feels Jung's history of individuation is 'so colored by masculinist categories that it cannot be of help in developing an alternative concept of individuation'.[131] Unlike Jung, Campbell concedes that heroes are not all men. 'The male usually does have the more conspicuous role', Campbell says in *The Power of Myth*, 'because of the condition of life.'[132] Moyers, Campbell's interlocutor, calls attention to the mother as hero, and the view that the new motherhood is a heroic journey. But most feminists, while accepting mothers as heroes, would argue that this acknowledgement is not enough. Annis Pratt in 'The Female Hero' has found in literature by women a female quest of individual development that she describes 'as markedly different from Campbell', and more social in nature.[133] In her essay in *The Journal of Analytical Psychology*, 'In Search of the Heroine', Coline Covington offers the idea of the hero and the heroine as both being part of the same spectrum of the self, and as both being aspects of the self. The hero seeks separation; the heroine seeks reintegration.[134]

As Covington is perhaps the closest to Le Guin as she accepts the Jung/Campbell heroic pattern as valid, but open to reinterpretation, I discuss her hero/heroine concept in more detail in Chapter Two on the reimagining of the monomyth. This reimagining, this revisioning, is key, I think, to how Le Guin sees and uses myth in her fiction, and it is through such use that myth for her becomes rhetorical. Patrick D. Murphy labels this 'feminist (re)mythopoiea'. Le Guin, according to Murphy, uses 'widespread revisioning of myth' that begins with a 'broader perspective than [simply including] women in myth'. Murphy describes her revisioning of the myth of Danae, 'Danae 46', as one in which she gives the other, the woman, a real and true voice: Danae becomes a speaking subject and not the object, Zeus' lover, Perseus' mother.[135]

Le Guin believes in the 'necessity of myth for culture' – for *our* culture – yet she recognizes that traditional myth and traditional definitions of myth, such as Jung's and Campbell's, have excluded women as speaking subjects, as heroes, as active – and that this exclusion has failed us. Her own 'poetic fabulations' she offers as 'part of the process of developing a new mythology for the future'.[136] In her essay 'Prophets and Mirrors: Science Fiction as a Way of Seeing' Le Guin argues first for story, then for fantasy and science fiction as essential for human understanding:

> We read books to find out who we are. What other people, real or imaginary, do and think and feel – or have done and thought and felt, or might do and think and feel – is an essential guide to our understanding of what we ourselves are and may become ... And a person who had never listened to nor read a tale or a myth or parable or story, would remain ignorant of his own emotional and spiritual heights and depths, would not know quite fully what it is to be human. For the story ... is one of the basic tools invented by the mind of man, for the purpose of gaining understanding.[137]

In the metaphors of science fiction stories, she argues – 'the spaceships faster than light, the weird worlds and alien beings, the intolerable or utopian societies, the dooms envisaged, the glories imagined' – we can find 'ways of seeing reality now. They are the medium used by certain serious artists to describe what all artists describe: this world, ourselves, the way we go.' (And, of course, the metaphors of fantasy – the wizards, the dragons, magic, rings of power, quests – also provide ways of seeing reality now.) That the reality seen may appear distorted is 'because the reality seen by the artist strikes him as distorted, as incredible'.[138] Science fiction, while dismissed as fantasies of the future, is really, Le Guin argues, intensely concerned with 'the here-and-now ... the present political-social-moral state of affairs':[139] it is a literature of ideas.

Le Guin's fiction – both her fantasy and her science fiction, and her mainstream – is exactly this, a literature of ideas. It is a literature that, while using the metaphors of science and technology, also uses the metaphors of myth. Le Guin says myth uses her to reveal its truth, and through her own revisioning and reimagining she revitalizes myth to contain its essential truths and the contemporary reinterpretations of such truths. Her use of myth becomes rhetorical as she argues for an alternative way of seeing, thinking and being that connects rather than separates, includes rather than excludes, gives voice rather than silences. She acknowledges the importance of myth, an importance that our Western culture seems to have forgotten. Our lack of it, Le Guin and others, such as Susanne Langer, argue, has made us lose touch with the irrational as a way of knowing, and thus lose touch with part of who and what we are. Jung sounds this warning in *Man and his Symbols:*

> Modern man does not understand how much his 'rationalism' (which has destroyed his capacity to respond to numinous symbols and ideas) has put him at the mercy of the psychic underworld. He has freed himself from super-stition (or so he believes), but in the process he has lost his spiritual values to a positively dangerous degree. His moral and spiritual tradition has disintegrated and he is now paying the price for this breakup in world-wide disorienta-tion and disassociation.[140]

Le Guin asks, instead, for reconnection, through one of the oldest ways to do so: stories. She asks us to respond to the still-numinous, albeit the revisioned. I will examine her rhetorical use of myth and the argument she is thereby creating through two myths, those of the Hero and the Quest, and of Utopia. The former is primarily concerned with the individual and how she interacts with and becomes part of her world; the latter is concerned with the world – or rather the community and how it works to allow this individual to exist and thrive. They both provide fertile ground for my investigation. From the myth I move on to the rhetoric, to the argument, and, at the end, I will explore Le Guin's community of the heart, the community her rhetoric is calling for – the community that we have made in our stories which have always been true.

Notes

1. Ursula K. Le Guin, *The Left Hand of Darkness* (New York: Walker & Co., 1969), p. 1.
2. Gerard A. Hauser, *Introduction to Rhetorical Theory* (Prospect Heights, IL: Waveland Press, 1986), p. 2.

3. Patricia Bizzell and Bruce Herzberg, 'Introduction to Kenneth Burke', in Patricia Bizzell and Bruce Herzberg, eds, *The Rhetorical Tradition: Readings from Classical Times to the Present* (Boston: Bedford Books, 1990), pp. 989–91.

4. Ursula K. Le Guin,'Why Are Americans Afraid of Dragons?', in *Language of the Night: Essays on Fantasy and Science Fiction,* ed. Susan Wood, rev. edn (New York: HarperCollins, 1992), pp. 39–40.

5. Ibid., p. 159.

6. Ursula K. Le Guin,'The Carrier Bag Theory of Fiction', in *Dancing at the Edge of the World* (New York: Grove Press, 1989), p. 170.

7. Edward Sapir, quoted in Susanne Langer, *Philosophy in a New Key: A Study in the Symbolism of Reason, Rite, and Art,* 3rd edn (Cambridge, MA: Harvard University Press, 1957), p. 126.

8. *Merriam-Webster Collegiate Dictionary,* 10th edn (Springfield, MA: Merriam Webster, 1993), p. 654.

9. Howard Gardner, *Frames of Mind: The Theory of Multiple Intelligences* (New York: Basic Books, 1983), p. 302.

10. Language is not, of course, limited to sound. Sign language is, as Oliver Sacks says in *Seeing Voices: A Journey into the World of the Deaf* (New York: HarperCollins, 1990), a 'completely visual language ... of an entirely different sort, a language that [serves] not only the power of thought (and indeed allowed thought) and perception of a kind not wholly imaginable to the hearing, [which serves] as the medium of a rich community and culture' (pp. xi, xii). What I want to note here is that again the commonality is that language is symbolic.

11. Anthony J. Cascardi, 'The Place of Language in Philosphy; Or the Uses of Rhetoric', *Philosophy and Rhetoric,* 16 (4) Fall 1983, p. 223.

12. Ernst Cassirer, 'Art', in Hazard Adams, ed., *Critical Theory Since Plato* (New York: Harcourt Brace Jovanovich, 1971), p. 997.

13. James Britton, *Language and Learning,* 2nd edn (Portsmouth, NH: Boynton/Cook, 1993), p. 5.

14. Susanne Langer, *Philosophy in a New Key: A Study of The Symbolism of Reason, Rite, and Art,* 3rd edn (Cambridge, MA: Harvard University Press, 1957), p. 135.

15. Langer, quoted in Britton, *Language and Learning*, p. 21.

16. Edward Sapir, *Language: An Introduction to the Study of Speech* (New York: Harcourt, Brace, and Co., 1949), p. 11.

17. Cassirer, quoted in Britton, *Language and Learning*, p. 13.

18. Britton, *Language and Learning*, p. 13.

19. Kenneth Burke, *Language as Symbolic Action: Essays on Life, Literature, and Method* (Berkeley: University of California Press, 1966), p. 5.

20. Gardner, *Frames of Mind*, p. 312.

21. Langer, quoted in Britton, *Language and Learning*, p. 21.

22. Ibid., p. 20.

23. Ferdinand de Saussure, *Course in General Linguistics*, trans. Wade Baskin, ed: Charles Bally and Albert Sechehaye (New York: Philosophical Library, 1959), pp. 111–12.

24. Lev Vygotsky, *Thought and Language*, rev. edn, trans. and ed. Alex Kozulin (Cambridge, MA: MIT Press, 1986), p. 79.

25. Ibid., p. 83.

26. Ibid., p. 82.

27. Ibid., p. 83.

28. Howard Rheingold, *They Have a Word for It* (Los Angeles: Jeremy P. Tarcher, 1988), p. 3.

29. Helen Keller, quoted in Britton, *Language and Learning*, p. 36.

30. Britton, *Language and Learning*, p. 289.

31. Langer, *Philosophy*, p. 28.

32. Ibid., p. 283.

33. Ann E. Berthoff, *The Making of Meaning: Metaphors, Models, and Maxims for Writing Teachers* (Montclair, NJ: Boynton/Cook, 1981), p. 70.

34. Britton, *Language and Learning*, p. 23.

35. Vygotsky, *Thought and Language*, p. 212.

36. Ibid., p. 219.

37. Ibid., p. 253.

38. Ibid., p. 256.

39. Ernst Cassirer, *An Essay on Man: An Introduction to a Philosophy of Human Culture* (New Haven, CT: Yale University Press, 1944), p. 134.

40. Vygotsky, *Thought and Language*, p. 173.

41. De Saussure, *General Linguistics*, pp. 111–12.

42. I. A. Richards, selections from *The Philosophy of Rhetoric*, in Bizzell and Herzberg, eds, *The Rhetorical Tradition*, pp. 982, 985.

I. A. Richards (1893–1979) taught English and moral philosophy at Cambridge, and is noted as a philosopher and a scholar of language and a 'leading figure in the development of modern literary criticism'. His fields of study and interest were broad: 'No field of study seemed foreign to him, and his many books and articles are marked by his continuing enthusiasm for psychology, linguistics, anthropology, information, and philosophy.' He developed the 'Basic English' project with C. K. Ogden, a project 'through which Richards hoped to improve international understanding' (Bizzell and Herzberg, eds, *The Rhetorical Tradition*, p. 964).

43. James Britton, *Prospect and Retrospect: Selected Essays of James Britton*, ed. Gordon M. Pradl (Montclair, NJ: Boynton/Cook, 1982), p. 96.

44. Ibid., p. 97.

45. Britton, *Language and Learning*, p. 40.

46. Bakhtin argues that even Story 1 is not simply 'the true account of a sequence of events' or a verbatim narrative. Even a list implies choice: some items are included, some are not. A recitation of events and the pertinent details also, Bakhtin suggests, implies choice and therefore

interpretation. Not every detail is included by the reciter. Offred, the primary character in Margaret Atwood's *The Handmaid's Tale*, explains all this very succinctly: 'It is impossible to say a thing exactly the way it was, because what you say can never be exact, you always have to leave something out, there are too many parts, sides, crosscurrents, nuances; too many gestures, which could mean this or that, too many shapes which can never be fully described, too many flavors in the air or on the tongue, half-colors, too many' (pp. 173–74). Even so, Story 1 is probably the closest we can come to pure factual truth.

47. Aristotle, *Poetics*, in *The Rhetoric and Poetics*, trans. W. Rhys Roberts and Ingram Bywater (New York: Modern Library, 1984), 1450b, 1451a.

48. Ibid., 1451a, 1451b.

49. Tim O'Brien, *The Things They Carried* (Boston: Houghton Mifflin, 1990), pp. 179–80.

50. C. Michael Curtis, 'Introduction', in Curtis, ed., *American Stories II: Fiction from* The Atlantic Monthly (San Francisco: Chronicle Books, 1990), p. xi.

51. Philip Sidney, 'An Apology for Poetry,' in Charles Kaplan and William Anderson, eds, *Criticism: Major Statements*, 3rd edn (New York: St. Martin's Press, 1991), p. 110.

52. Charles Kaplan and William Anderson, introduction to 'An Apology for Poetry', in Kaplan and Anderson, eds, *Criticism: Major Statements*, p. 108.

53. Robert Coles, *The Call of Stories: Teaching and the Moral Imagination* (Boston: Houghton Mifflin, 1989), p. 7.

54. Ibid., p. 24.

55. Ibid., p. 30.

56. Ibid., p. 68.

57. Ibid., p. 85.

58. Le Guin, *Left Hand of Darkness*, p. 1.

59. Augusta Baker and Ellin Greene, *Storytelling: Art and Technique* (New York: Bowker, 1977), p. 17.

60. Edith Nesbit, quoted in Baker and Greene, *Storytelling*, pp. 17–18.

61. Diane Wolkstein, 'Twenty-Five Years of Storytelling: The Spirit of the Art', *Horn Book*, 68 (6) November/December 1992, p. 708.

62. Baker and Greene, *Storytelling*, p. xiii.

63. Wolfgang Iser, *The Act of Reading: A Theory of Aesthetic Response* (Baltimore: The Johns Hopkins University Press, 1978), p. 107.

64. Ibid., p. 118.

65. Louise Rosenblatt, *The Reader, the Text, the Poem: The Transactional Theory of the Literary Work* (Carbondale, IL: Southern Illinois University Press, 1978), p. 10.

66. Ibid., p. 121.

67. Ibid., p. 76.

68. Walter Ong, 'The Writer's Audience is Always a Fiction', *PMLA: Publication of the Modern Language Association of America*, 90, 1975, p. 10.

69. Ibid., p. 12.

70. Ibid., p. 13.

71. Walter Fisher, *Human Communication as Narration: Toward a Philosophy of Reason, Value, and Action* (Columbia, SC: University of South Carolina Press, 1989), pp. 62–63.

72. Ibid., pp. xii, xiii.

73. Ibid., p. 64.

74. Mary Lee Coe, 'The Irresistible Loop of Story', *AWP Chronicle*, 28 (2) October/November 1995, p. 17.

75. Fisher, *Human Communication*, p. 5.

76. Ibid., p. 18.

77. Ibid., p. 6.

78. Coles, *The Call of Stories*, p. 191.

79. When Plato tells his myths of the Charioteer or the Cave he is using the word as *mythos* – 'word' or 'story'. He is not using the term myth as we would, in reference to the myths of the Olympians. But the fact that the word is also used by the Greeks to refer to the Olympians and the rest of their pantheon does suggest there is some overlap. The stories about the gods are efforts to make the divine mystery understandable, to make the numinous visible. They are stories that make 'available in words what by no other means is available'. Given this, Plato is actually using myth as simply story and as story to express what is available 'by no other means', his philosophic truths.

80. Robert Scott Stewart, 'The Epistemological Function of Platonic Myth', *Philosophy and Rhetoric*, 22 (4) 1989, pp. 275–76.

81. R. Hackforth, in Plato, *Phaedrus and Letters VII and VIII*, trans. Walter Hamilton (London: Penguin, 1975), p. 50.

82. Martha Nussbaum, *The Fragility of Goodness: Luck and Ethics in Greek Tragedy and Philosophy* (Cambridge: Cambridge University Press, 1986), p. 201

83. Plato, *Phaedrus*, in *Phaedrus and Letters VII and VIII*, 246.

84. Ibid., 253.

85. John Bierhorst, *The Mythology of North America* (New York: William Morrow, 1985), p. 5.

86. David Adams Leeming, *The World of Myth* (New York: Oxford University Press, 1990), p. 3.

87. Ibid.

88. Bierhorst, *Mythology of North America*, p. 6.

89. Rollo May, *The Cry of Myth* (New York: W. W. Norton, 1991), p. 15.

90. Bierhorst, *Mythology of North America*, pp. 1, 5.

91. J. F. Bierlein, *Parallel Myths* (New York: Ballantine Books, 1994), pp. xiii, 5.

92. Kees W. Bolle, 'Myth: An Overview', in *The Encyclopedia of Religion* (New York: Macmillan, 1987), p. 261.

93. Bierlein, *Parallel Myths*, pp. 6, 7.

94. Ibid., p. 6.

95. Carl Jung, *Psychology and Religion* (New Haven, CT: Yale University Press, 1938), p. 47.

96. June Singer, *Boundaries of the Soul: The Practice of Jung's Psychology* (Garden City, NJ: Doubleday, 1972), p. 84.

97. Steven F. Walker, *Jung and the Jungians on Myth* (New York: Garland, 1992), p. 10.

98. Ursula K. Le Guin, 'Myth and Archetype in Science Fiction', in *Language of the Night*, p. 75.

99. Walker, *Jung*, p. 4.

100. Carl Jung, *Memories, Dreams, Reflections*, ed. Aniela Jaffi, trans. Richard and Clara Winston (New York: Pantheon Books, 1963), p. 347.

101. Walker, *Jung*, pp. 10, 13.

102. Jolande Jacobi, *The Psychology of C. G. Jung*, rev. edn (New Haven, CT: Yale University Press, 1951), p. 62.

103. Walker, *Jung*, pp. 18, 19.

104. Ibid., p. 5.

105. Jung, *Memories*, p. 340.

106. Robert A. Segal, *Joseph Campbell: An Introduction* (New York: Garland, 1987), p. 130.

107. Jacobi, *Psychology of Jung*, pp. 63–64.

108. Ibid., p. 125.

109. Segal, *Joseph Campbell*, p. 125.

110. Joseph Campbell, *Transformations of Myth through Time* (New York: Harper & Row, 1990), p. 1.

111. Joseph Campbell, with Bill Moyers, *The Power of Myth*, ed. Betty Sue Flowers (New York: Doubleday, 1988), pp. 60–61.

112. Segal, *Joseph Campbell*, p. 111.

113. Ibid., pp. 119–20.

114. In *The Power of Myth* Campbell points out that for medieval people 'spiritual principles' informed society: the cathedral was the tallest and most important building in town. Today 'the tallest places are the office buildings'. This, for Campbell, means that modern man has 'lost touch with that kind of concern [the spiritual]. The goal of early life was to live in constant consciousness of the spiritual principle', or the mythic (pp. 118, 119, 120). This, Campbell says, is not the case for modern humanity, and as a result, modern life is lacking in meaning, purpose and connection.

115. Segal, *Joseph Campbell*, p. 132.

116. Ibid.

117. Campbell, *Power*, pp. 64–65.

118. Joseph Cambell, *The Inner Reaches of Outer Space: Metaphor as Myth and Religion* (New York: A van der Marck Edition, 1986), p. 18.

119. Segal, *Joseph Campbell*, pp. 26, 5.

120. Like Campbell, Le Guin professes she is not a Jungian. Indeed, she is adamant that she is not a Jungian 'in any sense of the word and dislike[s] being called so'. She explains: 'Jung's influence on my thought, though very strong for a brief period, was also very limited, both in time and scope. Unfortunately, during that period in which I first read Jung and was busy adding some of his ideas to my repertory – rifling his treasury for the bits I wanted – I wrote two or three essays in the enthusiasm of those discoveries, and they've sufficed, ever since, to convince people I was a follower. I just wish to repeat that I am not; and that what I personally find interesting in the mental relationship is that I arrived at "the shadow" – which is indeed very similar to Jung's concept of the Shadow – independently and in total ignorance of his writings. Convergence, not influence. A crossing of paths, not a joining of direction.' (Ursula K. Le Guin, letter to the author, 13 April 1998.)

121. Le Guin, 'The Child and the Shadow,' in *Language of the Night*, p. 58.

122. Le Guin, 'Is Gender Necessary/Redux,' in *Language of the Night*, p. 157.

123. Le Guin, 'Myth and Archetype in Science Fiction,' in *Language of the Night*, p. 69.

124. Ibid., p. 73.

125. Ibid., p. 74.

126. Ibid., pp. 75, 73.

127. Ibid., p. 75.

128. Daniel C. Noel, 'Revisioning the Hero,' in Christine Downing, ed., *Mirrors of the Self: Archetypal Images that Shape Your Life* (Los Angeles: Jeremy P. Tarcher, 1991), p. 207.

129. Mary Field Belenky, Blythe McVicker Clinchy, Nancy Rule Goldberger and Jill Mattuck Tarule, *Women's Ways of Knowing: The Development of Self, Voice, and Mind* (New York: Basic Books, 1986), p. 10.

130. Ibid., p. 229.

131. Michel Zimmerman, quoted in Noel, 'Revisioning the Hero', p. 126.

132. It is worth noting that Le Guin takes Campbell to task for this remark: '[His] statement, "The male usually does have the more conspicuous role, because of the condition of life," is probably the most fatuous remark he has ever made. Talk about begging the question! Translated into sense, what he said is, "The male has the more conspicuous role because the male chooses to make the male role conspicuous and to call that 'the condition of life'."'(Letter to the author, 13 April 1998.)

133. Annis Pratt, 'The Female Hero,' in Christine Downing, ed., *Mirrors of the Self: Archetypal Images that Shape Your Life* (Los Angeles: Jeremy P. Tarcher, 1991), pp. 213–14.

134. Coline Covington, 'In Search of the Heroine', *Journal of Analytical Psychology*, 1989, p. 253.

135. Patrick D. Murphy, 'The High and Low Fantasies of Feminist (Re)Mythopoeia', *Mythlore*, 16 (2) Winter 1989, pp. 26, 29.

136. Ibid., p. 29.

137. Ursula K. Le Guin, 'Prophets and Mirrors: Science Fiction as a Way of Seeing', *Living Light: A Christian Education Review*, 7, Fall 1970, pp. 111–12.

138. Ibid., p. 113.

139. Ibid., p. 114.

140. Carl Jung, ed., *Man and his Symbols* (Garden City, NJ: Doubleday, 1964), p. 94.

CHAPTER TWO
The Monomyth Reimagined

True myth, according to Le Guin, 'arises only in the process of connecting the conscious and the unconscious realms'. From this 'unconscious realm', myth releases 'the common darkness', familiar archetypal images: 'dragons, heroes, quests; objects of power, voyages at night and under sea'.[1] And we tell myths, stories, she says, 'for the purpose of gaining understanding' of what it means to be fully human.[2] But human experience, while personally a constant, as almost every human experiences birth, childhood, adolescence, maturity and death, is, for the species, in flux. We travel by air where we once walked or rode on horseback. The descendants of slaves are professors, doctors, lawyers and politicians. Instead of handwritten letters that took days to cross a continent, e-mail messages flicker across phone lines in seconds. Female astronauts, telephone lineworkers, lumberjacks and university chancellors are no longer novelties. Openly gay men and women serve in political and diplomatic posts. Those silenced a generation ago now speak loud and clear.

Because of this constancy and because of this change, myths need to be retold, over and over, to be useful. The needs and wants of the audience must be accounted for, as well as the purpose of the speaker. For each generation then 'the myths and tales we learned as children – fables, folktales, legends, hero-stories, god-stories' must be retold, rethought, revisioned.[3] This *revisioning* may be a shift in point of view, or bringing to the foreground people and things and creatures on the periphery, or in the background.

It is Le Guin's revisioning, reimagining, that I am interested in exploring here, especially what she does with the monomyth, the story of the Hero and the Quest, in *The Dispossessed* and the *Earthsea* tetralogy. It is my argument here that the reshaping of the Monomyth is progressive and increasingly more radical in form. Le Guin's progressive reshaping makes rhetorical use of the monomyth. By inverting the monomyth and redefining its hero, Le Guin both validates the ancient truths of the myth and asks the myth to be revisioned. To go from Shevek, the physicist as hero, who is the protagonist of *The Dispossessed,* to Tenar, a farmer's widow and the protagonist of *Tehanu,* is a statement of this revisioning, in terms of gender, social class and the nature of what a quest should be.

If Le Guin's purpose is rhetorical, as I argue, then in one sense she is arguing for the hero-myth's classical truth. As the myth tells the story of the hero and his journey, it is presenting a paradigm of human development: the growth of the self, the coming of age of the individual. Yet, as Le Guin's rhetoric celebrates the individual's growth, it asks the reader to question the myth: just who is this individual? Why is this person almost always male? She does not question the hero's courage, or the value of his quest; rather she asks for the rest of the story to be told. While the hero was off slaying the dragon, someone was back home cleaning the castle, minding the farm, looking after the children. Le Guin asks who this someone is, and calls attention to *her* deeds, asking the reader to consider *her* value and worth. She makes the reader see that these deeds, performed in private and with considerably less drama, are not of less importance. Through her rethinking, Le Guin asserts that there is more than one kind of courage, more than one way to be brave and heroic. For Le Guin to make one of her heroes a farmer's widow is to argue that there is more than one way to be a hero. To focus on the widow's daily life is to argue there is more than one way to be heroic, more than one kind of quest, outside the limelight as well as in public.

The Monomyth of the Hero and the Quest

But before examining Le Guin's heroes, their quests and her rhetorical use of the hero-myth, I want to review the monomyth by taking a closer look at the different elements that compose it: the hero; the different stages of the quest (separation, initiation and trial); and the journey and return. To define and explain these elements of the Hero's story I will draw upon two main sources: the works of Joseph Campbell, especially *The Hero with a Thousand Faces* and *The Power of Myth,* and the work of Swiss psychologist, Carl Jung. In particular, I want to use Campbell's definition of the monomyth, with its separate stages, and Jung's psychological approach through the use of archetypes. I will review here some of the material discussed in Chapter One, as it is vital that Campbell and Jung be understood. More attention will be given here, however, to the hero-myth itself, rather than myths in general.

Over the centuries, we have told and retold stories about heroes and their glorious deeds, stories that are as 'old as literature'. These stories, the hero-myths with their star character, are not, however, told merely to entertain. Human societies need and look for heroes. According to Campbell, in *The Power of Myth,* a society needs heroes 'because it has to have constellating images to pull together all these tendencies to separation, to pull them together in some intention'.[4] Or as W. B. Sanford explains in his introduction to Galinksy's *The Herakles Theme,* 'Every generation needs heroes and symbolic figures to embody its ideals and emotions.'[5] A hero then becomes something of a mirror to a people: his or her virtues, ideals and strengths reflect what a society deems to be of value at a particular time. And these values are what is celebrated in the hero's story. A prime example of the hero is Beowulf, whose story is one of the earliest extant myths in English – if not the earliest. Beowulf's life is an exemplar of the heroic society and its values and beliefs. He is the perfect king, the perfect lord in peace and war, the perfect shepherd of his people, and the perfect ring-giver, 'the gold-friend in peace, shield and helmet in war'.[6] According to Campbell, Beowulf is an early personification of a hero, who, whether we call him Hercules or Odysseus or the third son, is the same: 'there is but one archetypal mythic hero whose life has been replicated in many lands by many, many people'.[7]

To describe the hero as a recurring archetype is to suggest that heroes are not only mythic figures, but also a part of the human psyche, and that the human psyche has a certain commonality and is communal in nature. Jung called this commonality the collective unconscious, which is inborn and universal among all human beings, a universal 'common ground'. The collective unconscious, to reiterate Jung's definition, rises from the 'inward experience of the human body which is essentially the same in all human beings, with the same organs, the same impulses, the same conflicts, the same fears'.[8] Le Guin also believes in the collective unconscious, where 'we all meet … [in] the source of true community; of felt religion, of art, grace, spontaneity, and love'.[9]

Within this 'true community' is the source of such archetypes as the Hero and his Quest or Journey. The archetypes, or the 'cornerstones of myth', as Campbell calls them, are motives of behaviour. According to Jung:

Even dreams are made of collective materials to a very high degree, just as in the mythology and folklore of different peoples, certain motives repeat themselves in almost identical form. I have called these motives archetypes and by that I understand forms or images of a collective nature which occur practically all over the earth as constituents of myths and at the same time as autochthonous individual products of unconscious origin. The archetypal motives presumably stem from the archetypal patterns of the human mind which are not only transmitted by tradition and migration, but also by heredity.[10]

Archetypes are, Campbell adds, a priori forms of the mythic and the fantastic.[11] The hero is described by Jung in *Symbols of Transformation* as the 'finest of all symbols of the [human] libido'.[12] The libido, or 'psychic life-force', according to Jung, is symbolized by the sun, and is thus personified in 'figures of heroes with solar attributes':[13]

The heroes are usually wanderers, and wandering is a symbol of longing, of the restless urge which never finds its object, of nostalgia for the lost mother. The sun comparison can easily be taken in this sense: the heroes are like the wandering sun, from which it is concluded that the myth of the hero is a solar myth. It seems to us, rather, that he is first and foremost a self-representation of the longing of the unconscious, of its unquenched and unquenchable desire for the light of consciousness.[14]

Or in other words, the hero is an archetype of the self, of separation – the self seeking separation and eventually full individuation. The hero's story, the monomyth, or the Hero and the Journey or Quest, thus reflects human experience – in particular the individual's experiences of attaining maturity or coming of age – the actualization of the adult self.

This can be seen more clearly by briefly reviewing the heroic life-pattern of quest, boon, return,[15] or as Campbell defines it, this 'standard path of mythological adventure: separation, initiation, and the quest, which is both journey and return'.[16] This tripartite heroic life parallels the coming of age of the individual, 'the stage of human realization', as the individual separates psychically and eventually physically from his or her parents to seek the boon of adulthood through the quest of adolescence. In *The Origins and*

History of Consciousness, Erich Neumann, a Jungian, describes this coming-of-age pattern as 'the history of [the] self-emancipation of the ego struggling to free itself from the powers of unconscious to hold its own against overwhelming odds'.[17] The essential function of the heroic myth, then, as Joseph Henderson explains in *Man and His Symbols,* is 'the development of the individual's ego-consciousness'. The individual becomes aware of his own strengths and weaknesses in 'a manner that will equip him for the arduous tasks with which life confronts him ... The image of the hero evolves in a manner that reflects each stage of the evolution of the human personality.'[18] It is worth noting here that the language used by both Jung and Campbell indicates the *universality* of the myth and its psychological parallel. Gender is not mentioned, but as Le Guin notes in *Earthsea Revisioned,* the hero-tale, a human universal, is male-gendered: 'The hero is a man.' After all, until fairly recently, when a writer wrote of anything that was meant to be a human universal, the general pronoun used to include everyone was male. And as the hero's quest is typically a public event and on a large scale, little attention, if any, was paid to the small and the personal, and the feminine.[19]

The idea of the quest as being a universal coming-of-age story – adolescence, separation, individuation and maturity becomes problematic when parent–child relationships are given closer attention. According to Chodorow in *The Reproduction of Mothering* often a mother 'does not recognize or denies the existence of the daughter as a separate person'. The daughter comes to see herself as a 'continuation or extension of her mother', and the son, in contrast, separates and becomes the other.[20] The quest, as it has been traditionally defined, for *these* daughters would seem to fail as a paradigm for self-individuation. This different coming-of-age story does not necessarily discredit the myth. But it does suggest that the myth is more an ideal paradigm than a reality because it ignores certain realities of mother–daughter relationships. As an ideal, the quest becomes an *assumed* truth about the human experience of coming of age. Le Guin questions this assumption in her examination of the myth and expands its paradigm to include other kinds of quests, other ways to come of age, particularly female ways.

So, how do we believe people grow up and achieve individuality, and how is this belief expressed in the quest paradigm? The psychological coming-of-age story and the quest have several stages. Birth, the first experience that sets the child apart as a separate individual, is a unique and singular experience for each person. The hero, as a symbolic interpretation of human growth, is often marked from childhood as separate or different in some way from the rest of humankind as the 'makers of legend' have a 'tendency to endow the hero with extraordinary powers from the moment of birth, or even the moment of conception'.[21] These extraordinary powers, while often latent in the child, will become manifest in the young adult, as they are needed for the hero to pass his trials of initiation, or to successfully complete his quest. Frye, in *The Secular Scripture,* describes these extraordinary powers as a 'current of energy'.[22] Their appearance in the young adult suggests the onset of full social and sexual maturity. The individual is coming into his or her own, as a person distinct and separate from all others. Separation is now possible from the original community of the family, and the individual can explore other communities, other ways of living.

This step out of the family, in effect, allows the young adult to enter the ongoing adventure of adulthood: the making of a full and satisfying life. Thus familial separation becomes the next stage of the heroic life, the call to adventure: 'the call to every young person to leave [the] nest to make his or her order out of the world-chaos'.[23] This call 'signifies that destiny has summoned the Hero and transferred his spiritual center of gravity from within the pale of his society to a zone unknown'.[24]

In addition, the call usually gives the hero the object of the quest. There is a grail to seek, or a monster to overcome, or another dangerous and difficult task to complete. The task can be physical or spiritual:

> there are two types of deed. One is the physical deed, in which the hero performs a courageous act in battle or saves a life. The other kind is the spiritual deed, in which the hero learns to experience the supernormal range of human spiritual life and then comes back with a message.[25]

Once the call to adventure is finally accepted (or sometimes refused to the hero's detriment – witness the example of Jonah) and the object of the quest determined, the hero will encounter one or several guides or teachers to assist him in his journey. Such assistance often takes the form of a 'little old crone or old man', or sometimes an animal.[26] Often these guides will help the hero determine the deeds he must complete to achieve his quest. For the non-magical individual – the adolescent or the young adult, whose quest is the journey into adulthood – the deeds necessary to complete the quest are again physical or spiritual. The physical deed could be said to be the achievement of full physiological maturity, including the acceptance and practice of one's sexuality. But, to be a complete adult, psychic or spiritual maturity is necessary as well, and parents, teachers, coaches and friends all serve as the necessary guides for this journey.

When the direction and objective of the journey are established, and the hero's helpers are at his side, or the instructions are set in the hero's soul, the hero is ready to advance to the next stage: 'the crossing of the threshold', beyond which is the unknown. Once this threshold is crossed, and the separation is thus complete, the hero has set out on the 'road of trials'. He has begun his initiation: his preparation and testing for the coming quest. For the individual on the verge of adulthood, the lifelong quest for a fully realized self, adolescence itself serves as the initiation and the road of trials.

These trials for the hero occur beyond the familiar territory of his childhood. In this unknown territory, the hero may find himself in a 'dream landscape of curiously fluid ambiguous forms'.[27] This world of marvels and 'supernatural wonders' is a place in which the hero often encounters 'fabulous forces'.[28] (And if adolescence/ early adulthood isn't a world of 'curiously fluid ambiguous forms', then what is?) In *A Wizard of Earthsea*, the intellectual journey Ged takes with his teachers at the School for Wizards is beset with trials and tests of his spirit and mind, and his body as well, with each one transforming Ged into something other than who he was back on Gont.

It is this internal transformation that prepares the hero for the next phase of the quest, a phase more easily seen as akin to the process of self-individuation: the encounter with the goddess and atonement with the father. The encounter with the goddess is the 'bliss-bestowing goal of every Hero's earthly and unearthly Quest. [The goddess] is mother, sister, mistress, bride'.[29] This goddess is often benign: life-giving, maternal and nurturing. But there is equal likelihood that the goddess may be the temptress, or unattainable and forbidden. The hero may encounter the goddess three times, as she is often triune: maiden or young woman, mother and crone. In a word, the goddess is sexual knowledge: what one comes to know, in all senses of the word, as an adult. It is worth noting that the hero's encounter of a *goddess* at this point is proof of his maleness.

The atonement with the father is of a different nature. The father awaits the hero to see if he is truly ready for the quest. The father '[admits] to his house only those who have been thoroughly tested'.[30] He is the 'initiating priest through whom the young being passes on into the larger world'.[31] The use of the word 'atonement' bears examination here. In addition to suggesting reparation for sin, it suggests harmony, the latter meaning harking back to the Middle English meaning of 'to reconcile', to be 'at one'. This encounter with the father is, then, in essence an encounter with one's self or, as Campbell says, a reflection of one's own ego.[32] An excellent example of the atonement in popular culture, with decidedly mythic overtones, can be found in the original *Star Wars* trilogy. In *The Empire Strikes Back* Luke Skywalker finally meets Darth Vader, his father. Luke sees himself as he could be and might be, if he makes the same decisions his father did; and he sees himself as he is: darkness is inside all of us. And Luke, like Campbell's hero, must pass Vader, must defeat him, *and* Luke must accept Vader as his father – and therefore as part of himself – to be able to continue on.

With these meetings finished, all barriers overcome, the hero is now ready to take up the grail, Excalibur, the singing harp. But 'true journey is return', and the hero must come home with what he has achieved. He must return to the world from which he came with the 'ultimate boon' that will rejuvenate his people, 'the nation, the planet, or the ten thousand worlds'.[33] As the name of Campbell's work suggests, this mythic journey is universal. And as Peter Brigg says in his essay 'The Archetype of the Journey', the journey is a metaphor for human life, 'one of literature's great archetypal patterns'.[34]

It is worth examining the significance of some of the common-places of this journey. Quite often the journey is for a year and a day, which is the length of the courtly quest as Weston notes in *The Quest of the Holy Grail*.[35] A year is also one complete cycle of seasons, thus mirroring the cycle of a life, from birth to death. And quite often the Hero dies or is killed upon return from the quest – which, according to Jungians, is symbolic of the achievement of adult maturity.[36] That the journey is a day past a year suggests an incomplete circle, or a spiral. According to Northrup Frye, 'more frequently the quest romance takes on a spiral form, an open circle where the end is the beginning transformed and renewed by the heroic quest'.[37] The quests of Le Guin's heroes, particularly Shevek in *The Dispossessed* and Ged in the *Earthsea* cycle, are also open spirals. Shevek's return to Anarres does not neatly tie up matters, nor does Ged's return from the realm of the dead in *The Farthest Shore*. Things still need attention, problems still need solving. Life, messy, chaotic, disorganized, goes on – even though both Shevek and Ged have been transformed by their quests.

Transformation can be literal, as in the Grail Quest, when the quest's main object has been said to be the 'restoration to health and vigor' of an injured king, and through him the renewal of his kingdom.[38] And not only were the king and his country physically transformed, the Grail Questers were transformed through spiritual enlightenment as well.[39] The latter is the figurative enlightenment suggested by Campbell, for both the hero and his people, when he speaks of the journey as being a 'vision-quest' from which the hero brings home the ultimate boon:

> When the hero-quest has been accomplished through penetration to the source, or through the grace of some male or female, human or animal, personification, the adventurer still must return with his life-transmitting trophy. The full round, the norm of the monomyth, *requires* the hero shall now begin the labor of bringing the runes of wisdom, the Golden Fleece, or his sleeping princess, back into the kingdom of humanity, where the boon may redound to the renewing of the community ...[40]

But to renew, to be reborn, implies, as with the Grail king and his kingdom, death. In addition to the spiral and the renewal at journey's end, the 'last act of the biography of the hero is that of death or departure':[41] a journey into and back from the realm of the dead. There are countless examples, both literal and symbolic: Jesus' resurrection, Orpheus, Hercules' rescue of Alcestis, and Theseus and the Labyrinth, to name only a few. The psychological parallel for the development of the self is clear: the 'hero's journey to the underworld not only resembles both ancient, widespread initiation rites and a natural, probably almost universal human psychic experience, it satisfies a basic human need'.[42] A particular example may be when one emerges from a severe personal crisis – profound depression, a breakdown, extreme loss – 'refreshed, with new understanding'.[43] And so the hero returns, having faced and defeated the ultimate enemy, renewed, reborn and bringing the ultimate boon: knowledge. The 'experiential information' needed for this 'knowledge of and a way to reach the goal of life's voyage' has been obtained. Psychic wholeness has been achieved.[44] That this journey has become such a dominant and lasting theme and plot frame in all kinds of fiction is not surprising. The journey of the soul as fiction has the 'metaphorical significance of myth and the learning it engenders in both traveller and reader stands as a paradigm of all human experience'.[45]

Le Guin's early quests partake of the tradition to follow the psychic paradigm described by Campbell and Jung. But a paradigm could be said to be static – a model held up as example. Le Guin argues that the story is more than a model; rather it is a tool, 'one of the basic tools invented by the mind for the purpose of gaining understanding'. Le Guin is not just telling 'a tale or myth or parable'; she is using myth to tell stories of science fiction and fantasy. The mythic journey of the hero is a story which obviously attracts Le Guin – especially in the Jungian sense of the journey as psychic – 'the journey of self-knowledge, to adulthood, to the light'. She argues in her essay 'The Child and the Shadow' that the journey is the 'individual's need and duty' to make and that fantasy is the most appropriate fictional mode for telling the story of the journey and the hero-traveller:

> fantasy is the best medium suited to a description of that journey, its perils and its rewards. The events of a voyage into the unconscious are not describable in the language of rational daily life: only the symbolic language of the deeper psyche will fit them without trivializing them ... fantasy is the natural, the appropriate language for the recounting of the spiritual journey and the struggle of good and evil in the soul.[46]

Fantasy is, after all, as Le Guin says, the 'language of the inner self', and it is this language that speaks within the interior, and out, to the exterior, to the conscious self. This language is operating, then, primarily in the dream realm of the unconscious, and it uses the 'language of the unconscious – symbol and archetype'. This shifting of territories, so to speak, through the use of fantasy, within the unconscious and outward to the conscious, echoes the way life proceeds. We do not operate entirely within the rational world of daylight, of the touched, smelled, heard and seen. That we use language itself attests to this, as language is, according to Langer in *Philosophy in a New Key*, 'essentially an organic, functioning system of which the primary elements as well as the constructed products are symbols'.[47] Our experiences of the world may be direct, but it is language that allows us to 'construct a representation of what we experienced'.[48] When speaking of an experience, we use verbal symbols to make sense of what happened. Fantasy, then, as it describes the interior voyage (the dream, the daydream, the unconscious, the nightmare), gives us the language needed to describe what we do not experience through our senses, but what is even so still experienced. It is on this interior voyage, more often than not, that we find ourselves travelling with Le Guin's protagonists. And it is the language of fantasy and myth – expressed in the monomyth – that gives us the exterior shape to these journeys. But Le Guin is not simply retelling – she is reimagining the monomyth: by asserting that gender is a force in the quest, by making the personal and the public connect, by giving value to the small, the private, the feminine. The essential elements are all there, the journey, the quest and the hero, but as her reimagining subverts and inverts these elements, the monomyth becomes rhetorical. Or, in other words, to regender the myth, to leave it open-ended and to give value to both personal and private deeds as well as public ones, is to argue what has been changed is as much of worth as what has been taken out.

The Dispossessed: the Monomyth incompletely revisioned

The Dispossessed can readily and easily be identified as a version of the monomyth, a novel of the Hero and the Quest. Shevek's life, which is the essential story, is a series of journeys. In fact, journeys shape the novel's form, as Shevek's journeys to and from Urras begin and end the story: 'all the action in the Anarres sections ... leads up to the voyage in space of the opening chapter; similarly all the action in the Urras sections of the novel leads up to the voyage in the final chapter'.[49] Within each section there is a multiplicity of journeys, physical and mental. The greater encompassing journey, that of Shevek's life, contains all the others: the journeys of leaving home, of marriage, of self-discovery, of knowledge. As Elizabeth Cummins points out in *Understanding Ursula K. Le Guin*, all of Shevek's efforts 'to understand his personal and social functions in society and to find the equation for the general temporal theory' – Shevek's quest – 'are depicted as the familiar circular journey of discovery'.[50] Another journey sustained by the novel is that of the reader who, like Shevek, is asked to journey between Anarres and Urras, or rather between the sharply contrasted social philosophies of the two worlds. The novel's structure of the Anarres and Urras sections arranged in alternating chapters demands this participation.

It is during Shevek's many journeys that one can identify the other elements of the monomyth: separation, initiation and return; guides and teachers, helpful crones and old men; the call to adventure; the encounter with the goddess and atonement with the father; the journey to and from a symbolic realm of the dead, and so forth. But Le Guin reimagines the myth in ways that make the myth she creates an argument. Shevek, the Hero, is on a Quest like the traditional monomyth heroes. But he is seeking a doubled grail, which intertwines the personal and the public, the scientific and the social. Shevek has, since his childhood, pursued the truth as expressed in the sciences of physics and mathematics: 'so he turned his mind to the Square. It was made of numbers, and numbers were always cool and solid ... they had no fault.'[51] This is his vision of 'the balance, the pattern ... the foundation of the world'. Specifically he seeks a general temporal theory that could possibly allow faster-than-light travel.

The second part of this doubled grail is an ongoing personal and public exploration of the social philosophy that created Shevek's society, the Odonian promise of mutual solidarity and community and individual freedom. Shevek's task is to be true to Odonianism and to be true to himself and to his community. He must find a way to mediate between the needs of the community and individual needs, or as Selinger puts it: 'how to be isolated – in a private world which nourishes continuity and creativity largely by way of a private language – without having to be isolated from the other, the world of change and progress and people'.[52]

The connections between the two parts of the grail – Shevek's personal and scientific vision of the number, and his public and social promise of Odonianism – gradually become clear. To gain the necessary knowledge for advanced study, Shevek finds he has to deal with those who seek to control knowledge for their power and ego. To sustain himself emotionally and to anchor his life, so that he can pursue his work, Shevek finds he needs the partner, 'the bond ... now and for life', Takver. To publish his Principles of Simultaneity (the first step to the general temporal theory) he must compromise with men such as Sabul, 'the senior member of the

Abbenay Institute in physics', and other Anarresti power-seekers who pay only lip service to Odo's teachings. Indeed they invoke Odo's teachings as if they were laws, an anathema to Odo whose philosophy called for a society without laws.

To support the greater societal community, Shevek must be separated from his partner and his work for four years. When at last reunited with Takver, he finds he must journey to Urras, to a community of his scientific peers. Yet his society – which says the individual has absolute free choice – prohibits such travel. His society, which chose exile so that they could live as Odo taught, in a society without government, without laws, without ownership – a co-operative anarchistic community – says that for Shevek to travel to Urras will be the equivalent of an exile without hope of return. And it is Shevek's hope that, in addition to working on his research, he will end his people's self-imposed exile. Thus, Shevek's doubled grail is also a whole: to pursue his vision of scientific truth, Shevek must fully participate in community *and* he must insist his society keep its promise of individual freedom and initiative.

It is in the achievement of this double grail that Le Guin's reimagining becomes apparent. At first glance, both Shevek's quests could be described as failures. With the stimuli of Einstein's theories, he made his breakthrough to his general temporal theory, but it was not, as Shevek points out to Keng, the Terran ambassador, 'the instantaneous transferral of matter across space'. Shevek had also hoped, in addition to his scientific work, to share the idea of his society, 'an idea of freedom, of change, of human solidarity'.[53] This quest, the quest to bridge the gulf between the Urrasti and the Anarresti, ended in blood on the marble steps of the Directorate with Shevek fleeing like a hunted animal, allowed to go home only through the intervention of the Terrans and the Hainish. Shevek had finally made contact with the Urrasti underground and led a general strike, as his ancestors did two hundred years before, against social injustice and oppression. Two hundred years previously the strikers had been bought off with the Moon, with Anarres. This time, even with Shevek as a living symbol of a society without owners, without suppression, the government sends armed helicopters.

However, a second, more measured glance brings a different evaluation of Shevek as hero. As Elizabeth Cummins points out, Shevek's making his theory a gift demonstrates that 'exchange between individuals or societies need not be based on profit or power'.[54] And what his theory *will* produce is the ansible, 'a device that will permit communication without any time interval between two points in space'. Ideas and information will be shared across interstellar distances, and 'a league of worlds' will be possible. Indeed this league becomes a reality in Le Guin's future history, when the Hainish-based Ekumen, an interstellar community of the known human-settled worlds, comes into being. The communication, the end of exile that Shevek sought, which was one of his Grails, will be at last a reality, and on a much larger scale than just between Urras and Anarres.

Thus even as Shevek fails, he succeeds; he becomes the champion of the future, of 'things becoming'.[55] Shevek, an individual working within the context of his community, has become what Campbell would call a modern hero, 'the democratic ideal: the self-determining individual'.[56] According to Campbell, the deed of the modern hero 'must be that of questing to bring light again',[57] and he 'must not wait for his community to cast off its slough of pride, fear, rationalized avarice, and sanctified misunderstanding'.[58]

Rather than wait, Shevek defies the conventions of his society and crosses space to Urras. On Urras he defies their conventions of property and ownership, even of ideas, and forces a 'transmutation of the whole social order' on a multiplicity of worlds. His actions have changed him, and have also changed his home, and 'Shevek has breached the walls of his ambiguous utopia'.[59] Urras and Anarres will at last talk, the Ekumen lies in the future, and Shevek will never again be intellectually isolated. Thus, in the pain of his individual life, Shevek has served his society as hero. He has made the Anarresti recommit to the Odonian promise. This recommitment is the 'ultimate boon' of renewal, brought home by the hero. All these changes are the result of an individual life that matters, of individual actions that matter. The transformations Shevek sets in motion could only occur 'through one's personal journey and [only] through its sharing can the new society emerge'.[60]

That Le Guin has made her hero so unique an individual is the most important element of her reimagining. By making his life a succession of journeys she revalidates the mythic potency of the metaphor of journey for human life. Le Guin 'has reached the goal of explaining and contemplating the journey as it happens'. By humanizing the mythic experience, she 'has made potent the fact that the human journey is important for the way in which the experience happens and is understood'.[61] Le Guin thus validates

Campbell's statement in *Transformations of Myth through Time:* 'The material of myth is the material of our own life, the material of our body, and the material of our environment, and a living, vital mythology deals with these in terms that are appropriate to the nature of knowledge of the time.'[62] Through Shevek's story, Le Guin has confirmed that stories are argument and a way of understanding and making sense of the human experience. As Bittner says in *Approaches to the Fiction of Ursula K. Le Guin,* the generic conventions of the monomyth and its hero become 'heuristic devices used to constitute meaning'.[63]

To see Shevek as Hero, and his life as Quest, serves to validate the monomyth as a way of understanding the human experience of self-individuation, the coming of age. Le Guin's reimagining of the myth in *The Dispossessed* creates a rhetorical text, arguing for the idea of community based on mutual co-operation and solidarity, yet allowing for individual freedom and initiative. The constant multiple dialectics of the novel – between Anarres and Urras, Shevek and the conventions of his society, Shevek and the conventions of Urrasti society, the reader and the two worlds – become in and of themselves an argument for communication, talk, exchange – a society without the walls Shevek sought to tear down. That all of the novel's action is centred in and comes out of the initiative of one man argues again for the value of the individual life.

But the argument goes beyond that of the monomyth, which is solely concerned with the individual hero. Although Shevek's life *is* the novel, and his actions do provide its narrative drive, the Anarresti community – based on Odo's social philosophy of mutual solidarity, support and co-operation – is also the novel. Shevek is a citizen of this 'ambiguous utopia', after all. Part of his quest on Urras becomes an effort to extend the Odonian promise. And the choices he makes, the initiatives he takes, are all based on his Odonian values. The myth becomes, then, an argument for community as well. The monomyth, it would seem, has become a way to argue for more than self-individuation; and the hero and his deeds can now be seen as far more complex than once thought. The hero must be seen as a man, or a woman, who is part of a whole, the community, a whole that defines and shapes the hero as much as the hero defines and represents the community. Shevek is both a modern hero, as Campbell would define it, and a traditional hero, a male whose quest is public. And he is a hero of the reimagined myth as well.

Le Guin, interestingly enough, never calls Shevek a modern hero, or a hero of any kind for that matter. She argues in her essay 'The Carrier Bag Theory of Fiction' that 'the novel is a fundamentally unheroic kind of story' and that 'instead of heroes they [i.e. novels] have people in them'.[64] The initial image for *The Dispossessed* was that of a man, 'a scientist, a physicist in fact ... [with] a thin face, large clear eyes, and large ears'. His personality 'was most attractive – attractive ... as a flame to a moth'.[65] Her vision of Shevek suggests, however, that the definition of hero needs to be revised to be more inclusive and more embracing of all kinds of people. Shevek, after all, doesn't have a glamorous profession: physics is not sexy or heroic. Shevek's work is primarily mental, not physical. He has a partner and children; he isn't a romantic single male. Shevek's sexuality is somewhat ambiguous, as he has homosexual experiences as an adolescent and as an adult. Yet, Shevek is the hero.

Earthsea: The Monomyth Fully Revisioned

To go from *The Dispossessed* to the *Earthsea* fantasy cycle is initially somewhat surprising in terms of heroes. One finds, on first glance, in *A Wizard of Earthsea*, the first novel of the fantasy cycle, a hero far closer to the traditional than Shevek ever was. Ged, as the Wizard of Earthsea, fulfils the traditional definition of hero. But, as in *The Dispossessed*, Le Guin is not simply retelling and revalidating, but rethinking and reimagining. Ged, then, like Shevek, is more than the traditional hero. A dark-skinned man, he contradicts the too-familiar Western image of the white-skinned hero. And there is no apotheosis or funeral pyre or triumphant return. Return, for Ged, is loss of power, surrender and retreat. Le Guin takes us, in the spiral of Ged's life, beyond the traditional confines of the monomyth.

The essential metaphor of Le Guin's fantasy cycle, Earthsea, is the journey or the quest. She describes the story of the first book in the series, *A Wizard of Earthsea*, as being 'essentially a voyage, a pattern in the form of a long spiral'.[66] Raymond Thompson, in his essay 'Jungian Patterns in Ursula K. Le Guin's *The Farthest Shore*', concurs: 'In both *A Wizard of Earthsea* and *The Tombs of Atuan*, Ged's quest follows the basic pattern of the Monomyth outlined by Joseph Campbell in *The Hero with a Thousand Faces*.'[67] Thompson goes on to argue that while the structure of the third novel, *The*

Farthest Shore, is not as faithful to the monomyth as the first two, nevertheless it is still the story of a journey, of a quest, with Ged and Arren as the heroes.

Tehanu, 'the last book of Earthsea', was published in 1990, eighteen years after the 1972 publication of *The Farthest Shore.* There are no journeys into the realm of the dead, either literally or symbolically in *Tehanu,* as there are in the first three novels. Nor are there long voyages, spiral or otherwise – except from one Gontish town to another, a mere trip up and down the Gontish coast. Ged, the great Archmage of all Earthsea, has no more magic; and Tenar, the child-priestess he rescued from the tombs of Atuan, has grown up to be a farmer's wife, and is now a farmer's widow. *Tehanu* is a story of small things, private things: the small, regular, personal acts of daily life, the doings of those who only listened to or told the traditional hero-tale (such as Ged's story). And *Tehanu* is told from the perspective of Tenar, the farmer's widow.

One wonders, then, if the monomyth has been abandoned and the hero discarded with his quest unfinished. The answer is no, quite the opposite. What is happening is that, rather than being abandoned, the monomyth has been inverted and subverted, if not altogether turned on its head. If we read the entire *Earthsea* cycle, all four novels, as one long continuous metaphoric journey, the journey of Ged's life, with many quests – 'physical and psychological journeys for self-knowledge and objects of power' – then *Tehanu* is Ged's story after his return from the journey. It is the story of what happens when the hero has completed his tasks and, now tired and not as powerful as he once was, he goes home. That *Tehanu* is also just as much Tenar's story, perhaps even more so than it is Ged's, serves to make the monomyth a rhetorical device. As Le Guin feminizes the myth, she transforms it, and the resulting story becomes an argument for what was not told before.

Feminism is the key to Le Guin's transformation of the myth and its journey, as it is the key to her own transformation and to her own journey. The *Earthsea* cycle is not only the journey of Ged's life; it is also Le Guin's personal journey towards the revisioning of the myth. This personal transformation, according to Le Guin, is why she had to write *Tehanu:* 'My Earthsea trilogy is part [of the male tradition of fantasy] – that is why I had to write this fourth volume. Because I changed. I had to show the other side.' Le Guin acknowledges the tradition operating in the original trilogy as a 'great one, a strong one', but there was no escaping that it was a *male* tradition with set conventions as to who and what a Hero could be and do. To write in this tradition was to write from a male perspective, which was said to be inclusive of all humanity and so transcended gender. To do so was 'the only way to have one's writing perceived as above politics, as universally human'.[68] Men's writing, the male perspective and the male protagonist supposedly transcended gender; 'women's writing was trapped in it'.

Escaping this trap and subverting the male heroic fantasy tradition was an evolutionary process for Le Guin. She says in her essay 'The Fisherwoman's Daughter' that for some time she was not even aware she should change: 'I was free – born free, lived free. And for years that personal freedom allowed me to ignore the degree to which my writing was controlled and constrained by judgments and assumptions I thought were my own, but which were the internalized ideology of a male supremacist society.' She wrote her fiction about 'heroic adventure, high-tech futures, men in the halls of power', and 'men were the central characters, the women were peripheral, secondary'.[69]

Le Guin's women characters were brought in from the periphery when she learned 'what feminism, feminist literary theory, criticism, and practice had to give [her]'. Le Guin learned to write about women. Before this, she 'thought what men had written about women was the truth, was the true way to write about women'.[70] She began to question the traditional definitions of masculinity and femininity, and 'women readers [began to ask her] how come all the wise guys on the Isle of the Wise were guys?' No longer could she say that it didn't matter if Shevek was a man or not.[71] 'The artist who was above gender had been exposed as a man hiding in a raincoat. No serious writer could, or can, go on pretending to be genderless.' Before Le Guin could continue her hero-tale and complete Ged's journey, she had to wrestle 'with the angel of feminist consciousness'.[72]

The result of this evolutionary transformative wrestling was *Tehanu* which examines the mythic and heroic fantasy traditions from a feminist perspective, and as Michael Dirda says in his *Washington Post Book World* review: 'We are done with journeying and boys' adventures. This is a woman's world, a realm of socially imposed weakness and of male stupidity, of child abuse and evil with a human face.'[73]

The heroine, or the female hero, is different and yet akin to her better-known male counterpart, the hero. It should not be surprising that the monomythic hero, who seems to be 'inevitably, unfortunately macho', as a model of the self has come to be, for feminists, problematic at best. Daniel C. Noel, in his article 'Revisioning the Hero', cites Michel Zimmerman, a philosopher:

> Most feminists ... have concluded that Jung's and Neumann's history of individuation, despite its critique of the lopsidedness of patriarchal consciousness, is itself so colored by masculinist categories that it cannot be of help in developing an alternative concept of individuation.[74]

Annis Pratt offers one alternative concept of individuation, a female monomyth as it were, which she sees operating in literature by women. Pratt's female hero undergoes a social quest, whose stages are 'markedly different from Campbell'. This social quest is a search for self, 'in which the protagonist begins in alienation' and 'seeks integration into the human community to develop more fully'.[75]

This idea of integration marks Coline Covington's concept of the female hero which she explains in her article 'In Search of the Heroine'. Covington's concept needs to be described more fully, as it is the closest to what Le Guin is doing in *Tehanu*. Covington notes that the very concept of the heroine or female hero is relatively new and did not come into regular use until it appears at first 'in French and then in English classical language, where it evokes a classical world in which the concept would have been unknown'.[76]

Initially this female hero, according to Covington, might as well be male, as she is essentially a 'woman warrior whose battles take place within the male world. Although she is unusual in this respect, her sex is nevertheless incidental.' Prime examples of this type are such historical figures as Joan of Arc and Boudicca, the ancient British warrior queen. In addition to being warriors, female heroes are also 'characterized by sacrifice'. A familiar example is Antigone, 'who sacrifices her life to uphold patriarchy and [its supposedly] higher moral order'. That these women take action to preserve the old order make them heroic in the traditional monomythic sense.[77]

Another heroic role for the female hero is that of partner or partner-to-be of the real star, the hero. Penelope, the long-suffering wife of Odysseus, and Cinderella are two examples.[78] These are women who 'play a waiting role, resisting the flow of time, and whose aim is to be reunited with the hero'.[79] This role of the waiting partner is the one in which the reader first finds Tenar, the heroine of *Tehanu*. While the hero is out engaged in 'phallic activity' (as Covington puts it), what is the heroine doing at home or back at the castle – is she being 'anti-heroic'?

Covington asserts that having the king out and wandering around being heroic and the queen at home resting sets up a 'dynamic relation' between hero and heroine.[80] The hero, according to Covington, is seeking separation, or 'disintegration', as part of his process of individuation, of achieving self. The heroine is the counterbalance to this urge to separate: she is undergoing a 'process of individuation resulting in reparation and eventual reunion'.[81] The waiting process becomes, then, a time of 'incubation, in which inner processes are at work'.[82] At first this waiting time suggests dependence, but this dependency is transformed: the Heroine gains the capacity to make connections, to reintegrate.[83] And, of course, the heroine is not just sitting by the window; she is cooking, cleaning, caring for the children, tending the garden, telling stories – all of which are acts of connection, of reparation. Such acts are, of course, fairly traditional, but now they are visible. Their purpose and place and value are recognized: the Heroine is no less than the Hero.

The hero and the heroine, then, Covington argues, are mirror images of each other, two aspects of the self counterbalancing each other. Neither is truly only masculine or only feminine, and the 'importance of hero/heroine is that it can only be understood within a spectrum, the aspects functioning in dynamic inter-dependence. Both aspects must be valued together.' In the end, Covington argues against 'more of the "feminine" to counteract what is regarded as an imbalance of "masculine" consciousness'. Instead, she suggests that we need 'to incorporate the hero/heroine spectrum', and to acknowledge that, while nothing *seems* to happen while the hero is off slaying dragons, indeed things are happening for the heroine.[84]

Tehanu is, in essence, the story of what is happening while the hero is gone: it is the story of what the heroine does, 'the other side' of which Le Guin speaks. But it is more than that – as Le Guin uses feminism, not as it has been used all too often, in an exclusionary manner, but rather to include. Joanna Russ's female-only world of Whileaway in *The Female Man* is but one example. There are valid reasons, however, for an opposed group to choose exclusion as part of its mythos. Identity is one: an identity separate and distinct from the oppressor's. Recognition of obtained power is another: now the oppressed group *can* exclude; before it had to accept the beliefs imposed upon it. And why should the oppressed group trust the oppressor? Betrayal was too often included in the group's earlier mythos.

Le Guin, however, includes. Behind *Tehanu* and what happens to Tenar and Ged in the novel is all that has gone on before: Ged's quests across Earthsea, his freeing of Tenar from the tombs of Atuan, his struggles with the shadow, and journeys into and out of the realm of the dead, alone and later with Arren, the young prince whom Ged sends to Havnor to take a throne that has been empty for eight hundred years. The spiral of the journey uncurls in *Tehanu*, on the island of Gont, at the farmhouse of the widow of Farmer Flint, Tenar.

But is *Tehanu* just a case of Le Guin's feminism providing an answer to a traditionally male archetype, the hero? Is Ged the Wizard just one more face of the hero? In *Earthsea Revisioned*, Le Guin notes that even though she was, in the first three novels of the Earthsea cycle, working with the traditional monomyth, she was also pushing against its boundaries. She 'colored all the good guys brown or black' and 'only the villains were white'. Ged is dark-skinned, and by making him so she set him 'outside the whole European heroic tradition, in which heroes are not only male but white'. Ged was 'an Outsider, an Other ... like a woman', she says, like herself.[85] So, even though she used 'the pseudo-genderless male viewpoint of the heroic tradition',[86] Le Guin was beginning to subvert it, to take the myth and use it to advance an argument for her feminist perspective and the values associated with that perspective.

Ged's long spiral-shaped journeys dominate the first three novels – and here, in *Tehanu*, we have the end of the hero's journey, the return from the realm of the dead. But Ged is not returning in triumph to the island of Roke (the Isle of the Wise, where he was sent to school to learn the art-magic), where he is the Archmage of Earthsea, the island from which he began his last journey in *The Farthest Shore*; rather, Ged is coming home to Gont, the island of his birth, borne by a dragon, tired and bereft of all his power. He has come home to Gont, it seems, to die. Tenar thinks otherwise: 'Coming back from death must be a long journey – even on the dragon's back. It will take time. Time and quiet, silence, stillness. You have been hurt. You will be healed.'[87] Ged cannot see this: he tells her that he has no 'power, nothing'; he gave it all and now he is empty, at journey's end. She knows otherwise, that Ged's life hasn't ended. Rather it has been reduced in scale: from the entire world of Earthsea to one island, to one farm, to one widow and her burnt foster child, but still a life all the same.

The other journeys in *Tehanu* are the small journeys of life and death common to all. The novel opens with two such journeys. After seeing her daughter off to town, Tenar goes off 'down the lane' to the village with her friend Lark to see about the child left by the tinkers. Lark has taken the child into her house, severely burnt, beaten and raped. Tenar takes the child home to care for her, to raise the child as her daughter. The second such journey comes a year later, when a messenger comes to Oak Farm to tell Tenar that the Mage of Re Albi, Ogion, has sent for her. He is ill and needs her. Tenar sets off immediately with the child, whom she has named Therru:

> They went up the road [the messenger] had come down, northward and west into the hills of Gont Mountain ... They walked until the long summer twilight began to darken. They left the narrow road then and made camp in a dell down by the stream that ran quick and quiet, reflecting the pale evening sky between thickets of scrub willow. Goha[88] made a bed of dry grass and willow leaves, hidden among the thicket's like a hare's form ... When they woke the cold before the dawn, she made a small fire and heated a pan of water to make oatmeal gruel for the child and herself ... The east was brightening above the high, dark shoulder of the mountain when they set off again.[89]

At this journey's end, Tenar and Therru find Ogion ill in bed and dying. He doesn't need her care, but rather her help in dying: Ogion wants her to see him off on *his* last journey. The other journeys are the same: to see the new king, returning home on the king's ship, Ged coming back to save Tenar from the tinkers, Tenar going to see her friend Moss before she dies. There is the journey into sex as well, because until now Ged, as a mage, has been celibate. Tenar is Ged's guide and it is a journey they take together, as they journeyed together years before, in the tombs of Atuan: 'They were not at the fire. They were in the dark – in the dark hall. The dark passage. They had been there before, leading each other, following each other, in the darkness underneath the earth.'[90]

These small, private journeys, whether in the light or the dark, stand in sharp contrast to the great adventurous journeys in the first three Earthsea novels, journeys which now, in *Tehanu*, have become stories to be told and remembered, and in due time, myths. Shevek's journey-quest in *The Dispossessed*, while a personal act by a private individual, was done in public, and with public consequences. This is not the case in *Tehanu*. All Tenar's journeys, and Ged's now, are small, private and, in the greater scheme in which previous journeys operated, unimportant – or are they? As Le Guin puts it in *Earthsea Revisioned*, Tenar's journeys, and her actions related to them, aren't so much unimportant as 'invisible' – they are women's work:

> Women's work, as usual, is the maintenance of order and cleanliness, housekeeping, feeding and clothing people, childbearing, care of babies and children, nursing and healing of animals and people, care of the dying, funeral rites, those unimportant matters of life and death, not part of history, of story.[91]

Through her subversion of the typical hero, Le Guin argues for attention to be paid, for credit and recognition to be given, to the fact that life does go on while the men go off to battle. Otherwise life might not be there waiting for them when they return. Such work is essential and vital – without these 'obscure' acts, human life would be chaos. Pay attention, *Tehanu* argues; these acts are extremely important – and perhaps more so than rescuing a damsel in distress or recovering a grail.

But what of the Quest, and the sought-for grail? Shevek's grails are clear: the general temporal formula, the end of his people's exile and the renewal of his society's revolutionary promise. While seeking no promise to be renewed, Ged is seeking, in *The Tombs of Atuan*, the other half of the ring of Erreth-Akbe, with which he can make whole the Bond-Rune, 'the sign of dominion, the sign of peace'. Unless the rune is made whole, 'no king could rule well', and since the ring was lost, 'there have been no great kings in Havnor'.[92] In *The Farthest Shore*, Ged seeks the answer to the loss of magic and the testing of the prince to be this great king in Havnor, where no king has ruled over all of Earthsea for centuries. And in *Wizard*, Ged seeks to undo the evil he caused, to find the shadow he set loose and to come of age as a wizard.

Noble, heroic deeds, worthy of legend all. The king, Lebannen,[93] comes in search of Ged, to have at his coronation his companion

into and out of the realm of the dead. The mages on Roke seek a
new Archmage, with only one clue, 'a woman on Gont'. But Tenar
seeks to comfort the dying, to rescue the injured child, and to take
in and love the man (Ged) who saved her from the darkness of the
Tombs of Atuan twenty-five years ago. She seeks, as Covington
suggests, to reintegrate Ged into life, into her life, and she into his.
Their sexual union is the private reintegration, and the public is the
telling of Clearbrook and the other tenants of Oak Farm that she
has replaced '"the old master" with a hired hand'.[94]

Is this reintegration the grail of the story? Is it Therru's discovery
that she is more than the burnt, raped foster child Tenar has given a
home? One might argue that all of them – Tenar, Ged and Therru –
find a grail at the end, but I don't think so. True, Tenar and Ged,
who have fallen afoul of an evil mage, a follower of Cob whom Ged
defeated in *The Farthest Shore*, are rescued by Therru when she calls
Kalessin, the eldest of the dragons. And that the child is able to
summon the dragon is proof she could be the 'woman on Gont' for
whom the mages of Roke seek. But they did not find her – she
found herself. Therru has achieved recognition of who she really is:
she knows her true name, Tehanu. But while knowing one's true
name is of vital importance in Earthsea, even this was not a
particular goal sought by the child or either Ged or Tenar. What Le
Guin is doing is rescuing the monomyth, with its valuable
metaphors, from its patriarchal origins. She is, in effect, making the
myth of the Hero and the Quest into a human myth, and not an
exclusively male one.

So it is with the rest of the conventions of the monomyth: they,
too, have been overturned. As Le Guin says in *Earthsea Revisioned*:

> Certainly if we discard the axiom *what's important is done by
> men*, with its corollary *what women do isn't important*, then
> we've knocked a hole in the hero-tale, and a good deal may
> leak out. We may have lost quest, contest, and conquest as
> the plot, sacrifice as the key, victory or destruction as the
> ending; and the archetypes may change. There may be old
> men who aren't wise, witches who aren't wicked, mothers
> who don't devour. There may be no public triumph of good
> over evil, for in this new world what's good or bad,
> important or unimportant, hasn't been decided yet, if ever.
> Judgment is not referred up to the wise men. History is no
> longer about great men.[95]

Nor has history ever been so, Le Guin would argue – rather it has been told *by* men *about* men. And, as Le Guin is presenting in *Tehanu*, 'The important choices and decisions may be obscure ones, not recognized or applauded by society.'[96]

By calling attention to these obscure choices and decisions, performed by the invisible in a book that subverts the traditional male role, Le Guin is also suggesting that such acts aren't – except for childbearing and nursing – the exclusive domain of women. As Nancy Chodorow points out in *Reproduction of Mothering*, the reason that women are the ones who mother, who are the primary care-givers, is not biological. Mothering, fathering – 'sex, as we know it – gender, identity, sexual desire and fantasy, concepts of childhood' – are all social products. Our sex-gender system is an artificial construct, 'a set of arrangements by which the biological raw material of human sex and procreation is shaped by human social interventions and satisfied in a conventional manner'.[97] Traditional gender roles can be seen, then, as fiction, a myth, a construct, which can overturned, revised, subverted and eventually rejected, through feminism:

> Therru, the burned child, will grow up to be fully sexed, but she's been ungendered by the rape that destroys her 'virtue' and the mutilation that destroys her beauty. She has nothing left of the girl men want girls to be. It's all been burned away. As for Ged and Tenar, they're fully sexed too, but on the edge of old age, when conventional gendering grants him some last flings and grants her nothing but modest grandmotherhood. And the dragon defies gender entirely. There are male and female dragons in the earlier books, but I don't know if Kalessin, the Eldest, is male or female or both or something else. I choose not to know. The deepest found-ation of the order of oppression is gendering, which names the male normal, dominant, active, and the female other, subject, passive. To begin to imagine freedom, the myths of gender, like the myths of race, have to be exploded and discarded.[98]

Of course, the monomyth is no less 'a construct, which may be changed; an idea which may be rethought, made more true, more honest'.[99] And at the end of *Tehanu* Ged and Tenar have renounced the heroism of the old tradition 'and have discarded something of the old male and female roles'. Doing so leaves them helpless

'against the defenders of the old tradition'.[100] The evil new mage of
Re Albi has ensorcelled both of them and is leading them, as if they
were dogs, up into the hills, to be killed. But in somewhat of a *deus
ex machina* fashion (this is a fantasy, after all), Therru has called to
the dragon Kalessin and he has come. The evil is cleansed by fire,
thus completing the overturning of the old order: a woman, a girl-
child, has the power once only held by the male wizards and she
has used it to destroy those who would deny such power is possible
in a woman.

The standard conclusion to fairy tales, 'and they lived happily
ever after', is not, of course, the conclusion for Tenar and Ged and
Therru – rather it is only a possibility. They do form a family and
settle in the house left vacant by the death of Ogion, who was the
mentor and teacher for both Tenar and Ged years before. As Tenar
says, 'I think we can live there.' But more than just the creation of
this tiny community has happened. The new Archmage has been
found – and she is a girl-child, 'the woman of Gont' in the future –
or is she? In the short novel *Dragonfly,* Le Guin provides a postscript
which indicates Earthsea's future is even more open that *Tehanu*
suggests. The title character is the daughter of a once-rich family
fallen on hard times, on the island of Way. The local witch, Rose,
who gives Dragonfly her true name, Irian, tells the young woman
she has a power in her, but of what kind and what she is to do with
it, the witch does not know.

Some years after Dragonfly is named, a failed wizard, Ivory, finds
her and persuades her to go to Roke, to the Great House, the School
of the master mages, and there she can find out who she is and
what this unknown power is. Ivory thinks to do this to get revenge
on the mages for failing him, as no woman is allowed inside the
School: 'A she-mage! Now that would change everything, all the
rules!'[101] After all, these are uncertain times in Earthsea. It was just
last autumn that, contrary to all custom, the king crowned himself,
as the old Archmage, Ged, bereft of his power, wouldn't come.
Does this mean the king doesn't 'rightly hold the throne'? And
what of this 'woman on Gont'? Since the mages on Roke cannot
answer this riddle, does this mean the 'dark years [will] come
again, when there was no rule of justice and wizardry was used for
evil ends'?[102]

Ivory foregoes his plan for revenge and tells Irian how she can
enter the Great House, disguised as a man. At the door, he leaves
her and, as Irian gives her name to the Doorkeeper and enters, the

magical disguise 'dropped away like a cobweb'. A woman has entered the School, causing immediate dissension among the nine master mages; she is a young woman, as the Doorkeeper and the village witch both noticed, with an incomplete name. Irian is only part of her true name. When the Doorkeeper is challenged by the Changer as to why, the answer is that not only is she here to find out what she needs to know, but 'also what [the mages] need to know'.[103] Irian stays, living in the Grove of the Patterner, and as the mages split in disagreement, the Summoner takes action to drive her out: 'that there may be peace and order, and for the sake of the balance of all things, I bid you now to leave this island'.[104]

But there is no going back, no undoing the changes. The Summoner is destroyed, and Irian is revealed, as Tehanu was, to also be a dragon, and it is to them she must go to seek her other name. The doors of the Great House are to be opened to men *and* to women. Female magic has been (or soon will be) recognized as 'necessary and life-giving', and the world of Earthsea will be shaped and named by a woman – whether she is Irian or Tehanu remains to be seen. '[A] new world seems dawning', for sure.

In this new world, unlike the traditional monomyth, neither hero nor heroine is dominant at the end – rather the new relationship will be one of interdependence, on both public and private levels. In *Dragonfly*, it is public: the School on the Isle of the Wise will be open to all, and thus even the definition of the Wise will change for all of Earthsea. In *Tehanu*, the interdependence is personal: Tenar and Ged will rely on each other. And Tenar and Ged and their dragon-child are where Le Guin says she wanted them to be, not safe, but free.[105] Like Shevek, who returns to an Anarres unlike the one he left, Tenar and Ged find themselves in a world in which there are 'new things to be learned, no doubt'. Things have been turned upside down, as Shevek tells Ketho, the Hainishman who asks to accompany Shevek planetside:

> Things are ... a little broken loose, on Anarres. That's what my friends on the radio have been telling me about. It was our purpose all along – our Syndicate, this journey of mine – to shake up things, to stir up, to break some habits, to make people ask questions. To behave like anarchists! All this has been going on while I was gone. So, you see, nobody is quite sure what happens next. And if you land with me, even more gets broken loose.[106]

But Shevek has been essentially alone on his quest, with its double grail; Takver, his partner, remained behind with their children as he followed his hero-path. While in many ways Shevek is working against the standard mythic conventions, he is still operating within the general framework, as Ged does in the first three Earthsea novels. The subversion of the monomyth is incomplete in both *The Dispossessed* and *A Wizard of Earthsea, The Tombs of Atuan* and *The Farthest Shore*. That Shevek does, to some degree, fit Campbell's description of the modern hero attests to this: a man, acting alone to transform his society, as he 'carries the cross of the redeemer – not in the bright moments of the tribe's great victories, but in the silences of his personal despair'.[107]

But Ged and Tenar are fundamentally different, and their actions, and those of Therru and Irian, *are* going to transform their world of Earthsea. Campbell speaks of a man, alone. In *Tehanu*, there is a man and a woman, not alone, but interdependent, together. Thus the more complete retelling and rethinking of the monomyth is *Tehanu:* a heroine and a hero, small journeys of the mundane, a defeated and powerless wizard, and an abused girl-child who is possibly the new Archmage. *Dragonfly*, Le Guin's postscript, adds and reinforces this retelling and rethinking: doors once closed are open, what was once a male-only community is transformed. Thus, while true journey is return, what one returns to is *not* the place from which the journey began. There is no circle to be closed, but an open-ended spiral that leads on, even though it is not finished. That Le Guin has a postscript to Earthsea, with an indefinite and open ending, attests to this. Whether she will write another Earthsea story is uncertain; even so, the characters, their lives, their world continues. Actions have consequences, which will be played out. Process becomes what is important, not product. There is no 'happily ever after', no Edenic new world. Le Guin has more than broken things loose; rather she has broken them apart and has rearranged them. The monomyth thus becomes a way to argue for what before has been off-stage, unimportant, invisible, and for what it has always argued for, the true journey into the self, into knowledge.

Notes

1. Ursula K. Le Guin, 'Myth and Archetype in Science Fiction', in *Language of the Night: Essays on Fantasy and Science Fiction*, rev edn, ed. Susan Wood (New York: HarperCollins, 1992), pp. 74–75.

2. Ursula K. Le Guin, 'Prophets and Mirrors: Science Fiction as a Way of Seeing', *Living Light: A Christian Education Review*, 7, Fall 1970, p. 112.

3. Ursula K. Le Guin, *Buffalo Gals & Other Animal Presences* (New York: Dutton, 1994), p. 75.

4. Joseph Campbell, with Bill Moyers, *The Power of Myth*, ed. Betty Sue Flowers (New York: Doubleday, 1988), p. 163.

5. W. B. Sanford, Foreword, in G. Karl Galinsky, *The Herakles Theme: The Adaptions of The Hero in Literature from Homer to the Twentieth Century* (Totowa, NJ: Rowman & Littlefield, 1972), p. ix.

6. Michael Alexander, Introduction, in *Beowulf*, trans. Michael Alexander (London: Penguin, 1973), pp. 15–16.

7. Campbell, *Power of Myth*, p. 166.

8. Ibid., p. 60.

9. Le Guin, 'The Child and the Shadow', in *Language of the Night*, p. 59.

10. Carl Jung, *Psychology and Religion* (New Haven, CT: Yale University Press), pp. 63–64.

11. Joseph Campbell, Editor's Introduction, in Carl Jung, *The Portable Jung*, ed. Joseph Campbell, trans. R. F. C. Hull (New York: Viking, 1971), p. xxxi.

12. Carl Jung, *Symbols of Transformation*, trans. R. F. C. Hull, 2nd edn (Princeton: Princeton University Press, 1956), p. 171.

13. Ibid., p. 202.

14. Ibid., p. 205.

15. Shirley Park Lowry, *Familiar Mysteries: The Truth in Myth* (New York: Oxford University Press, 1982), p. 78.

16. Joseph Campbell, *The Hero with a Thousand Faces* (Princeton: Princeton University Press, 1968), p. 30.

17. Erich Neumann, quoted in Daniel C. Noel, 'Revisioning the Hero', in Christine Downing, ed., *Mirrors of the Self: Archetypal Images that Shape Your Life* (Los Angeles: Jeremy P. Tarcher, 1991), p. 206.

18. Joseph Henderson, 'Ancient Myths and Modern Man', in Carl Jung, ed., *Man and His Symbols* (Garden City, NJ: Doubleday, 1964), p. 112.

19. Ursula K. Le Guin, *Earthsea Revisioned* (Cambridge, MA: Children's Literature New England, 1993), pp. 4–7.

20. Nancy Chodorow, *The Reproduction of Mothering: Psychoanalysis and the Sociology of Gender* (Berkeley: University of California Press, 1978), p. 103.

21. Campbell, *Hero*, p. 319.

22. Northrup Frye, *The Secular Scripture: A Study of the Structure of Romance* (Cambridge, MA: Harvard University Press, 1976), p. 67.

23. Lowry, *Familiar Mysteries*, p. 88.

24. Campbell, *Hero*, p. 58.

25. Campbell, *Power*, p. 152.

26. Campbell, *Hero*, p. 319.

27. Ibid., p. 97.

28. Ibid., p. 101.

29. Ibid., p. 111.

30. Ibid., p. 133.

31. Ibid., p. 136.

32. Ibid., p. 129.

33. Ibid., p. 193.

34. Peter Brigg, 'The Archetype of the Journey', in Joseph Olander and Martin Greenberg, eds, *Ursula Le Guin* (New York: Taplinger, 1979), p. 36.

35. Jessie L. Weston, *The Quest of the Holy Grail*, reprint of 1913 edn (New York: Haskell House, 1973), p. 18.

36. Jung, ed., *Man and his Symbols*, p. 112.

37. Frye, *Secular Scripture*, p. 174.

38. Jessie L. Weston, *From Ritual to Romance* (Garden City, NJ: Doubleday, 1957), p. 20.

39. Weston, *Quest*, pp. 2–3.

40. Campbell, *Hero*, p. 193.

41. Ibid., p. 356.

42. Lowry, *Familiar Mysteries*, p. 121.

43. Ibid., p. 120.

44. Brigg, 'Archetype', p. 36.

45. Ibid.

46. Le Guin, 'The Child and the Shadow', in *Language of the Night*, pp. 61–62.

47. Susanne Langer, *Philosophy in a New Key: a Study in the Symbolism of Reason, Rite, and Art*, 3rd edn (Cambridge, MA: Harvard University Press, 1957), p. 135.

48. James Britton, *Language and Learning*, 2nd edn (Portsmouth, NH: Boynton/Cook, 1993), p. 12.

49. Bernard Selinger, *Le Guin and Identity in Contemporary Fiction* (Ann Arbor, MI: UMI Research Press, 1988), p. 125.

50. Elizbeth Cummins, *Understanding Ursula K. Le Guin*, (Columbia, SC: University of South Carolina Press, 1990), pp. 109–10.

51. Ursula K. Le Guin, *The Dispossessed* (New York: Harper & Row, 1974), p. 27.

52. Selinger, *Le Guin and Identity*, p. 111.

53. Le Guin, *The Dispossessed*, pp. 300, 301.

54. Cummins, *Understanding Le Guin*, p. 120.

55. Campbell, *Hero*, pp. 218, 243.

56. Ibid., p. 387.

57. Ibid., p. 388.

58. Ibid., p. 391.

59. Cummins, *Understanding Le Guin*, p. 122.

60. Dennis C. Sullivan and Larry L. Tifft, 'Possessed Sociology and Le Guin's *The Dispossessed:* From Exile to Anarchism', in Joe DeBolt and Barry N. Malzberg, eds, *Ursula K. Le Guin: Voyager to Inner Lands and Outer Space* (Port Washington: Kennikat Press, 1979), pp. 196–97.

61. Brigg, 'Archetype', p. 63.

62. Campbell, *Transformations of Myth through Time* (New York: Harper & Row, 1990), p. 1.

63. James W. Bittner, *Approaches to the Fiction of Ursula K. Le Guin* (Ann Arbor, MI: UMI Research Press, 1984), p. 6.

64. Ursula K. Le Guin, 'The Carrier Bag Theory of Fiction', in *Dancing at the Edge of the World: Thoughts on Words, Women, Places* (New York: Grove Press, 1989), pp. 168, 169.

65. Le Guin, 'Science Fiction and Mrs Brown', in *Language of the Night*, p. 108.

66. Le Guin, 'Dreams Must Explain Themselves', in *Language of the Night*, p. 46.

67. Raymond Thompson, 'Jungian Patterns in Ursula K. Le Guin's *The Farthest Shore*', in William Coyne, ed., *Aspects of Fantasy: Selected Essays from the Second International Conference on the Fantastic in Literature and Film* (Westport, CT: Greenwood Press, 1986), p. 189.

68. Le Guin, *Earthsea Revisioned*, p. 6.

69. Le Guin, 'The Fisherwoman's Daughter', in *Dancing*, pp. 233–34.

70. Ibid., p. 234.

71. The seeds of this change are, however, visible in *The Dispossessed*. The founder of Odonianism, the social philosophy of Anarres, Shevek's world, was a woman, Odo. Gvarab, a physicist and one of Shevek's teachers in Abbenay, was a woman. Her ideas on simultaneity were crucial in the development of Shevek's general temporal theory. And, of course, Anarresti women were not the second-class citizens their sisters were on Urras, the homeworld.

72. Le Guin, *Earthsea Revisioned*, p. 11.

73 . Michael Dirda, 'The Twilight of an Age of Magic', *Washington Post Book World*, 25 February 1990, p. 9.

74. Michel Zimmerman, quoted in Noel, 'Revisioning the Hero', p. 207.

75. Annis Pratt, 'The Female Hero', in Christine Downing, ed., *Mirrors of the Self: Archetypal Images that Shape Your Life* (Los Angeles: Jeremy P. Tarcher, 1991), p. 213.

76. Coline Covington, 'In Search of the Heroine', *Journal of Analytical Psychology*, 1989, p. 243.

77. Ibid.

78. Ibid., pp. 243–44.

79. Ibid., p. 244.

80. Ibid., p. 246.

81. Ibid.

82. Ibid., p. 247.

83. Ibid., p. 251.

84. Ibid., p. 253.

85. Le Guin, *Earthsea Revisioned*, p. 8.

86. Ibid., p. 12.

87. Ursula K. Le Guin, *Tehanu: The Last Book of Earthsea* (New York: Bantam Books, 1990), p. 79.

88. In Earthsea, it is customary to have a use-name, which is commonly known and used by all, and a true name. The use-name usually is that of an animal or a geographical feature that has some connection to the individual. The true name is given 'by one of true power, a wizard or a mage, because that is their power, naming'. The true name is only given in 'utmost need and trust' (*Tehanu*, pp. 10–11). Knowing a person's true name could give power to the knower. Only a rare few, such as the king, used their true names openly. Tenar's use-name on Gont is Goha, which is also the name of a 'little white web-spinning spider', thus acknowledging that Tenar is 'white-skinned and small and a good spinner of goat's wool and sheep-fleece' (p. 1).

89. Le Guin, *Tehanu*, pp. 7–8.

90. Ibid., p. 197.

91. Le Guin, *Earthsea Revisioned*, pp. 15–16.

92. Ursula K. Le Guin, *The Tombs of Atuan* (New York: Bantam Books, 1971), p. 110.

93. Arren is the young prince who, in *The Farthest Shore*, accompanies Ged on his journey into the realm of the dead. Upon Arren's coronation as King of all the Isles, the King of Earthsea, he chooses to use his true name, Lebannen, publicly.

94. Le Guin, *Tehanu*, p. 212.

95. Le Guin, *Earthsea Revisioned*, p. 13.

96. Ibid.

97. Chodorow, *Reproduction of Mothering*, p. 8.

98. Le Guin, *Earthsea Revisioned*, p. 24.

99. Ibid., p. 17.

100. Ibid., p. 19.

101. Ursula K. Le Guin, *Dragonfly*, in Robert Silverberg, ed., *Legends: Short Novels by the Masters of Modern Fantasy* (New York: Tor, 1998), p. 355.

102. Ibid., p. 361.

103. Ibid., p. 368.

104. Ibid., p. 394.

105. Le Guin, *Earthsea Revisioned*, p. 26.

106. Le Guin, *The Dispossessed*, p. 336.

107. Campbell, *Hero*, p. 391.

CHAPTER THREE
Which Way to Eden?

According to Janice Antczak, in *Science Fiction: The Mythos of a New Romance*, science fiction 'gives clear expression to the inter-connectedness of myth and literature' in that 'the conventions of the science fiction story express the mythic archetypes of the quest in the idiom of the space age'. Antczak is arguing that, as a genre, science fiction is displaying 'the elements of the monomyth of the hero and the quest'.[1] But in equating the entire genre with the monomyth, it does seem Antczak paints with a rather broad brush. As seen in Chapter Two, there are other myths at work in science fiction, and in fantasy, as Le Guin illustrates in *The Dispossessed* and in *Earthsea*. In addition to the monomyth, of which *Earthsea, The Dispossessed* and *Always Coming Home* are all expressions, there is a much older myth being expressed in the latter two novels: the myth of utopia.

Before examining *The Dispossessed* and *Always Coming Home* as contemporary expressions of the utopian myth, it is necessary to look first at utopia both as myth and as literary genre. With both aspects of utopia defined, I will examine the connections between myth and genre (in this instance, science fiction, which many have said evolved from utopian literature). Because the author is creating an alternative society as a critique of his or her own, a literary utopia is inherently rhetorical. Given this, I will examine Le Guin's utopias,[2] with particular emphasis given to *Always Coming Home* as it is the most recent and the closest to what she believes a utopia should be. It is my contention that Le Guin's choice of sources for her alternative societies becomes part of her argument. Furthermore, as she did with the monomyth, Le Guin is again working inside and against the established generic conventions of utopian literature. This subversion and inversion again will become part of her argument as the myth itself becomes rhetorical.

The Myth of Utopia

The root myth of utopia is the myth of the Golden Age, when humans supposedly inhabited a perfect world as a gift from the gods.[3] Utopian narratives are human constructs attempting to recapture this mythic perfect world, the ideal human past – each one rhetorical, an argument to convince the reader that this is the way to recover lost Eden, and more importantly, this is what is wrong with the way things are now. Utopian narratives thus are very much things of their time, as they reflect each age's interpretation of the perennial human longing for an ideal society. According to Robert Elliott, in *The Shape of Utopia: Studies in a Literary Genre*, both the Golden Age and utopian narratives are 'projections of man's wishful fantasies, answering to the longings for the good life which have moved him since history began'.[4] The very term 'utopia' itself, used by St Thomas More in 1516 for *his* utopian narrative, suggests the fantastical fictional quality of the concept. Utopia is from the Greek: 'eu topos' or good place, and 'ou topos', no place – no good place, except in human fantasies and myths of the Golden Age.

The Golden Age as myth incorporates a complex of other ideas including the Islands of the Blessed, Earthly Paradise, the Happy Otherworld and the Fortunate Isles.[5] In all these versions of Eden, human life is perfect: there are no wants, no cares, no unfulfilled desires: 'And out of the ground the Lord God made to grow every tree that is pleasant to the sight and good for food …' (Genesis 2:9).[6] There are *some* responsibilities: humankind has to till the garden and name and care for the cattle, the birds of the air and the beasts of the field, but even so, it is the perfect life. The garden requires no preparation, no sowing of seed, no breaking of ground. Nor is humankind separate from the divine: they can walk and talk together 'in the garden in the cool of the day'. It is this, this total belonging to the entire universe that is longed for and evoked in the stories of lost paradise.

But paradise, the Golden Age, exists 'outside of history, usually before history begins'.[7] Utopia is different; as Robert Elliott says, even though it is connected to the Golden Age myth:

> Utopia is the application of man's reason and his will to the myth [of the Golden Age], … is man's efforts to work out imaginatively what happens – or what might happen –

> when the primal longings embodied in the myth confront
> the principle of reality ... In this effort man no longer merely
> dreams of a divine state in some remote time; he assumes
> the role of creator himself.[8]

In utopia, men and women are not just garden and wildlife
stewards, having merely to reach up and pull breakfast from the
nearest tree. Rather, the world, with all its messiness, still exists,
still needs and demands attention. Indeed, the world is 'a necessary
condition of utopia's existence'.[9] There has to be a non-utopian
society, as it were (often our own – or certainly the writer's own),
against which utopia is juxtaposed as the better, more humane,
alternative.

To present this juxtaposition of utopia and the less-preferred
'real world', a dialectic in and of itself, utopian narrative has
developed certain generic conventions. According to Elizabeth
Cummins, in *Understanding Ursula K. Le Guin*, the story usually
begins with a journey and a traveller. The journey may be through
time or space, over the sea or across a desolate region of the world.
It is often accidental: the traveller, who is from contemporary
society, may run afoul of a natural disaster, pirates, or a faulty plane
or spaceship. Regardless of what happens to the traveller, for him
or her the journey has ended apparently in More's 'ou topos'. He or
she is far removed from the real world,[10] and is an outsider in this
new society.[11]

To understand this new society, the traveller invariably encounters a utopian citizen who becomes her guide. The tour of utopia,
so to speak, becomes the bulk of the narrative. Using expository
passages, like those between the traveller and the guide, the
utopia is presented and explained.[12] Utopia is, of course, a better
society than the one from which the traveller came, and it is to
this understanding that the guide converts the traveller.[13] This
conversion is usually amicable. While the traveller may exchange
arguments with her guide, there is little conflict or real disagreement. Utopia *is* better; how could it not be? In essence, as Jean
Pfaelzer says in her article 'Response: What Happened to History?',
the traditional utopian narrative presents a didactic picture, a
sociopolitical parable.[14] Utopia, then, is not a 'prescription for
immediate consumption', but rather 'a statement about a kind of
life that would be better than the one we have – one which could
be achieved if people have the will to achieve it'.[15] Utopia is,

however, more than a statement; it is a dialogue, a dialogue between the traveller and the guide, between utopia and the traveller's society. In a utopian narrative, dialectic is not only a rhetorical device, it is a trope, a metaphor for utopia itself – an answer to what ails us, reached through dialogue.

These dialogues, these utopian narratives, pre-date the term's sixteenth-century coinage, with More's classical predecessors generally considered to be Plato's *Republic* and *Critias*, Xenophon's *Cryopaedia* and Plutarch's *Lycurgus*. Less well-known in the West are such contemporary works as Confucius's fifth century BC *LiChi*, about a Grand Commonwealth, presenting a typical utopian conception of the just state. Other notable non-Western works include the *Tao Te Ching*, which contains a 'formula for the development of the ideal community', the fourth-century *Mo Tzu*, with its ideal of good government, and the more modern *Great Commonwealth* of Kang Youwei (1889). Even twentieth-century rivals Mao and Chiang Kai-shek could be said to be advocating utopian ideal states.[16]

Of course, we may be more familiar with the utopias in the Western literary tradition. More's successors included Tommaso Campanella's *City of the Sun* (1602), Bacon's *The New Atlantis* (1627) and Swift's *Gulliver's Travels* (1726). Like More, his successors use narrative, a different rhetorical approach from Plato's use of a fictional structured dialogue with a physical setting.[17] These and other utopian narratives of the seventeenth and eighteenth centuries 'made great use of itinerant sailors' and 'previously unknown islands or barely explored continents'. They were further distinguished by 'their attempt to explicate the past or to criticize the present, not anticipate the future'.[18] In the nineteenth century, utopian writers began a tradition of anticipating the future. Samuel Butler's *Erewhon* (1872), Edward Bellamy's *Looking Backward* (1888) and William Morris's *News from Nowhere* (1890) are prime examples of this approach to utopia.

At the turn of the century, H. G. Wells further revised utopian narratives by displacing his utopias in time, with *The Time Machine* (1895) as perhaps the most famous example, followed by *A Modern Utopia* (1905), *Men Like Gods* (1922) and *The Shape of Things to Come* (1933). More contemporary examples include Aldous Huxley's *The Island* (1962), Robert Heinlein's *Farnham's Freehold* (1964) and Frederick Pohl's *The Age of the Pussyfoot* (1969). Utopias on other planets include Arthur C. Clarke's *Against the Fall of the Night* (1953), Le Guin's *The Dispossessed* (1974) and Russ's *The Female Man* (1975).[19]

Wells is also credited with introducing the anti-utopian or dystopian narrative with his *When the Sleeper Awakes* (1899), a cautionary tale warning against the concentration of money and power in the hands of the few. This element of warning against the evil that may be coming is prevalent in such dystopic works as Zamyatin's *We* (1921), Huxley's *Brave New World* (1932), Orwell's *1984* (1949), Bradbury's *Fahrenheit 451* (1953), John Brunner's *Stand on Zanzibar* (1968) and Atwood's *The Handmaid's Tale* (1986). Many of these twentieth-century dystopias caricatured the 'corrected' state, which is stable and complete, and in which nothing happens that is not designed or expected. Often the stability and happiness come at the cost of human freedom.[20] Others, in particular those by Brunner, present the state or society without stability, without control, and as one in which any planning has been done without sufficient thought. Many of these 'unstable state' dystopias appeared in the 1960s and 1970s as ecological disaster tales, warning of the perils of such twentieth-century problems as overpopulation, the green-house effect and pollution. The 1970s and 1980s saw a revitalizing of the form. Novelists such as Le Guin and Lessing put the story ahead of the theory, creating human drama and less dogma. Lessing and Le Guin wrote post-dystopian or critical utopias, or open-ended utopias, and overcame the narrative stasis traditionally associated with utopian fiction through 'ambiguity, contradiction, and fragmentation'.[21] They present a dynamic society in process and, more importantly, create in the form an experience of change recognizable by its complexity and pain.

As Dominic Baker-Smith says in his article 'The Escape from the Cave: Thomas More and the Vision of Utopia', utopian fiction is 'fundamentally concerned with the relation between imagined and experienced worlds'.[22] Thus the connection between utopian fiction and science fiction comes as no surprise. According to Darko Suvin in *Positions and Presuppositions in Science Fiction*, utopian fiction is a root of science fiction.[23] Their meanings and territories overlap, as Suvin illustrates in his singular prose:

> [Utopian fiction is] a literary genre or verbal construct whose necessary and sufficient conditions and the presence of a particular quasi-human community whose sociopolitical institutions and norms and individual relationships are organized by a more perfect principle than in the author's community, this construction based on estrangement arising

out of an alternative historical hypothesis ... Utopias do not have to be perfect places, rather more perfect.[24]

Utopia is an historically alternative wishful construct ... out of this world.[25]

[Science fiction is] a literary genre or verbal construct whose necessary and sufficient conditions and the presence of a particular quasi-human community whose sociopolitical institutions and norms and individual relationships are the presence and interaction of estrangement and cognition, and whose main device is an imaginative framework alternative to the author's implied empirical environment.[26]

Utopian and science fiction definitely blur, blend and overlap. Since utopia, by definition, is supposed to be 'remote or well-isolated from the real world to which it proposes an alternative',[27] then, today, utopia has to be found in science fiction – in the future or the past, or on another planet. Writers no longer have the luxury of the unexplored vastness of Africa or Antarctica, or lost Pacific islands. Suvin goes on to argue that utopia, which is indeed a putative ancestor of science fiction as a literary genre, can now be said to be 'the sociopolitical subgenre of science fiction'. Utopian fiction is now often thought of as part of social science fiction – 'science fiction restricted to sociopolitical analysis'.[28] A look at the *utopian intention,* as defined by Annegret Wiemer in her essay 'Utopia and Science Fiction: A Contribution to their Generic Description', supports this view. The utopian intention is 'the explicit or implicit gesture of social critique the utopia is directing toward its contemporary world'.[29] Science fiction, Wiemer argues, is also seen as being social commentary or didactic literature, with science the added element.[30] As utopian fiction, she says, science fiction 'summons a whole array of additional rhetorical devices in order to enhance the pseudo-authenticity of its fictional design'.[31] It seems that contemporary utopian fiction has become, willy-nilly, part of science fiction. The generic boundaries define the same territories.

It is in this common territory that Le Guin operates, particularly in a subgenre, the feminist science fiction utopia. But as she did with the monomyth, Le Guin is using the generic conventions of the utopian narrative and the assumptions of the utopian myth as a way to invert and subvert them, to make them serve her argument. She makes this point in the introduction to *The Left Hand of Darkness* in which she speaks of one of the metaphors used by science fiction as being the alternative society. Utopia for her is a metaphor for science fiction, a way to describe a thought-experiment. Le Guin explains this by example: 'Let's say (says Mary Shelley) that a young doctor creates a human being in his laboratory; let's say (says Philip K. Dick) that the Allies lost the Second World War ... Such a thought-experiment, such a use of metaphor, is not meant to predict the future.' Rather, Le Guin argues, it describes 'reality, the present world'.[32] She notes that *The Left Hand of Darkness*, while set many centuries from now, isn't meant to suggest that 'in a millennium or so we will all be androgynous', but rather that 'at certain odd times of the day in certain weathers we already are'.[33] Le Guin, then, is using the feminist utopia to describe and comment on how she sees us as we are and by reimagining and rethinking the utopian myth, what we might be or should be and perhaps are becoming.

Both of Le Guin's utopian novels, *The Dispossessed* and *Always Coming Home*, are considered to be feminist utopias, the latter more so than the former.[34] Both are also, I would argue, rhetorical texts. Of course, all utopian fiction is rhetorical, as it is social critique, commentary and argument. But what I want to examine here is the particular argument that Le Guin is making – an argument that evolved from *The Dispossessed* in 1974 to *Always Coming Home* in 1984. As feminist thought transformed her use of the monomyth in the *Earthsea* cycle and *The Dispossessed*, so it transformed her use of utopian myth. Both transformations make the myths rhetorical: they become arguments for what Cornel West describes succinctly as a society based on 'nonmarket values – love, service to others', a 'love ethic'.[35] Such a society would reject binary thinking, excessive competition and inherent inequality; it would embrace alternative answers, co-operation, collaboration and community. As Roslynn Haynes says in her essay 'Science, Myth and Utopia', such a society's goal would be the 'establishment of *communitas* ... capable of nurturing individuals in their individual freedom'.[36]

Le Guin's use of utopian myth, more so than her use of the monomyth, is an overt argument for this alternative to the late twentieth-century American way of life. In addition to utopia, she is working rhetorically with certain American cultural myths, particularly in *Always Coming Home*. But as she does with the monomyth, Le Guin first subverts the myth and its conventions, and then reimagines and reinterprets its meaning. By doing so, she asks questions. What is a utopia? What journey are we to take to get there? How will this journey change us? How will we understand ourselves as human beings once this journey to this other utopia has been made?

In *The Dispossessed*, Le Guin inverts the traditional conventions of utopian narrative. Shevek, the protagonist, is not a traveller to utopia; instead he travels away from and then back to utopia. He is the heart of the novel, not, as in traditional utopian narrative, the traveller from the outside. Le Guin further subverts the traditional narrative in that it is utopia that is in danger and suffering internal conflict. In the traditional utopian narrative, there is little or no conflict. The long expository passages of dialogue between the traveller and guide are usually very amiable. The traveller's conversion is through agreement, not coercion.

The Dispossessed

While Le Guin is obviously, as science fiction author and critic Brian Aldiss notes in *Trillion Year Spree: The History of Science Fiction*, writing 'explicit social commentary ... utopian fiction in a specific tradition – that of anarchist utopianism from Thoreau to Paul Goodman, the anti-centralized state', she is not presenting *The Dispossessed* as Eden.[37] The novel's subtitle, 'An Ambiguous Utopia', emphasizes that this is not a guide to Eden, and the conditions on Anarres – drought, austerity, rationing, power struggles, voluntary labor drafts necessitating long familial separations, and so on – paint an equally non-Edenic picture. Indeed, as Keng, the Terran ambassador points out to Shevek, Urras, the oppressive capitalist mother-planet the Anarresti fled generations ago, is far more like Eden: 'Urras is the kindliest, most various, most beautiful of all the inhabited worlds. It is the world that comes as close as any could to Paradise.'[38]

This encounter with the Terran ambassador is one of the key places where Le Guin uses inversion of the utopian generic conventions to make her argument. The traveller from utopia has met another traveller, albeit one from a dystopia, as the ambassador's Terra is far from paradise. Her Earth

> is a ruin ... A planet spoiled by the human species ... There are no forests left on [her] Earth. The air is grey, the sky is

grey, it is always hot ... it is still habitable, but not as this world [Urras] is. This is a living world, a harmony. [Hers] is a discord ... Odonians chose a desert ... Terrans made a desert ...[39]

The only way the Terrans survived this nightmare, the ambassador tells Shevek, was the only 'way it could be done: by total centralization. Total control over the use of every acre of land, every scrap of metal, every ounce of fuel. Total rationing, birth control, euthanasia, universal conscription into the labor force.'[40]

Total centralization, with the super-state in total control of all aspects of life, has been, of course, advocated both as a utopia and a dystopia in the genre's history. As Aldiss describes the Platonic ideal state in *Trillion Year Spree*, Plato's *Republic* was not a benign democracy. There is a stratified class structure, with the virtuous philosopher-kings in control, served by a guardian class of public officials, workers and tradesmen, and the slaves. 'Private property has been abolished and the state controls marriage and child-bearing.'[41] The individual is not Plato's concern; rather it is the city: 'Our purpose in founding the city was not to make any one class in it surpassingly happy, but to make the city as a whole as happy as possible.'[42]

More's *Utopia* is no more benign – indeed to our twentieth-century sensibilities, it sounds totalitarian, as 'citizens have to fit into its pattern as into a town plan'. More's Utopians all wear the same cloak of the same color when they go outside. All the cities on the island are exactly alike: 'whoso knoweth one of them knoweth them all'. Licences are required to travel from one city to another and all 'dice-play and such other foolish and pernicious games they know not'. In exchange for loss of personal freedom, More's island has 'sane laws and is wisely ruled'. Moreover, 'The citizens have fine gardens and hospitals. Bondsmen perform all the drudgery, mercenaries fight all the wars.'[43]

Ironically, what Plato, More and others thought utopias, we would use and have used to describe dystopias. Examples of these totalitarian dystopic states can be found in Orwell's *1984*, Zamyatin's *We*, Huxley's *Brave New World* and London's *The Iron Heel*. Le Guin presents in *The Dispossessed* a dystopic Earth, ruined by all-too-familiar humans, a planet that requires co-operation for survival, juxtaposed against Anarres, another world on which human survival necessitates co-operation – with the key difference that the Anarresti co-operation, even in times of severe drought and near-famine, is voluntary. Juxtaposed to Anarres is the rich, lush Urras, the Terran ambassador's Paradise, 'a living world, a harmony'. Yet Urras is dominated by oppressive nation-states.

This ongoing dialectic, in particular that between Urras and Anarres, supplants the expository passages between the traveller and the familiar guide in the traditional utopian narrative. This is especially true in that the dialectic is presented through Shevek, who is a traveller and an insider and outsider on both planets, Anarres and Urras. Thus, in a sense, Shevek is in dialectic with both cultures – a traveller in each. Given this, Shevek as utopian traveller is constantly engaged in explication, in an attempt to understand and make sense of the worlds in which he lives. His conversations as a teenager with his friends Bedap, Tirin and the others; his encounters with his teachers at Northsetting; his struggle with the narrow-minded Sabul in the Institute in Abbenay – all of Shevek's life is an attempt to explicate the world he is in and a part of, and yet outside of, be it Anarres or Urras. And it is part of Le Guin's inversion of the utopian conventions that both worlds – given that they are both utopias and dystopias, depending on one's perspective – present, not constant extremes, but the ambiguity of human life. Shevek encounters the smallness and greatness of being human on both worlds, in both cultures.

Le Guin is thus using utopia to argue, in effect, for both its imaginary state and its reality. Regardless of the amount of human energy expended, utopia can never exist as a finished product, as it is in the *Republic* or *Utopia* or even in Clarke's *Childhood's End*.[44] As Shevek hopes to convince the Anarresti, revolution is an ongoing process; it can't be allowed to sink into custom and convention. Odo's wisdom can't be quoted as if it was laws written in stone. Rather, utopia and its promised Golden Age of an improved and improving human existence must be achieved elsewhere, in the heart. Shevek's speech on the steps of the Directorate is a passionate statement to this end:

> 'We know that there is no help for us but from one another, that no hand will save us if we do not reach out our hand. And the hand you reach out is empty, as mine is. You have nothing. You possess nothing. You own nothing. You are free. All you have is what you are, and what you give.
>
> 'I am here because you see in me the promise, the promise

that we made two hundred years ago in this city – the promise kept. We have kept it on Anarres. We have nothing but our freedom. We have nothing to give you but your own freedom. We have no law but the single principle of mutual aid between individuals. We have no government but the single principle of association. We have no states, no nations, no presidents, no premiers, no chiefs, no generals, no bosses, no bankers, no landlords, no wages, no charity, no police, no soldiers, no wars. Nor do we have much else. We are sharers, not owners ... If it is Anarres you want, if it is the future you seek, then I tell you that you must come to it with empty hands ... You cannot buy the Revolution. You cannot make the Revolution. You can only be the Revolution. It is in your spirit, or it is nowhere.'[45]

Here is the Golden Age, the fulfilment of the utopian myth for which Le Guin is arguing as she inverts the traditional generic conventions, thus questioning these conventions as valid approaches to the myth. This Golden Age is the reality Le Guin says we should be seeking – and no amount of clean, well-ordered streets and gardens, with the trains running on time will truly get us there. Rather by the removal of the paradisal conditions associated with a traditional utopia, Le Guin is asking if they are necessary. As Judah Bierman argues in his essay 'Ambiguity in Utopia: *The Dispossessed*', 'to call a land without a green leaf a utopia is surely to cast ambiguity over the term, over the whole idea'.[46] Not only is the 'meaning of plenty' called into question, as Bierman suggests, but also what is needed to make a utopia. And removal of a verdant paradise forces attention on the primary resource left, the human one.

Another assumption of the utopian myth that Le Guin questions and subverts is that in the ideal social form individuals will have full freedom, which is the promise of Odonianism, the philosophy on which Anarres is founded. 'Utopias make good citizens, good soldiers, but when have they shown us flourishing geniuses other than founders?'[47] One might argue that John Savage in *Brave New World* could aspire to be a great philosopher, but he commits suicide. Winston, in *1984*, chooses Julia to be with the rats, rather than revolution. Shevek, to achieve his own personal promise, needs the community of his scientific peers and it is this community his utopian anarchist society would deny him. Utopia becomes then, not the realized state, but the effort, the continued process, as Shevek insists his people recognize. Utopia is the means, the action, the thought, and the people who think, act, process, not the product.

As Le Guin admits, *The Dispossessed* is an intentionally didactic novel. 'The sound of axes being ground is', as she says, 'occasionally audible.' Yet, what transcends the idea, the utopian themes, Le Guin insists, is that 'at the heart of it you will not find any idea, or an inspirational message, or even a stone ax, but something much frailer and obscurer and more complex: a person … Shevek … the Other, a soul, a human soul, the spirit we live by'.[48] Utopia, to be utopia, must be human and be about humans.

By placing Shevek at the heart of *The Dispossessed* Le Guin embodies idea in character, and thus makes character a rhetorical device. Shevek *is* a rhetorical statement: he is an argument for Odonian values and beliefs, and for utopia as being human. Character is not the only traditional fictional element used rhetorically; such stylistic devices as metaphor and structure are also used to make Le Guin's argument. The primary controlling metaphors of *The Dispossessed* are the journey, the wall and the promise. The journey as metaphor in *The Dispossessed* (and the *Earthsea* cycle) is rhetorical in that it argues for a way to understand human life as process. That the individual's journey of coming of age parallels and mirrors the hero's journey suggests that to set up the hero as a paradigm is to argue for certain values and beliefs in the myth. Le Guin, of course, questions and reinterprets these values and beliefs as she reimagines the myth. She uses its original structure to argue for different values and beliefs other than the traditional.

As structure the journey is also rhetorical in that it creates the novel's utopian dialectic. The journeys that make the story are the journeys within the greater journey of Shevek's life, from childhood to adulthood, and then the physical journeys from Northsetting to Abbenay, away from Takver during the drought and his return, and to Urras and back. Shevek's soul is also journeying, as much of his life is an attempt to mediate the tension between the individual and the community, between personal freedom and serving the community. Shevek's intellectual journey in search of the general temporal formula parallels his social journey in search of a place for himself in his community as he seeks the renewal of the Odonian promise that brought his people to Anarres. In the end, the resolution of Shevek's return journey to Anarres, accompanied by Kethoe, the Hainish crewman, is left open and unsettled. This ambiguity serves to underscore what I consider Le Guin's journey structure and metaphor to be: life as process, not product. There is no return to square one to begin the cycle all over again.

The novel itself is structured as a journey that also creates the utopian dialectic. It is organized into chapters alternating between Urras and Anarres, between the journey of Shevek's year on Urras seeking the formula and trying both to end his people's exile and to reconcile them with the Urrasti, and the journey of Shevek's coming of age on Anarres. Each section ends in a journey, to Urras, and the return to Anarres in the end. As is Ged's journey in *Earthsea*, this journey is an open spiral. The circle does not close as Shevek is still journeying, he is still in transit, waiting for the landing craft to take him down to Anarres.

The metaphor of the wall is also part of Le Guin's rhetoric. The most important wall on Anarres is the one enclosing the 'barren sixty-acre field called the Port of Anarres'. The wall is a physical barrier, providing a space in which Urrasti spaceships can land and take off. But, as Le Guin says, the wall is more:

> The wall shut in not only the landing field, but also the ships that came down from space and the men on the ships and the worlds they came from, and the rest of the universe. It enclosed the universe, leaving Anarres outside free.
>
> Looked at from the other side, the wall enclosed Anarres: the whole planet was inside, a great prison camp, cut off from other worlds and other men, in quarantine.[49]

Shevek makes the unbuilding of the wall (and its psychic equivalent in the Anarresti and the Urrasti) his goal. The walls coming down become an argument for co-operation, for greater community, for freedom of the mind and of individual initiative.

The third metaphor, the promise, becomes the underlying foundation of the structure of the novel's argument. It is the Odonian promise – community, human solidarity, mutual aid, co-operation and fidelity to each other – that creates the social movement that results in the colonization of Anarres. With this promise at the heart of the social philosophy that operates Anarresti society, Le Guin then presents those people who keep these promises and those who break them. Shevek does both – as he negotiates with Sabul to get his work published, as he returns again and again to his partner, Takver, regardless of the time and distance of separation, and as he insists his society let him travel to Urras. As Shevek's actions to renew the promise become the novel's driving force, Le Guin can be said to be making the promise a metaphor for Anarres itself – and a metaphor for the utopian ideal it represents.

Thus this utopian ideal, this utopia as all-too-human people who must choose and rechoose it, is a promise which must be renewed. Thus, utopia is more than just an idea; it is a process as well. This insistence that utopia is more than its idea is given even more weight when one considers the source of the originating philosophy of Anarres, Odonianism, is a woman, Odo. This female source has created a culture in which women are accepted as full equals – a feminist society. This makes, according to Joanna Russ in her article 'Recent Feminist Utopias', Le Guin's *The Dispossessed* a feminist utopia, one which is contemporaneous with the rise of the women's movement in the early 1970s. *The Dispossessed*, Russ notes, is similar to other feminist utopias, such as her own *The Female Man*, Delaney's *Triton*, Bradley's *The Shattered Chain* and Charnas's *Motherlines*. That Le Guin's society is built on 'communitarian anarchism' is secondary, according to Russ, to its being feminist.[50] But while Russ argues for *The Dispossessed* as a feminist utopia, Le Guin argues otherwise, especially in comparison with what she considers is a truer feminist utopia, *Always Coming Home*.

Le Guin, Feminism, and Yin and Yang Utopias

For Le Guin, feminism is as transformative for utopian myth as it was for the monomyth. Le Guin's thinking for *The Dispossessed* began with, as she says, 'Scraps of More, fragments of Wells, Hudson, Morris. Nothing.' Once Shevek had appeared and uncertainly answered her question as to who he was with 'I am a citizen of Utopia', she began what she says was 'years of reading and pondering and muddling, and much assistance from Engels, Marx, Godwin, Goldman, Goodman, and above all Shelley and Kropotkin ... ' In the process of finding out 'who and what Shevek was', Le Guin 'found out a great deal else ... about society, about [her] world'. The result is 'a Utopia, of sorts'.[51]

But as with *Tehanu* and the monomyth and the hero, Le Guin

came to realize that, even though she had created a utopian vision which advocated feminist values and ideals, the vision itself was (as with Ged's story) still masculine, or as she explains in her essay 'A Non-Euclidean View of California as a Cold Place to Be', yang:

> The major utopic element in my novel *The Dispossessed* is a variety of pacifist anarchism, which is about as yin as a political ideology can get. Anarchism rejects the identification of civilization with the state, and the identification of power with coercion; against the inherent violence of the "hot" society it asserts the value of such antisocial behavior as the general refusal of women to bear arms and other coyote devices ... The structure of the book may suggest the balance-in-motion of the Tai Chi, but its excess yang shows: though the utopia was (both in fact and fiction) founded by a woman, the protagonist is a man; and he dominates it in, I must say, a very masculine fashion.[52]

Le Guin had done, in other words, exactly what she had done with the monomyth – accepted the utopian myth as it was and inverted its conventions – yet she had not questioned some of its basic assumptions. She discovered that

> Utopia has been euclidean, it has been European, and it has been masculine ... Utopia has been yang. In one way or another, from Plato on, utopia has been the big yang motorcycle trip. Bright, dry, clear, strong, firm, active, aggressive, lineal, progressive, creative, expanding, advancing and hot.[53]

And yang utopias were not getting us anywhere. Yang or rationalist utopias, Le Guin argues, were power trips, with the premise of *progress*, not *process*.[54] But big isn't always better. As E. F. Schumacher notes in *Small is Beautiful: Economics as if People Mattered*, we need to turn away from the notion that bigger is better and stronger. Small, according to Schumacher, is 'free, efficient, creative, enjoyable, enduring'. He ties it to anarchism, which embraces the 'communal, handicraft, tribal, guild, village lifestyles', lifestyles that the Kesh (Le Guin's fictional people in *Always Coming Home*) exemplify.[55] Schumacher answers bigness and big-thinking with 'Buddhist' economics, in which the function of work 'gives man a chance to utilize and develop his faculties; enables him to overcome his ego-centeredness by joining together in a common task; and brings forth the goods and services needed for a becoming existence'.[56]

Civilization should not multiply wants, but purify character, which is formed by a man's (or a woman's) work. And work should be in done in 'conditions of human dignity'.[57] Schumacher calls for an 'entirely new system of thought ... a system based on attention to people, and not primarily to goods ... [There] should be production by the masses, not mass production.'[58] Our persistence in thinking antithetically to Schumacher has, Le Guin insists, led us into a 'really bad mess and we have to get out'.[59] Mass markets, a consumer society, a nation's worth measured by its productivity – to Le Guin, all this needs reconsideration, rethinking. As Cornel West argues in *Race Matters,* this sort of thinking threatens the African-American community with pervasive and pernicious nihilism. Le Guin would argue that it is not just the African-American community that is being threatened.

To counter the big is better, money-oriented thinking, more than a new economic theory is needed. Le Guin's answer is feminist or yin utopias. A yin utopia, according to Le Guin, is 'dark, wet, obscure, weak, yielding, passive, participatory, circular, cyclical, peaceful, nurturant, retreating, contracting, and cold'.[60] She finds an example in Austin Tappan Wright's 1940 utopian novel, *Islandia,* in which a 'deliberate choice is made to get no hotter' and the concept of progress as being a forward motion is rejected. 'Persevering in one's existence' is accepted as a 'completely worthy social goal'. *Islandia* goes sideways, and to Le Guin, side trips and reversals are 'precisely what it is minds stuck in forward gear most need'.[61]

Such an unstuck society would not be devoid of technology: as Le Guin points out in *The Dispossessed,* Odo was all too aware that the decentralized society she advocated would need modern transportation, communications and manufacturing. Technology should support Le Guin's yin utopia:

> a society predominantly concerned with preserving its existence; a society with a modest standard of living, conservative of natural resources, with a low constant fertility rate, and a political life based upon consent; a society that has made a successful adaptation to its environment and has learned to lived without destroying itself or the people next door.[62]

Technology is presented through sentient computers in the Na Valley in *Always Coming Home*. There is an internet of sorts, the 'City of the Mind', which the Kesh do use when they need to: 'Some eleven thousand sites all over the planet were occupied by independent, self-contained self-regulating communities of cybernetic devices or beings – computers with mechanical extensions.'[63] Anyone can access it, collect information, ask questions. The City, despite its being somewhat 'outside the world', further extends the idea of connection, as it becomes a thin electronic web linking the globe together. Even the language used by humans originally to talk just to the City, TOK, becomes a lingua franca of the Valley.

Connection is considered characteristic of feminism and its rhetoric, as Belenky makes clear in *Women's Ways of Knowing*.[64] Women are urged to network, to collaborate, to find meaning in sisterhood and community. As it did with the myth of the quest, feminist thought has reshaped Le Guin's original thinking on utopia. But feminist thought is not the sole theoretical and philosophical basis for the Kesh. Le Guin also draws upon Native American (in particular the California Indians) religious beliefs and social practices, and American cultural myths. These sources, used to construct the yin utopia of *Always Coming Home*, all become rhetorical. By choosing feminist theory, Native American culture and American cultural myths to be the building blocks of her utopian vision, Le Guin is using them to rhetorically support and advance her argument.

Always Coming Home

In *Always Coming Home*, Le Guin uses frame, structure and form rhetorically. The traditional form of the utopian narrative is present, albeit in reimagined form. In the traditional narrative, there is one narrator, the traveller to utopia, the outsider to whom the utopian guide must explain how his or her paradise on earth came to be and continues. Le Guin has two. One is the self-conscious anthropologist and ethnographer, Pandora, who constantly comments to and questions herself and the reader as she collects social data on the Kesh. Stone Telling, a Kesh woman whose autobiographical story can be said to be a novel embedded within the novel, is the second narrator. The stories told by both narrators bear some examination in that each is an example of what I call utopian dialectic – between the better life offered by the mythic vision and the less-preferred other life. This utopian dialectic becomes rhetorical in that, for example, the sharp contrast between the lives of the Kesh, the people of Stone Telling's mother, and the lives of the Condor,[65] the people of her father, is, in part, an argument for feminist values.

Le Guin is once again inverting the traditional utopian narrative in *Always Coming Home*. This is evident in the fact that Stone Telling's autobiography, which is presented in the traditional narrative form of a journey and return, is only a hundred pages in a novel of more than five hundred pages. The rest of the book, as Peter Fitting notes in his article 'The Turn from Utopia in Recent Feminist Fiction', is presented as ethnographic data (gathered by the other narrator, Pandora): poems, songs, stories, a chapter from *Dangerous People*, a typical Kesh novel, life stories, discussions of death practices, language, children's games and the like. The novel is, as Fitting suggests, something of a kit:[66] non-linear, fragmented, with Stone Telling's story itself (and the other stories collected) as ethnographic data.[67] These fragments, then, as artefacts of this culture, become ways to present the culture's values and beliefs. This, in effect, puts the reader into a dialectic with the novel: here, take these pieces, and assemble the story of the Kesh in the Na Valley.[68] The reader's participation in this utopian vision becomes, then, a process in and of itself.

That the novel is fictionalized ethnography allows Le Guin, as Ron Scollon says in 'In Defense of Writing: The Contemporary Merger of Ethnography and Fiction', to give no one single vision of Stone Telling's world.[69] What the multiple visions do, being both story and ethnographic data, is to make arguments for both as ways of understanding reality through experience. The entire world of the Kesh, from children's games and rituals of death and dying to coming-of-age ceremonies, becomes as Scollon says, text.[70] To understand their world, then, we have to attempt to understand it in context. It is only then that the value-systems of a people, of the fictional Kesh or of our own, can have meaning. As ethnographic data, then, these fragments present the culture through living example. As such, there is no covert argument to present a particular practice as preferable; rather the data are presented as just the way the Kesh are. Since the information is foreign to the reader and to the ethnographer-narrator, explanation is necessary. Such explanation becomes rhetorical as the reader compares the Kesh's practices with her own.

As examples of Le Guin's rhetorical use of ethnographic data, I want to look briefly at three 'fragments' or cultural artefacts: a discussion of a children's game, a transcript of a community discussion of the Warrior Lodge and the excerpt from *Dangerous People*, a Kesh novel. The children's game is, in effect, a metaphor for Kesh society, which stresses collaboration over competition. The goal of 'hish' is to keep the 'swallow' aloft in a 'regular swift pattern of exchanges'. That the ultimate goal is not victory but the beautifully executed completion of a pattern suggests again the value of process over product, and the benefit of collaboration over competition. The transcript of the discussion of the Warrior Lodge underscores the fact that the Kesh do not make a choice between either/or or binary thinking. The Kesh are concerned that the warlike Condor have infected them, through the Warrior Lodge, with the 'sickness of man'. After a heated argument from both sides, the either/or choice of forcing the Warriors to leave or be cured is refused. The Kesh go home, leaving the choice to the Warriors. The third piece of ethnographic data, the excerpt from *Dangerous People*, argues for the value of process over product as well as the rejection of binary thinking. Like *Always Coming Home*, this novel-within-a-novel is circular and recursive; it rambles and meanders. Nothing much really seems to happen except talking. This excerpt exemplifies 'the life that keeps moving, here and there, backward and forward, in whatever way is necessary for the good of the individual and the community'.[71] There is no single right or wrong way; rather there is a multiplicity of ways to live – there is no either/or. The emphasis is on the connections between people, the link from one relationship to the next.

The overall pattern and metaphor of *Always Coming Home* that illustrates this connecting and linking is the hinge, the 'heyiya-if', used by the Kesh. In the novel excerpt the pattern is that of two people meeting, turning apart and then going on to the next person. This meeting and turning apart is repeated over and over, until there is a great invisible chain of hinges, linking everyone together. Everyone is connected. At the conclusion of the excerpt, a once-sick boy, feeling better, leaves in search of his mother (it is her disappearance that began this great chain, with his father seeking her). The boy is accompanied by a dog that once knew his mother – another connection with another person (dogs are people in the Valley, too). 'So they went out of town, northwestward, into the willow flats along the River, and alongside the water, going upstream.'[72] Or in other words, the boy and the dog follow the uncurled spiral of the hinge, and move into a 'never-ending fluid process between individual and community, and between person and nature, all in a spiralling network of relationships'.[73]

Le Guin thus has gone beyond the open spirals of *The Dispossessed* and *Earthsea*. The spiral has been pulled even further open, into a continually uncurling spiral, an ongoing continuous process of journey, of becoming. This opened and extended spiral, the hinge, is repeated constantly in *Always Coming Home*. Section openings and closings are marked with the hinge in one form or another throughout the book. Le Guin writes in her essay 'A Non-Euclidean View of California as a Cold Place to Be' that the hinge epitomizes the Native American philosophy from which she has drawn much of the Kesh's world-view. She gives as one source for the hinge the Cree saying, 'Usa puyew usu wapiw!' which is translated as 'Back round once more/He goes backward, looks forward.'[74] Adoption of such a way of looking at the world, Harper notes, is what Le Guin is offering as a means to save us from the binary either/or thinking in which Le Guin sees the West as being trapped:[75]

> In order to speculate safely on an inhabitable future, perhaps we would do well to find a rock crevice and go backward. In order to find our roots, perhaps we should look for them where roots are usually found ... With all our self-consciousness, we have very little sense of where we live, where we are right now ... If we did – if we really lived here, now, in this present – we might have some sense of our future as a people. We might know where the center of the world is.[76]

As in *The Dispossessed*, where utopia is ambiguous and uncertain, and is, as Shevek insists his people see it, an ongoing process, so the hinge suggests utopia in *Always Coming Home*. The hinge itself is ambiguous with its multiple meanings and connections. As I. A. Richards notes, 'the more important a word [or symbol or idea], and the more central and necessary its meanings are, the more ambiguous ... the word will be'. These ambiguities become 'the hinges of thought'.[77] And as Ann E. Berthoff argues in *Making of Meaning*, such ambiguities serve to open the reader and the student to the 'possibility of other meanings'.[78] And it is these other meanings, the alternative solutions past the either/or, that Le Guin is arguing for in *Always Coming Home*, that she repeatedly calls to our attention. In *Always Coming Home*, as the games, the hinge and the novel illustrate, we have an alternative approach, 'a variety of solutions to the problem of structuring reality'. *Always Coming Home* becomes, then, a 'personal vision of life where one may refuse to participate in either/or thinking'.[79] The Kesh are a process-oriented alternative. They seek, and the novel argues for, as C. S. Peirce advocates in his philosophy, a third way.

In addition to the rhetorical use of ethnographic data in *Always Coming Home*, Le Guin also uses the stylistic device of the narrator rhetorically. She does this through the types of narrator she makes Stone Telling and Pandora, and through cultural juxtaposition. Like Shevek, Stone Telling is both insider and outsider in each culture she explores, the Kesh and the Condor. This dual status places her as narrator in utopian dialectic with each culture, and her comparisons become, in effect, rhetorical. That Stone Telling chooses the Kesh over the Condor also becomes rhetorical, because this choice, when made, is a value judgement. There is a further dialectic created by Stone Telling as narrator in that she is telling the story of both cultures to the reader – or, in other words, her presentation and observations become rhetoric: this is what I saw *here* and *there,* and *this* is better. Again like Shevek, she becomes, as Wayne Booth defines the term in *The Rhetoric of Fiction,* a narrator-agent. More than mere observer, the narrator-agent produces 'some measurable effect in the course of events'.[80] Shevek's development of the general temporal formula which produces a communication device, the ansible (which allows for instantaneous interstellar communication), affects not just Anarres and Urras, but all of humanity. And it is Shevek's journey – physically and spiritually – that creates the cultural dialectic through juxtaposition. Furthermore, it is his choice, to go Urras and to return to Anarres, that becomes the central argument of the novel.

Stone Telling as narrator-agent and as insider/outsider has a similar profound effect that is 'measurable … in the course of events'. Being an outsider places her in dialectic with her own culture, which as a young woman she found unsatisfactory and boring (a warning to the reader: utopias can be just as lacking as dystopias). Stone Telling chooses to go back with her father to the Condors. Her experiences in the city of the Condor, with the Dayao,[81] the people of her father, creates yet another dialectic and argument for the Valley and its way of life. Almost immediately upon leaving the Valley with her father, Stone Telling learns of the hierarchical superior/inferior structure of Dayao society. She learns that one of her father's servants is a 'hontik' (foreigner), and as such can't read or write – such arts are sacred and not for the lesser folk, those fit only to serve the Dayao. When she reaches the Condor city, she learns it is not only the hontik who do not read or write; women are not to have this knowledge either. Only by virtue of being her father's daughter does Stone Telling have any status in Dayao society, with its rigid hierarchical structure. Women do not have souls and 'have no part in the intellectual life of the Dayao people; they are kept in, but left out'.

Stone Telling tries to become a true Condor Woman. She marries a True Condor, becomes his second 'pretty wife', and bears him a daughter. But even so, as a woman trying to assimilate, she cannot help but see the Dayao as a sick culture, a sick people, doomed to die of its own weight. Her position in this culture and the position of other women, indeed of any other – non-Condors, foreigners, slaves, women – again serve as a way for Stone Telling to better understand the Dayao and the Valley. The Dayao think, as Stone Telling puts it, in terms of everyone being 'either this or that' – binary thinking carried to an extreme conclusion.

Eventually Stone Telling can try no more to be a Dayao: they were a people 'going the wrong way'. She knows, when she has this epiphany, that her journey is only half-made, and that to complete it she must return, as Shevek learns when he is on Urras. According to Fitting, her departure and return are the literal re-enactment of the symbolic choice each member of the Kesh must make, to choose their way of life and thus accept it, and work to maintain it.[82] 'Utopias do not exist', as Fitting says, 'simply for us to wander into and then live happily ever after; the novel tells us they must be built and renewed constantly and chosen again and again.'[83] Stone Telling's choice to return and her choice of a new name, Woman Coming Home, again underscores Le Guin's idea of utopia as process – we must always come home, we must always choose home, we must always remake and renew home.

The other primary narrator of the novel, Pandora, the anthropologist-observer and the traveller-visitor to utopia, is also engaged in choice: what Kesh data to record and present, how to present them, how much interpretation is necessary, and so forth. She is, as Booth defines it, also a narrator-agent: her data collection, presentation and interpretation create *Always Coming Home*. She is also a self-conscious narrator: she knows she is recording and presenting a utopia. Her commentary, even more so than Stone Telling's, is rhetorical. Her interviews and conversations, her musings to herself and to the reader, all become part of an ongoing and multiple utopian dialectic.

Through these multiple dialectics with this self-conscious narrator, Le Guin asks the reader for even more participation than other utopists in the understanding and creation of utopia. Through Pandora, Le Guin is asking if it is indeed possible to imagine utopia, a task Franko argues is both impossible and very possible. Writers such as 'Russ, Le Guin, Piercy, Delany', according to Franko, use a self-reflexive narrator for 'simultaneously destroying and transforming utopia', and thus transform utopia into an 'open-ended' creation. [84]

Pandora also becomes the interface, between the reader who is making the Kesh world out of Pandora's collected fragments and the novel itself, a whole evocation of an imaginary world. In the first section of the novel Pandora worries about her presentation of this culture: should it be as a whole, or in pieces – will patterns be complete? In addition, Pandora asks, can a utopian culture be presented at all by a citizen of dystopia?

> I know about war and plague and famine and holocaust … Am I not a daughter of the people who enslaved and extirpated the people of three continents? Am I not a sister of Adolf Hitler and Anne Frank? Am I not a citizen of the State that fought the first nuclear war? Have I not eaten, drunk, and breathed poison all my life … Do you take me for innocent, my fellow maggot, my colluding Reader? I knew what was in the box my brother-in-law left here.[85]

Just who is this narrator? Is she a time-displaced worrying archaeologist? Is she Le Guin? Pandora, after all, is 'originator, first woman, goddess, troublemaker' and, here, she is 'scatterer of utopian and dystopian fragments, the inclusive, all-embracing encompassing multiple narrative voices'.[86] In the section in which Pandora converses with the archivist of the Library of the Madrone Lodge at Wakwaha-na, this ambiguous narrator mocks the entire utopian literary tradition. Their conversation, Pandora says to the archivist, 'is the kind they always have in utopia. I set you up and then you give interesting, eloquent, and almost entirely convincing replies. Surely we can do better than that?'[87]

What Le Guin is doing here, it seems, is opening up the box by evoking the 'conventional dialogue between visitor to utopia and utopian guide', and thus demonstrating her fictional roots and at the same time how far she has come in reshaping and reimagining this myth. And to underscore this reshaping, the archivist, in a very untraditional move, asks Pandora questions about *her* culture: how is its information organized, retrieved, accessed? 'How do you keep information yet keep it from being the property of the powerful?' Pandora tells the archivist she hates 'smartass utopians' who are 'always so much healthier and saner and sounder and fitter and kinder and tougher and wiser and righter ... People who have the answers are boring ...' The archivist's response is that she doesn't have the answers and this isn't a utopia; it is a 'mere dream dreamed up in a bad time, an Up Yours to the people who ride snowmobiles, make nuclear weapons, and run prison camps by a middle-aged housewife, a critique of civilisation possible only to the civilised ...'[88]

At the end, this seems to be true, when, after six of these meditative, self-conscious sections by Pandora, Pandora and Le Guin seem to merge as Pandora/Le Guin thank the real people who helped in the book's making. Yet, can author and self-conscious narrator be equated? After all, to write down one's own voice is to reinterpret, to make fiction, to tell a story. Is this more of the broken, fragmentary rhetoric of Le Guin's text, 'created to give us the feel of a utopia that is not a dead thing, a static system to be emulated [as so many of its predecessors were], but rather a living, changing relation to us as readers'?[89]

Le Guin asks us, Khanna insists, to read as participants, to take this novel-as-kit, novel-as-assemblage, and if the reader 'lets her mind play with its scraps (text), [she] may piece together a vibrant quilt of utopian thought, one not to be admired, but lived with'.[90] This quilt is one made up of the traditional utopian mythic narrative, with its generic conventions, changed by Le Guin to have multiple narrators and multiple perspectives. Examining the utopia as an anthropologist/ethnographer would further multiply these perspectives, as such an examination, through the fragments, creates a whole, detailed culture. These multiplicities all work to create the utopian dialectic – here we are, now, and here we could be, if we use what we have now in a different way. That this utopia demands the reader to examine, juxtapose and re-juxtapose makes it something that is a continual process, a continual journey, a spiral, an open hinge. As Khanna says, 'The journey of Le Guin's utopia is, of course, endless and cannot be made without the questing reader, for women's utopias are not places or even times, but states of mind'.[91]

Feminist Utopian Thought

To look at feminist utopian influences on *Always Coming Home* and Le Guin's use of myth, I want to first consider how Le Guin fits into and derives from the feminist utopian tradition. Khanna cites the following attributes for Le Guin's Kesh as being similar to other fictional feminist utopian people: 'more attention is paid to relationship than achievement' (or in other words, process over product); animals and the natural environment are highly valued to the point that our relationship with them is ritualized; the natural cycle of life is followed with 'appreciative ceremonies' for 'birth, coming of age, marriage, death'; and the paramount values are 'individual moral and intellectual growth, community, harmony'.[92]

Marleen Barr elaborates on these values and concepts as part of feminist utopian thought in her book *Lost in Space: Probing Feminist Science Fiction*. One area on which she places special emphasis is the notion of sexuality in the feminist utopia. Often in these fictional worlds, there are 'well-characterized, likeable women [who] can get along without men'.[93] The sexuality presented is frequently permissive and without 'violence and exploitation'. There are often elaborate scientific, genetic and "historical" explanations as to why men are absent and not needed for reproduction, or why gender roles have been so radically altered. Parthenogenesis, eugenics, surrogacy, in vitro pregnancy and cloning are some of the ways such conditions are created.

Barr cites Joanna Russ's essay 'Recent Feminist Utopias' and her explanation of 'why this literature is characterized by sexual permissiveness': 'not to break taboos but to separate sexuality from questions of ownership, reproduction and social structure'.[94] Russ's explanation for male exclusion and 'the sanctioned presence of lesbianism' is equally to the point. Lesbianism, of course, is real and present and *does* offer women freedom from men. At times when men are present, they are sometimes genetically altered to be able to nurse, or to be less aggressive. But perhaps more telling (as it is more possible), in addition to biological transformation, both men and women are raised in these alternative cultures to value collaboration and co-operation over competition, gender equality, pacifism over aggression, mutual solidarity and interdependence, community over the individual, and so forth.

In *Always Coming Home*, Le Guin does not prescriptively present a society that echoes all of these attributes of feminist utopian

thinking as part of her vision. It is clear, however, that she intends
the Kesh to be feminists. As I mentioned earlier, according to
Khanna in 'Utopias: New Worlds, New Texts', the Kesh are very
similar to other feminist utopian people in their relationships with
each other, the animals and the environment, and their adherence
to the natural life-cycles. They are fully integrated into their world
to the point that the most important part of Kesh education is
'learning to manage the three basic energies of life: cosmic, social,
personal'.[95]

When Stone Telling undergoes a coming-of-age ceremony – a
solitary journey into the wilderness – as an eight-year-old, she is
fully aware she is in a full relationship with her environment:

> Everything that came to me I spoke to by name or saying
> heya, the trees, fir and digger pine and buckeye and
> redwood and manzanita and madrone and oak, the birds,
> blue jay and bushtit and woodpecker and phoebe and hawk,
> the leaves of chamise and scrub oak and poison oak and
> flowering thorn, the grasses, a deer's skull, a rabbit's
> droppings, the wind blowing from the sea.[96]

She speaks to the water and asks it for directions, sleeps in Coyote's
house, and asks for and gives blessings to the deer, to the
waterskater. Everything is seen as part of everything. Animals and
humans are thus seen as related, as different kinds of people. The
word 'pet' is not used – rather 'commensal', 'which better trans-
lates the Valley term meaning people living together'. As the Kesh
saw things, 'the domestic animals consented to live and to die with
human beings'.[97] Social relationships between human people in
this non-patriarchal culture were also based on voluntary consent.
Stone Telling's grandfather lives most of the time with his mother's
people – which is all right with her grandmother.

That the Kesh culture is non-patriarchal is clear. But non-
patriarchal does not equal matriarchal. Rather, the Kesh are the
third way: women and men are equal. Women are not possessions
solely for sex, status and the producing of heirs, and they are full
participants in a society that includes and works not to exclude. As
a result, the emphasis is on relationship, on connection, between
other humans, between other living beings. There are, Le Guin
asserts, no Kesh matriarchs.[98] This third way is the preferred, more
human way, as Stone Telling's choice indicates, when she decides
to come home, having experienced the patriarchal Dayao. In such a

'third' society, in which no gender is dominant over the other, children are taught to enjoy and respect their sexuality, and to be fully sexual beings as adults.

Sexuality for the Kesh calls for a 'realistic and undemanding attitude ... avoiding excess both of indulgence and abstinence, [with] a style of control and self-control [of] ease, not of rigidity ... Boys and girls by the age of ten knew all the uses of contraceptives, and most of them had used them – for children's sexual play was taken altogether for granted, indulged, and even encouraged.'[99] Adolescents, in what at first appears to be a contradiction, are expected to 'live on the Coast' or, for a time, be sexually celibate. The beginning of this time is marked with ritual (as are almost all events in a person's life). The reason is for them to learn to balance all the energies of being human: the personal (sex, mind, work and play), the cosmic and the social ('the community of being, the fabric of interdependent existences ... of relationship'). 'Living on the Coast, then, was the beginning of living mindfully ... From it would arise the work of being a person, itself part of the work of relationship.'[100] As adults, sexual permissiveness comes as part of ritual dances, such as the Moon Dance, an occasion similar to contemporary Mardi Gras, times during which anything goes: 'It's all backwards, it's a reversal, you see. It's sex without anything that belongs to sex – responsibility, marriage, children.'[101] Preceding the dance are rituals of purification, and sex occurs during the dance, in the dance, in the full moonlight.

Thus it is within feminist thought on how life should be lived that Le Guin grounded the utopian society of her fictional Kesh. The Kesh world is one of connection and community, of collabora-tion and co-operation, and yet a world demanding individual freedom and accountability. Their sexuality, which to many of us might be considered loose and unrestrained, instead should be seen to be demanding maturity, respect and responsibility. Through their sexual practices and in the rest of their lives, the Kesh remain connected to the world, its rhythms and cycles, and to each other. The rituals of puberty, of sexual maturity, weddings, funerals – all remind one of and make the connections to each other, to the tribe, the Valley and beyond. This is how I see feminism: a way of thinking that links rather than separates, and that creates a *communitas* 'capable of nurturing individuals in their individual freedom'. The Kesh are neither matriarchal or patriarchal – and again this is what true feminism calls for – and have an equality that celebrates differences, rather than denies them or uses them to hurt or exploit. After all, as Kenneth Woodward states in his essay 'Gender and Religion', the purpose of feminism, in its healthiest manifestation, is 'not female domination, but the liberation of men and women from androcentrism and its attendant evils ... sexism, racism, clericalism, ageism, classism, conflict, leadership by hierarchy – even the rape of the environment'.[102] Choose, Le Guin argues, the third way.

Native American Practices and Beliefs

Closely parallel to feminist thought and as present in *Always Coming Home* are the social customs and behaviours of Native Americans. This evocation of Native American practices and beliefs is, of course, no surprise. Le Guin has clearly modelled Kesh religious and social customs rather closely on those of the Native Americans, particularly those of California, the latter thoroughly studied by her anthropologist parents, Alfred and Theodora Kroeber. Theodora Kroeber describes the California Indian as a 'true provincial', who was 'also an introvert, reserved, contemplative, philosophical ... [They] lived at ease with the supernatural and the mystical which were pervasive in all aspects of life.'[103] As Richard Slotkin puts it in his work on the myth of the frontier in early American colonial history, *Regeneration through Violence: The Mythology of the American Frontier, 1600–1800,* the Indians worshipped the world 'as-it-is'.[104] The California Indians, as did their spiritual and literary descendants, the Kesh of the Na Valley, lived in a numinous world, a world in which there was 'no need to differentiate mystical truth from directly evidential or material truth, or the supernatural from the natural: one was as manifest as the other within [their] systems of values and belief'.[105]

Another Kesh custom easily traceable to the California Indians is that of naming their houses. This custom, Alfred Kroeber argues in his influential work *Handbook of the California Indians,* is indicative of the 'intense localization of life' for the Yurok tribe.[106] Le Guin underscores this when she notes that in California, before the white man, 'Every hill, every valley, creek, canyon, gulch, gully, draw, point, bluff, beach, bend, good-sized boulder, and tree of any character had its name, its place in the order of things.'[107] This intense sense of place and locality and connectedness to place is demonstrated in *Always Coming Home* when Stone Telling reports what the people of the Finders Lodge say about leaving the Valley: 'there is a pain in their heart, or a voice singing in their ears, or a whitening, or a sense of falling – always some sign'.[108] Return is no less emotional, as shown when Stone Telling, in the last section, speaks of returning to the 'Valley of her being'. And, of course, the Kesh named their world as thoroughly and closely as did the California Indians – even taking names for different times in an individual's life, to indicate that the different ages are different places in a life as well.

These naming practices are integral to Native American culture. As Samuel Gill notes in *Native American Traditions* names are not simply labels. '[Names] often are consciously used and understood as shaping and reflecting the very identity and character of a person. Often individuals receive a succession of names in a lifetime,'[109] as do the Kesh. This Native American practice is one which Le Guin uses effectively as part of the novel's rhetoric and John Algeo discusses this in his essay 'Magic Names: Onomastics in the Fantasies of Ursula K. Le Guin'. To match a name specifically to a particular time in one's life means the name, in some way, must reflect who the person is or is becoming, what traits are manifest now that weren't before. Such names Algeo calls 'trait names' or 'traditional characterizing names' – 'charactonyms' – which are appropriate to and revealing of a character.[110] Le Guin, when she chooses these names, is, according to Algeo, inviting the reader to 'interpret them'.[111] Stone Telling's childhood name, North Owl, as is true for many Kesh babies, is that of a bird, as 'they are messengers'. And Stone Telling, in effect, becomes the messenger – to the Condor, to the reader and to the Kesh – of how she has lived her life and the choices she has made. Her middle life name, Woman Coming Home, is pure rhetoric: utopia must always be chosen, one must always return to it, one must always come home to it if utopia is to have any reality at all. The name she takes for the last part of her life, Stone Telling, is because, as she says, 'I have a story to tell of where I went when I was young; but now I go nowhere, sitting like a stone, in this ground, in this Valley. I have come where I was going.'[112]

The allusions are multiple and in a way summarize the novel's philosophy. Stone Telling is integrally connected to the Valley, to the world: it is a part of her and she of it. Stones, like everything else, 'live in the Five Houses of the Earth' – everything is part of the whole. And as with her middle life name, this name indicates choice of utopia: it is return, and yet it is the spiral, as she is changed by her journeys. Story itself becomes part of the rhetoric: as it becomes her way of making meaning of her life, and as the novel is the story of a people, so it attempts to make meaning of their life, while it argues for the value and worth of their way of life.

Naming practices are but one Native American custom Le Guin uses to great effect in *Always Coming Home*. However, it is not my purpose here to play a matching game with the social customs, beliefs and values of the California Indians and the social customs, beliefs and values of the Kesh. It is obvious that Le Guin took full advantage of the experiences of her anthropologist parents. Le Guin has interpreted both feminist utopian thought and the Native American way as being almost synonymous, if not parallel. Both argue for a way of life that is, as Le Guin says, yin and not yang. There is no center in which power can adhere, as there were (and are) 'centers of the world all over California' (and everywhere else). For the Native Americans and the feminist utopias, a preferred government would be decentralized and community-based: the tribe. The survival of the community, the tribe, the family takes precedence over the individual. Even so, they still were 'concerned … with discovering the readiest way to reconcile personal freedom with individual and collective survival'.[113] With all this, they were able to obtain a 'delicate equilibrium' with the environment, necessitating an ongoing effort to be in harmony and co-operation with the natural world. That Le Guin can easily equate feminist utopian thinking with Native American thinking lets her argue that this way to utopia is achievable: it has already been done, and the choice can be made again.

Le Guin does not, of course, ignore the warfare and military aggression – a decidedly non-feminist activity – practised by the California Indians. The Kesh have engaged in previous skirmishes and battles, such as the summer war with the Pig People. Moreover, there are also the Warrior and Lamb Lodges, which both focus on the art of war. But the Kesh choose, over and over again – as Le Guin insists they must, as utopia is always process, always coming home – not to wage war, declaring that war is sickness. Fighting itself is something for children and adolescents, as Clear of the Yellow Adobe testifies in 'A Commentary on the War with the Pig People':

I am ashamed that six of the people of my town who fought this war were grown people. Some of the others were old enough to behave like adults, too ... It is appropriate for children to fight, not having yet learned how to be mindful, and not yet being strong ... It is appropriate that adolescents, standing between childhood and adulthood, may choose mindfully to risk their strength in a game, and they may choose to throw their life away, if they wish not to go on and undertake to live a whole life into old age. That is their choice. In undertaking to live a whole life, a person has made the other choice. They no longer have the privilege of adolescence. To claim it in grown life is mindless, weak, and shameful.[114]

Le Guin does not identify Clear Adobe as either a woman or man. I think this is important because all too often feminism is equated with being female. This is simply not the case – there *are* feminist men. Perhaps there should be another term for this way of thinking: unfortunately 'humanist' has already been opted. That Clear Adobe can be of either gender is further argument for feminism as inclusive, as community-making, a community in which men and women can both be mindful.

To be mindful and to choose to be so is the Kesh way of life. The Kesh become a powerful argument, then, for a way of life thought to be fanciful – yet one that has already been and is. This way of life wasn't and isn't perfect – the violence of the North Americans attests to this, as do the extreme excluding anti-male forms of feminism.

American Cultural Myth, Native Americans and Utopia

In one sense, Americans have already admitted to valuing this less aggressive yin way of life – if not in practice, at least in American cultural myth, which expresses what they believe themselves to be and what they tell themselves they value, their world-view. Native Americans occupy a special place in their cultural myth, so large that they have come archetypal. The notion of America as the Promised Land of milk and honey, as Eden, the Golden Land, as utopia, is equally special. California itself occupies a very special place in this last myth, for as Le Guin says, it is called the 'Golden

State not just for the stuff Sutter found but for the wild poppies on
its hills and the wild oats of summer ...' To the Anglos, she goes on
to say, California has always been utopia:

> the Golden Age made accessible by willpower, the wild
> paradise to be tamed by reason; the place where you go free
> of the old bonds and cramps, leaving behind your farm and
> your galoshes, casting aside your rheumatism and your
> inhibitions, taking up a new "life-style" in a not-here-not-
> now where everybody gets rich quick in the movies or finds
> the meaning of life or anyhow gets a good tan hang-
> gliding.[115]

One only has to look at *The Grapes of Wrath* to see the power of this
mythic California on the American psyche, and what it can do to
those who believe it.

It is the weight and power of these cultural myths – of America
as Eden, with California the last hope for Eden, and of the Native
Americans as archetype – that Le Guin brings to *Always Coming
Home*. These universal archetypes are 'essential to myth since all
myth to be credible must relate the problems and aspirations of
particular cultures to the fundamental conditions of human
existence and human psychology'.[116] Or, in other words, for there
to be a myth specific to a particular culture, to be local, as it were,
then that myth and its archetypes must connect first to the
universal, to the Jungian collective unconscious. The myth of the
Hero and the Quest is an example that Slotkin argues is 'the most
important archetype underlying American cultural mythology'.[117]

The stories of these quests and their heroes, taken from
American history, 'have acquired through persistent usage the
power of symbolizing [American] ideology and of dramatizing [its]
moral consciousness'. These stories become 'deeply encoded' in the
national psyche, and become deeply 'resonant set[s] of symbols'.[118]
All these stories become cultural myth, the national narrative of
Americans' history that recapitulates who they are, what they
believe and how they got to where they are. Universal archetypes –
the hero, the Noble Savage, the Golden Land – have become local
American archetypes, incorporated into the American national
myth. Americans have, through their 'development of traditional
metaphors (and the narratives that express them)' moved from
'archetypal paradigm[s] to the creation of acculturated, even
idiosyncratic metaphor'. The stories, the archetypal narratives,

have been reimagined and reinterpreted, as they have been told and retold, and thus reflect the Americans' 'characteristic approach to life'. [119]

These stories that comprise the American national mythology do not, however, remain static, even as they become peculiarly American and distinct from the universal. As historical circumstances change, as a culture assimilates and integrates other cultures, the stories change:

> If the first American mythology portrayed the colonist as a captive or a destroyer of Indians, the subsequent acculturated versions of myth showed him growing closer to the Indian and the wild land. New versions of the hero emerged, characters whose role was that of mediating between civilization and savagery, white and red – yeoman farmer, explorer, surveyor, naturalist. [120]

With this in mind, I want to look first at the myth of America as utopia, as Eden. I would even argue that the American people as a whole are on a quest, for the dream America represented to the Europeans: Eden, the Promised Land, the Kingdom of God here on Earth. And the only way to reach this grail is through separation from the old, and purification through the trials and tribulations of colonization, of conquest, of western advance, and continual belief in the American dream. America's identification with this myth began early. According to Slotkin, the European response to the discovery of the New World was in 'conventional terms of utopian treatise, arcadian poetry, and the chivalric romance epic'. [121] As Arcadia, America was the new garden without walls, an Eden without 'the serpent and forbidden trees'. It offered the hope and promise of renewal, of 'new physical and sexual vigor, of the power of the heart and sentiment, through a return to a more natural, less civilized ... mode of life'. For those like More, who set his *Utopia* in an imaginary American Indian empire, the renewal is somewhat different: 'moral and intellectual: the expansion of knowledge through discovery gives men the power to reform social and religious institutions'. [122] One only has to consider the motives of the various groups that colonized America both to understand ideas of renewal and to see how they merge together. They came to begin again, to start over, without the corruption and sin and lack of grace of the Old World, to worship God in a place pure of the taint of old sin. There was hope of redemption, the second chance, of achieving what they could only see others achieving: land, house, riches. Seeing America this way, as renewal, as the second chance, is to see America as the pastoral ideal. As Leo Marx explains in *The Machine in the Garden*, here, in America, humans might realize their poetic fantasy, 'a new beginning for Western society', an improved, better society, paradise regained.[123]

The myth of America as Eden[124] was modified once the European colonization began in earnest. America turned out to be both Eden and 'hideous wilderness'.[125] Edenic America offered harmony, grace, redemption and second growth. Wilderness America had to be tamed and conquered; its savages had to be killed. The wilderness-needing-conquest image, and its corollary, that the wilderness could become an Edenic garden, dominated. This image became, by the eighteenth century, a utopian vision, such as the 'undefiled green republic' of Jeffersonian agrarianism. Even into the twentieth century, this vision lasted, with the American imagination 'dominated by the idea of transforming the wild heartland into a Garden of the New World'. The westward movement had the effect of displacing the garden until it resided in California. As Charles Crow points out in his essay 'Homecoming in the California Visionary Romance', California has 'always been linked to the possibility of a fully realized life in harmony with an inviting and nurturing landscape'. Coupled with this dream has been a sense of urgency: California is the 'last stop, the end of the road'.[126] This is the California of the American dream.

And as this vision of America as Eden has changed and shifted and condensed to California, so has the vision of Eden's original inhabitants. Also, with this double image of America as wilderness and garden, there are double images of the Native Americans: the Noble Savage, God's innocents, the natural children of the deep woods; and the Bloodthirsty Savage, murderous creatures, barely more than animals. These two conflicting archetypes are seen side by side again in their fictional and perhaps more lasting and influential forms in *The Last of the Mohicans*. Uncas is 'Nature's gentleman' and his father Chingachgook *is* the Noble Savage: 'the expanded chest, the full-formed limbs, and grave countenance of this warrior would denote that he had reached the vigour of his days'.[127] Magua, of the evil Hurons, whom 'you can never make anything of ... but skulks and vagabonds', is introduced by the colours of his warpaint, 'blended in dark confusion around his fierce countenance [rendering] his swarthy lineaments still more savage and repulsive ... His eye which glistened like a fiery star amid lowering clouds, was to be seen in its state of native wildness.'[128]

Thus, thanks to James Fenimore Cooper, 'these are the world's images of the Red Man'. John McWilliams, in *The Last of the Mohicans: Civil Savagery and Savage Civility*, credits Cooper's novel with making these two images, 'the opposed faces of one figure', the dominant ones in 'white thinking about the character of the Indian from Cooper's time to now'.[129] Neither is, of course, accurate, and neither, in the end, is positive. As McWilliams points out the Noble Savage is still less than the white man: he is a child needing protection. Noble Savages are still illiterate, still susceptible to alcohol, and are very easily duped by their love of trinkets. For all that the Noble Savage's culture is closer to nature, it is still inferior to 'white civilization'. That the 'bad Indian's' culture, that of the 'barbaric, polytheistic, scalping torturer', is inferior goes without saying.[130]

The Noble Savage and the Bloodthirsty Savage, America as a utopian vision, the parallel social values and beliefs of Native Americans and feminist utopian thought, the use of multiple utopian dialectics, ethnography as fiction, Buddhist economics, the traditional conventions of utopian literature, and the myth of utopia, of the Golden Age – all these various elements have gone into Le Guin's yin utopia, *Always Coming Home*. That they define and shape this utopia makes them rhetorical: they are part of the argument she is making to and with the reader.

By inverting the utopian conventions in both of her utopian novels, *The Dispossessed* and *Always Coming Home*, Le Guin calls utopia itself into question. Her travellers, both citizens of utopia, are the ones to suggest utopia is not and cannot be finished and perfect. Utopia must always be process, and always be chosen again and again, as the traveller must do, whether he or she returns or stays. Neither utopia is truly paradisal. Anarres is a water-hungry, resource-starved moon, and the Valley has the toxins, radiation and genetic damage as its legacy of the past, and both are arguments for utopia as only being obtainable here, now. Eden is not needed, the Golden Age never was. Choice becomes for Le Guin a rhetorical device, and a way of initiating the utopian dialectic. Besides Stone Telling's and Shevek's choosing to return and thus choosing utopia, this is nowhere more apparent than in Le Guin's utopian parable, 'The Ones Who Walk Away from

Omelas'. She presents in this story an idyllic paradise, a society without want and restraint, with total freedom. Yet, there is a price for utopia: the abused child hidden in the cellar, who must remain there or paradise will fall. For the Omelans, there is the knowledge of the child and the Faustian bargain it represents, and then, there is the choice: to stay, to accept or to leave. To make the choice becomes rhetorical: choose a paradise that is literally rotten at the base, or choose true freedom, with responsibility and compassion. The dialectic is thus set in motion: here, then, are things as they are, and here are things as they might be. Choose.

To choose for *Always Coming Home* the parallel social customs and beliefs of the Native Americans and contemporary American feminist utopian thought again argues for utopia as a state of the mind rather than 'no good place' removed from here in space and/ or time. Such beliefs work – the Native Americans have already done it. Here again is the argument for process. Neither the lifestyle of the Native Americans nor feminist philosophy is perfect and a cure-all. Native Americans knew all about war and violence before the whites came. It is, as the Kesh put it, the 'sickness of man', a sickness against which we must always contend, a way of seeing the world that we must not choose again and again. The Kesh are an adult people – not the 'children of the wood'. And feminism, as Le Guin points out in her essay 'The Fisherwoman's Daughter', can stand some criticism of its own, as it can be just as exclusive as the patriarchal culture it seeks to change.

To place her utopia in a future California, in America, becomes, I think, an argument for the truth in the American national myth. By this I mean, regardless of how far short they fall of it, Americans do live as if they believe the world can be made better, as if there are other choices to make. They do live in process – America is not finished, or it shouldn't be. The Golden Land can't be found here anymore, not in the mythic sense of Eden, but, as Le Guin argues, it is already here.

Le Guin's choice of structure for *Always Coming Home* – a fictionalized ethnography, with its multiplicity of voices: utopian, observers, outsiders – becomes, I think, perhaps her greatest argument for utopia as process, as becoming. By having the reader assemble the Kesh culture out of a disparate collection of parts, Le Guin insists that we participate and consider the various arguments, the ongoing utopian dialectics between cultures, peoples and their differing ways of life. She insists we take the values she argued for in her reimagining of the myth of the Hero and the Quest (the small, the private, the worth of the work done back at home by the ones the Hero left there – women, children and the old) and make them local; these values can be part of a utopia. Such a utopia, Le Guin argues, can only be reached by not going in a straight line:

> I don't think we're ever going to get to utopia again by going forward, but only roundabout or sideways; because we are in a rational dilemma, an either/or situation as perceived by the binary computer mentality, and neither the either nor the or is a place where people can live.[131]

And it is this 'either' *and* this 'or', the third place, the choice mediating between the first two, these places where a people can live, these communities of the heart, to which Le Guin's fiction is leading us.

Notes

1. Janice Antczak, *Science Fiction: The Mythos of a New Romance* (New York: Neal-Schuman, 1985), p. 3.

2. As I discuss later in this chapter, utopia as a theme can be said to be integral to science fiction. For Le Guin, utopian thinking, utopia as a theme, a motif, has always been part of her work, with, I am arguing, *The Dispossessed* and *Always Coming Home* being the two primary and most important examples. Her story 'The Ones Who Walk Away from Omelas' is, arguably, one of the most famous examples in short fiction; this is particularly so in that it is included in many high school literature texts and many freshman composition readers. I would like to note here other examples of Le Guin's utopian or utopian-related science fiction, examples that come both before and after *The Dispossessed*. That *The Lathe of Heaven* (Avon Books, 1971) is the story of George Orr and his world-transforming dreams makes it clearly utopian. Orr dreams of making the world a better place, a place, as the back cover blurb says, that is a 'better reality, free from war, disease, overpopulation, and all human misery'. The catch is that to make one change sets a whole series of changes in motion, with unpredictable and, in the novel, disastrous results. Utopia here, as Le Guin clearly defines it in *The Dispossessed* and *Always Coming Home*, needs to be seen as process and not product. Le Guin's 1978 novel, *The Eye of the Heron*, is something of a more didactic and shorter version of *The Dispossesssed*. The colony planet Victoria is where Earth has dumped both a group of pacifists, the People of Peace, fictional kin of the Odonians,

and a group of criminals, who control the City. The pacifists – or rather their descendents – are also related to the ones who walk away from Omelas as this, in the end, is how they deal with the power-seekers in the City. Rather than fight and thus increase the likelihood of becoming like the oppressors, the oppressed seek utopia elsewhere, knowing that it still must be within as without. *The Beginning Place* (1980) is more akin to fantasy, as its two protagonists, Hugh and Irene, find Tembreabrezi, their haven of peace on the mountain, not another world, but through a threshold between here and there. Again, utopia must be more process than product, more a state of mind that a physical state, as Tembreabrezi proves to have horror as well as peace. This awareness, as I will discuss later in the chapter, is the same as that of Stone Telling in *Always Coming Home.* Stone Telling returns to her home, chooses it again; so do Hugh and Irene return home, to this reality and not the other. Utopia is already here. I selected *The Dispossessed* and *Always Coming Home* for examination here as they are, in my opinion, Le Guin's most fully realized utopias.

3. While there are clear and definite distinctions between traditional utopian literature with its conventions and the myths of the Golden Age, the time before history in which mankind lived in a perfect world, it seems that the terms can be used interchangeably here. This is because the utopian narrative is the human attempt to recreate the conditions of the myth, and in doing so, the narrative becomes another myth of the perfect world.

4. Robert Elliott, *The Shape of Utopia: Studies in a Literary Genre* (New York: University of Chicago Press, 1970), p. 7.

5. Ibid., pp. 3–4.

6. This quotation is from *The New Oxford Annotated Bible,* Revised Standard Version (New York: Oxford University Press, 1973). This version will be used for all biblical quotes in the text.

7. Elliott, *The Shape of Utopia*, p. 9.

8. Ibid., pp. 8–9.

9. Ibid., p. 7.

10. Elizabeth Cummins, *Understanding Ursula K. Le Guin* (Columbia, SC: University of South Carolina Press, 1990), p. 106.

11. Carol Franko, 'Dialogic Narration and Ambivalent Utopian Hope in Lessing's *Shikasta* and Le Guin's *Always Coming Home'*, *Journal of the Fantastic in the Arts*, 2 (3), 1990, p. 24.

12. Cummins, *Understanding Ursula K. Le Guin*, p. 106.

13. Franko, 'Dialogic Narration', p. 24.

14. Jean Pfaelzer, 'Response: What Happened to History?', in Libby Falk Jones and Sarah Webster Goodwin, eds, *Feminism, Utopia, and Narrative* (Knoxville, TN: University of Tennessee Press, 1990), p. 191.

15. Frederick Pohl, Martin Greenberg and Joseph Olander, 'Utopias and Dystopias', in Patricia Waricke, Martin Greenberg and Joseph Olander,

eds, *Science Fiction: Contemporary Mythology. The SFWA-SRA Anthology* (New York: Harper & Row, 1978), pp. 396–97.

16. Ibid., pp. 394–95.

17. Annegret Wiemer, 'Utopia and Science Fiction: A Contribution to their Generic Description', *Canadian Review of Contemporary Literature*, 19, March/June 1992, p. 150.

18. Pohl et al., 'Utopias and Dystopias', p. 395.

19. Ibid., pp. 395–96.

20. Naomi Jacobs, 'Beyond Stasis and Symmetry: Lessing, Le Guin, and the Remodeling of Utopia', *Extrapolation*, 29 (1), Spring 1980, p. 36.

21. Ibid., p. 37.

22. Dominic Baker-Smith, 'The Escape from the Cave: Thomas More and the Vision of Utopia', *Dutch Quarterly Review of Anglo-American Letters*, 15 (3), 1985, p. 158.

23. Darko Suvin, *Positions and Presuppositions in Science Fiction* (Kent, OH: Kent State University Press, 1988), p. 38.

24. Ibid., pp. 35–36.

25. Ibid., p. 34.

26. Ibid., p. 37.

27. Chris Ferns, 'Dreams of Freedom: Ideology and Narrative Structure in the Utopian Fiction of Marge Piercy and Ursula K. Le Guin', *English Studies in Canada*, 14 (4), December 1988, p. 453.

28. Suvin, *Positions and Presuppositions*, p. 38.

29. Wiemer, 'Utopia and Science Fiction', pp. 180–81.

30. Ibid., p. 184.

31. Ibid., p. 187.

32. Ursula K. Le Guin, 'Introduction to *The Left Hand of Darkness*', *Language of the Night: Essays on Fantasy and Science Fiction*, ed, Susan Wood, rev. edn (New York: HarperCollins, 1992),p. 151.

33. Ibid., p. 153.

34. Joanna Russ, 'Recent Feminist Utopias', in Marleen Barr, ed., *Future Females: A Critical Anthology* (Bowling Green, OH: Bowling Green State University Popular Press, 1981), p. 71.

35. Cornel West, *Race Matters* (New York: Vintage Books, 1994), pp. 27, 29.

36. Roslynn Haynes, 'Science, Myth and Utopia', in Kath Filmer and David Jasper, eds, *Twentieth-Century Fantasists: Essays on Culture, Society, and Belief in Twentieth-Century Mythopoeic Literature*, eds. (New York: St. Martin's Press, 1992), p. 16.

37. Brian Aldiss, *Trillion Year Spree: The History of Science Fiction* (New York: Avon, 1986), p. 480.

38. Ursula K. Le Guin, *The Dispossessed* (New York: Harper & Row, 1974), p. 303.

39. Ibid.

40. Ibid., p. 304.

41. Aldiss, *Trillion Year Spree*, pp. 75–76.

42. Plato, in Aldiss, *Trillion Year Spree*, p. 75.

43. More, quoted in Aldiss, *Trillion Year Spree*, p. 76.

44. Some might argue that Arthur C. Clarke's 1953 novel is not utopian. However, I agree with Frederick Pohl, Martin Greenberg and Joseph Olander who present it as utopian in their introductory essay 'Utopias and Dystopias' in *Science Fiction: Contemporary Mythology. The SFWA-SRA Anthology* (1978). At the novel's conclusion the human race, under benign alien tutelage, evolves to merge with the Universal Mind, an ideal state of existence.

45. Le Guin, *The Dispossessed*, pp. 261–62.

46. Judah Bierman, 'Ambiguity in Utopia: *The Dispossessed*', *Science-Fiction Studies*, 2, 1975, p. 250.

47. Ibid.

48. Ursula K. Le Guin, 'Science Fiction and Mrs Brown', in *Language of the Night*, p. 109.

49. Le Guin, *The Dispossessed*, p. 2.

50. Russ, 'Recent Feminist Utopias', in *Future Females*, p. 71.

51. Le Guin, 'Science Fiction and Mrs Brown', in *Language of the Night*, pp. 108, 109.

52. Ursula K. Le Guin, 'A Non-Euclidean View of California as a Cold Place to Be', *Dancing at the Edge of the World: Thoughts on Words, Women, Places* (New York: Grove Press, 1989), p. 95.

53. Ibid., pp. 89, 90.

54. Ibid., p. 87.

55. E. F. Schumacher, *Small is Beautiful: Economics as if People Mattered* (New York: Harper & Row, 1973), p. 4.

56. Ibid., p. 51.

57. Ibid., pp. 51, 52.

58. Ibid., p. 70.

59. Le Guin, 'A Non-Euclidean View of California', in *Dancing*, p. 98.

60. Ibid., p. 90.

61. Ibid., pp. 94, 95.

62. Ibid., p. 96.

63. Ursula K. Le Guin, *Always Coming Home* (New York: Harper & Row, 1985), p. 149.

64. Mary Field Belenky, Blythe McViker Clinchy, Nancy Rule Goldberger and Jill Mattuck Tarule, *Women's Ways of Knowing: The Development of Self, Voice and Mind* (New York: Basic Books, 1986), pp. 102–03.

65. Condor is the name given to Stone Telling's father's people by the Kesh. The Condor call themselves the Dayao, a name which Stone Telling doesn't use until she is living with her father's people.

66. It is interesting to note that the word "kit" can be used quite literally with *Always Coming Home* as the edition I have came with a

cassette tape of Kesh music and poetry. On the cassette wrapper are songs and poems in Kesh and English. I would argue that this again is an element of Le Guin's rhetoric in the use of the myth of utopia, particularly as she has chosen to create her utopia from an ethnographic and anthropological perspective. The tape provides yet more voices to serve as witnesses to Kesh culture and to suggest that to know a society one must know more than its written texts.

67. Peter Fitting, 'The Turn from Utopia in Recent Feminist Fiction', in Libby Falk Jones and Sarah Webster Goodwin, eds, *Feminism, Utopia, and Narrative* (Knoxville: University of Tennessee Press, 1990), pp. 151–52.

68. The Na Valley, the home of the Kesh, is California's Napa Valley some centuries in the future, after the disastrous collapse of our contemporary civilization. Setting a utopia at a distance from the author's and the reader's own culture is part of the traditional generic conventions – whether the distance is geographical or temporal. To do so, of course, is to make the time and place rhetorical – the future is a better place than the present because *now* we believe and do this; *then*, if we see the light, we will believe and do something else. *Here* we believe and do this; *there*, far from the corruption and wrongness of *here*, they (and possibly us) believe and do something else. Geographical and/or temporal distance also underscores the fantastic mythical qualities of the utopia: all the Golden Lands – Atlantis, the Isles of the Blessed, Tir na n-Og, and the rest – are forever far from us in space and time. California itself, as I will discuss in more detail when I talk about Le Guin's use of cultural myth, was for a long time America's Golden Land for very similar reasons.

69. Ron Scollon, 'In Defense of Writing: The Contemporary Merger of Ethnography and Fiction', *Redneck Review of Literature*, 20, Spring 1991, p. 35.

70. Ibid., p. 37.

71. Mary Catherine Harper, 'Spiraling around the Hinge: Working Solutions in *Always Coming Home*', in Barbara Howard Meldrum, ed., *Old West, New West: Centennial Essays* (Moscow, ID: University of Idaho Press, 1993), p. 253.

72. Le Guin, *Always Coming Home*, p. 338.

73. Harper, 'Spiraling around the Hinge', p. 252.

74. Le Guin, 'A Non-Euclidean View of California', in *Dancing*, p. 84.

75. Harper, 'Spiraling around the Hinge', p. 241.

76. Le Guin, 'A Non-Euclidean View of California', in *Dancing*, pp. 84–85.

77. I. A. Richards, *How to Read a Page* (1942; repr. Boston: Beacon Press, 1959), p. 24.

78. Ann G. Berthoff, *The Making of Meaning: Metaphors, Models and Maxims for Writing Teachers* (Montclair, NJ: Boynton/Cook, 1981), p. 71.

79. Harper, 'Spiraling around the Hinge', pp. 245, 241.

80. Wayne Booth, *The Rhetoric of Fiction*, 2nd edn (Chicago: University of Chicago Press, 1982), pp. 153–54.

81. As I noted earlier, Stone Telling did not use the name Dayao until she went to live with her father's people. Even with this distinction, which is made clear in the text, the usage of the names Condor and Dayao is 'complicated', as Stone Telling explains: 'We call them the Condor people; their name for themselves as distinct from all other people is Dayao, One-People. I shall call them that in the story now, because the way they use the word Condor, *Rehemar*, is complicated. Only one man whom they believe to be a messenger from One to them, and whom they all serve, is called The Condor. Certain men belonging to certain families are called True Condors and others like them are called, as I said, One-Warriors. No other people are called Condors ... Women of these families are called Condor Women and most serve Condor men ...' (Le Guin, *Always Coming Home*, p. 193). I have tried to follow Stone Telling's usage as closely as possible.

82. Fitting, 'The Turn from Utopia', p. 152.

83. Ibid.

84. Franko, 'Dialogic Narration?', p. 57.

85. Le Guin, *Always Coming Home*, pp. 148–49.

86. Lee Cullen Khanna, 'Women's Utopias: New Worlds, New Texts', in Falk Jones and Webster Goodwin, eds, *Feminism, Utopia, and Narrative*, p. 134.

87. Le Guin, *Always Coming Home*, p. 315.

88. Ibid., p. 316.

89. Khanna, 'Women's Utopias', in *Feminism*, p. 139.

90. Ibid., p. 138.

91. Ibid., p. 136.

92. Ibid., p. 131.

93. Marleen S. Barr, *Lost in Space: Probing Feminist Science Fiction and Beyond* (Chapel Hill: University of North Carolina Press, 1993), p. 40.

94. Russ, quoted in Barr, *Lost in Space*, p. 41.

95. Khanna, 'Women's Utopias', in *Feminism*, p. 131.

96. Le Guin, *Always Coming Home*, p. 20.

97. Ibid., pp. 419, 420.

98. Ursula K. Le Guin, letter to author (13 April 1998).

99. Le Guin, *Always Coming Home*, p. 488.

100. Ibid., pp. 489, 491.

101. Ibid., p. 243.

102. Kenneth L. Woodward, 'Gender and Religion', *Commonweal*, 123 (20), 22 November 1996, p. 10.

103. Theodora Kroeber, *Ishi in Two Worlds: A Biography of the Last Wild Indian in North America* (Berkeley: University of California Press, 1976), p. 24.

104. Richard Slotkin, *Regeneration through Violence: The Mythology of the Frontier, 1600–1800* (Middletown, CT: Wesleyan University Press, 1973), p. 44.

105. Kroeber, *Ishi in Two Worlds*, p. 24.

106. Alfred L. Kroeber, *Handbook of the Indians of California* (New York: Dover Publications, 1976), p. 12.

107. Le Guin, 'A Non-Euclidean View of California', in *Dancing*, p. 82.

108. Le Guin, *Always Coming Home*, p. 189.

109. Samuel Gill, *Native American Traditions: Sources and Interpretations* (Belmont, CA: Wadsworth, 1983), p. 88.

110. John Algeo, 'Magic Names: Onomastics in the Fantasies of Ursula K. Le Guin', *Names: Journal of the American Name Society*, 30 (2), June 1982, pp. 59, 62.

111. Ibid., p. 62.

112. Le Guin, *Always Coming Home*, p. 7.

113. Slotkin, *Regeneration through Violence*, p. 45.

114. Le Guin, *Always Coming Home*, pp. 133–34.

115. Le Guin, 'A Non-Euclidean View of California', in *Dancing*, p. 81.

116. Slotkin, *Regeneration through Violence*, p. 14.

117. Ibid., pp. 14, 10.

118. Richard Slotkin, *Gunfighter Nation: The Mythology of the Frontier in Twentieth-Century America* (New York: Atheneum, 1992), p. 5.

119. Ibid., pp. 14, 15.

120. Ibid., p. 21.

121. Ibid., pp. 29–30.

122. Ibid., p. 30.

123. Leo Marx, *The Machine in the Garden: Technology and the Pastoral Ideal* (New York: Oxford University Press, 1964), p. 3.

124. I think it would be useful here to examine the word Eden itself. Its root in Hebrew is uncertain. A connection with the Sumerian-Akkadian *ediner* word meaning 'wilderness' or 'flatland' is possible. On the other hand, the Septuagint derived Eden from a Hebrew word meaning 'to delight', hence the 'garden of Eden' is translated as the 'garden of delight'. Eden thus becomes paradise. 'Eden occurs 13 times in the singular, undetermined form to designate a location. In three places, Genesis 2:8, 10, and 4:16, it refers to a geographical land in which a garden is placed: the garden *in* Eden. A shift in meaning occurs in Genesis 2:15 and 3:23–24, which speak of the garden *of* Eden ... Man was driven from the garden on account of his disobedience, because Eden symbolized the state of unbroken fellowship between God and man' (B. S. Childs, 'Eden', in George Arthur Buttrick, Thomas Samuel Kepler, John Knox, Herbert Gordon May, Samuel Terrien and Emory Stevens Burke, eds, *Interpreter's Dictionary of the Bible* (4 vols, New York: Abingdon Press, 1962), pp. 22–23).

125. Marx, *The Machine in the Garden*, p. 43.

126. Charles L. Crow, 'Homecoming in the California Visionary Romance', *Western-American*, 24 (1), May 1989, p. 1.

127. James Fenimore Cooper, *The Last of the Mohicans: A Narrative of 1757* (Albany: State University of New York Press, 1983), p. 29.

128. Ibid., p. 18.

129. John McWilliams, *The Last of the Mohicans: Civil Savagery and Savage Civility* (New York: Twayne, 1995), pp. 54, 12.

130. Ibid., pp. 52, 53.

131. Le Guin, 'A Non-Euclidean View of California', in *Dancing*, p. 98.

CHAPTER FOUR
American Romantic/Pragmatic Rhetoric

These communities of the heart, to which Le Guin has been leading us through her rhetorical use of myth, are not newly discovered territories. As Robert Coles points out, both in *The Call of Stories* and in his 6 April 1995 address at UNC Greensboro, the potential for such communities already exists and can begin in a classroom. Such classrooms, Coles argues, would have a teacher who 'is willing to reach out to students in a moral way, that mixes head and heart'. Such classrooms, he insists, will have rigorous intellectual standards and acknowledge the value of the cognitive and of the affective. In this way classrooms become a part of a greater community – the school, the neighbourhood, the city – and teaching becomes integrated into how people live and work.[1] That such communities can and do exist in the classroom is particularly appropriate for Le Guin as her protagonists quite often are anthropological observers, such as Genly Ai in *The Left Hand of Darkness* and Havzhiva in *Four Ways to Forgiveness*. Karen Sinclair, in her essay 'Solitary Being: The Hero as Anthropologist', describes these protagonists as 'social anthropologists who [operate] as both cultural translator and social commentator. [Their] main purpose is to gather knowledge, and by standing in the threshold between two different cultures, to try (and usually fail) to explain each culture to the other.'[2] Even when, as with Shevek in *The Dispossessed*, the protagonist isn't a trained cultural observer, he or she is still attempting to explain one culture to another. Thus, many of Le Guin's protagonists are teachers, with classrooms of varying sizes.

As Hephzibah Roskelly and Eleanor Kutz point out in *An Unquiet Pedagogy: Transforming Practice in the English Classroom*, there is a 'common school culture', with its own rituals and structures, such as 'IQ and achievement tests, homogenous "ability" groupings, [and] academic and vocational tracks'. Individual schools have their own cultures, Roskelly and Kutz argue, with their own ways of knowing and using language, and their particular codes of behaviour, which both teachers and students must know.[3] Like their classroom counterparts, Le Guin's teacher-heroes are attempting to teach one culture and community the ways and mores of another. At the same time, sadly unlike many of their classroom counterparts, these fictional teacher-heroes must learn ways and mores they themselves do not know. Ai teaches the Gethenians of the Ekumen, and he learns about the Gethenians – their unusual sexuality, their customs and mores, their language – to more effectively work with them and to explain Gethen to the Ekumen. Teaching, learning-teachers, students, classrooms – and the communities that include both and that both make together – become interconnected and interrelated. Even the reader becomes a part of these interconnections – and explicitly so in *Always Coming Home.* That the teaching and learning are done through story, that a society is being taught and learned through story – on both personal and public levels – becomes an argument for story as a way to teach, as a way to make community. As Coles says:

> How to encompass in our minds the complexity of some lived moments in a life? How to embody in language the mix of heightened awareness and felt experience which reading a story can end up offering to the reader? ... The whole point of stories is not 'solutions or resolutions' but a broadening or even a heightening of our struggles ...[4]

To be able to connect, to understand a lived moment in another life, to have our own struggles resonate in another, is to create community. Story achieves this aim.

For Le Guin, this use of story, of myth in particular, is rhetorical, as it both leads us to and persuades us of the efficacy of community. The boon of her fictional quest is community. In *Tehanu,* the community is small and local: the family that consists of Tenar and Ged with Therru-Tehanu, the burnt child. In *The Dispossessed,* we find ourselves in more than one kind of community – again, the family, and yet a larger one, that of a society and a people, and something still larger, the species. *Always Coming Home*'s community is similar to that of *Tehanu:* a family, a society, a tribe.

By leading us to community, Le Guin is also arguing for what she incorporates as part of her rhetorical use of myth: the small, the private, the local. Using myth in this way is also an acknowledgement that humans are 'sensual, emotional, appetitive, ethical beings'.

All these, she argues, are valid and true ways of knowing and making meaning and perceiving the world, as valid as the Cartesian, the linear, the rational. When Le Guin presents an alternative or companion belief system to the Cartesian, she is placing herself squarely in a particular philosophy and its particular rhetoric: American pragmatism and American romantic rhetoric, or to use the combined term, as coined by Roskelly and Ronald, American romantic/pragmatic rhetoric.[5]

It is my contention that Le Guin's fiction is an expression of both pragmatism and romantic rhetoric. Her most recent work, the story collections *A Fisherman of the Inland Sea, Four Ways to Forgiveness, Unlocking the Air,* and *Old Music and the Slave Women* and *Dragonfly,* two recent novellas, and some selected short stories not yet collected, can be read as statements of American romantic/pragmatic rhetoric, and as realizations of her vision and idea of true community. Furthermore, I think her entire Hainish cycle[6] can be seen as a greater statement of community. To explain this interpretation of her work, I will first review American pragmatic philosophy and American romantic rhetoric. Then, having established this context, I will take a broad overview of Le Guin's work – in particular, her Hainish universe – and also examine selected stories in Le Guin's later story collections as expressions of this philosophy and its rhetoric. I conclude with a discussion of myth as rhetoric and story as a way of knowing, a way of teaching and making meaning--with a particular emphasis on science fiction. I will argue that to use myth, to use story, rhetorically and pedagogically, as Le Guin does, is to revalidate and make new a very old method of discovering truth and knowledge. This approach is as equally valid as the Cartesian and I am convinced it is more in tune with how humans really think and feel and come to know.

American Romantic/Pragmatic Rhetoric and Philosophy: The Past

Le Guin's use of American romantic/pragmatic rhetoric mirrors the historical evolution and merging of the former into the latter. To see this, we need first to look back to American pragmatism's nineteenth-century roots in Ralph Waldo Emerson's (1803–82) American romanticism. According to Cornel West in *The American Evasion of Philosophy: A Genealogy of Pragmatism,* Emerson 'prefigures the dominant themes of American pragmatism', as he saw a way to embody the 'ideal in the real'.[7] As Roskelly and Ronald argue in *Reason to Believe: Romanticism, Pragmatism, and the Possibility of Teaching*, 'Emerson's romanticism meant that he took his ideals for realities, believed them to be part of real and possible action'.[8] Emerson saw an 'inseparable link between thought and action, theory and practice'[9] – a cardinal connection later reiterated in pragmatic philosophy by Peirce, James,[10] and Dewey.

In 'The American Scholar', an essay often noted for its declaration of American intellectual freedom from Europe, Emerson advocates that the ideal becomes real, becomes action in the scholar's life: 'The one thing in the world of value, is the active soul'.[11] Scholars are not to be 'recluses' in 'ivory towers' – 'Action is with the scholar subordinate, but it is essential … Life is the dictionary of the scholar.'[12] He must be educated by 'nature, by books, by action'. He is 'Man Thinking', whose duties are 'to cheer, to raise, to guide men by showing them facts amidst appearances'.[13] Or in other words, Emerson is calling for a scholar to be connected to and part of his world – to its past in books, to the natural environment, and to life itself – a life of participation, in which one's actions have meaning and purpose. The scholar lives in a greater community, in which, as Roskelly and Ronald describe it, the 'powers of the individuals are not separable from the powers of the group, of the culture in which the individual resides'.[14] Or, as Emerson says, 'A Nation of men will for the first time exist, because each believes himself to be inspired by the Divine Soul which also inspires all men.'[15]

The self, that celebrated aspect of American romanticism, is connected, is a part of a whole and is integrated into a whole made up of other selves, all of whom have affected and changed each other. The action of one, the experiences of one, affect and resonate in others' experience. Life's continuum of experience – past into present, the contemplative and active – becomes, according to Emerson, the basis of knowing. Nature is as celebrated a part of American romanticism as is the self, and has acquired mystical overtones as a source of truth. Nature is 'the symbol of the spirit', and a 'metaphor for the human mind'.[16] But despite the otherworldliness these descriptions suggest, Emerson again is concerned with the individual in the community and what is connecting the two. The essay 'Nature' itself was composed on Boston Common, and is thus emblematic of the individual in the community and in nature. Nothing is isolated and separate: 'A leaf, a drop, a crystal, a moment of time, is related to the whole, and partakes of the perfection of the whole. Every particle is a microcosm, and faithfully renders the likeness of the world.'[17]

This unity in duality, this connection between self and other, between community and individual, is 'a guiding principle' in American romantic/pragmatic rhetoric. This is, as Roskelly and Ronald describe it, something of a paradox:

> Self-reliance itself builds upon that paradox, that one finds community in self and self in community. The simultaneous inward and outward search is a function of rhetoric, of knowing the self in order to know others and understanding others in order to understand the world inhabited by the self. And it's deeply a part of American romanticism, steeped in the inward turning of religious thought and outward yearning for a new community where such thoughts are given nourishment.[18]

It was in the working out of such paradoxes, and the putting into practice of the ideas that make them, that American pragmatism began to flower. The Sage of Concord, however, was not the one to test out his ideas to see if they worked, which is an important tenet of American pragmatism (as distinct from American romanticism). The best-known attempt to test out Emerson's ideas was that of his most famous disciple, Henry David Thoreau (1817–62), who 'takes Emerson's prescription in "The American Scholar" to heart and retreats to Walden Pond to become "man thinking"'.[19] Along with Thoreau, there are two other significant practitioners of Emerson's ideas I want to discuss here: Margaret Fuller, whose 1843 *Summer on the Lakes* could be considered a feminist version of *Walden*, and Walt Whitman, whose life and work are permeated by Emerson's philosophy.

Thoreau's *Walden* is often considered to be a symbol of the 'romantic vision of the isolated and egoistic poet', in full retreat from a loud and intruding world. It can, however, be seen as rather the opposite: a 'pragmatic experiment ... testing theory and suggesting a program for possible action'.[20] The goal of this pragmatic experiment was to bring men and women to a greater understanding of the truth of what it means to be human.

Walden becomes, then, Thoreau's rhetorical vision of how one might 'live in the world' – he is attempting to 'persuade readers to a new vision of consciousness and change'. That *Walden* is often read as a celebration of 'ego, nature, and retreat' is to ignore Thoreau's creation, as Roskelly and Ronald argue, of a romantic rhetoric that is dialectical.[21] The form of *Walden* becomes, in effect, an evocation of American romantic/pragmatic rhetoric, as Thoreau seeks, through his exploration of his self alone and his self as a part of the surrounding world, to mediate the tensions inherent in this rhetoric: between self and other, community and individual, public and private, big and small, linear progression and circular, contingent growth. *Walden* is not a straight, chronological, linear account of Thoreau's two-year sojourn by Walden Pond. Rather, *Walden* is an account of Thoreau's reflections of those two years, and the topics on which he reflected – economy, reading, sounds, solitude, visitors and so on – could be easily rearranged. These are his thoughts as he thought them, their order contingent on his inspiration and effort. *Walden* becomes an argument for a life of action and consequences, a life connected, not isolated and cut off. As Thoreau argues for the self as an agent of change, discovery and knowledge, he is also arguing for a self that is connected and part of a community, of a natural experiential world in which villages are universities, and such villages would 'stagnate if it were not for the unexplored forests and meadows' surrounding them. Everything is part of the whole and the whole contains everything.[22] *Walden*, rather than being an evocation of the romantic solitary poet communing with nature, becomes more significantly an evocation of C. S. Peirce's American pragmatism.

And as is *Walden,* so is *Summer on the Lakes, in 1843,* by Margaret Fuller (1810–50), who was as profoundly influenced by Emerson as Thoreau was. By 1843 she was 'already established as an important member of the Transcendental circle along with Emerson and Thoreau' and 'had been working with Emerson on editing the *Dial*[23] since 1840'.[24] Fuller is also known for her early advocacy of women's rights, particularly so in *Women in the Nineteenth Century,* in which she argues for women, in true romantic/pragmatic fashion, 'to direct their energies to exploring the self, developing autonomy, and expanding their intellectual and personal horizons'. Women, as a group, needed to 'raise themselves out of their condition of dependence to one of self-reliance'. Fuller saw women as needing a balance in their lives between their Minerva- and Muse-like qualities. To be Minerva-like was to develop 'intellectual discipline, critical intelligence, and self-awareness'. Women, Fuller argued, were 'overdeveloped' in their 'emotional, intuitional, divinatory, or Muse-like qualities'. To bring Minerva and the Muse into balance 'would endow woman with the power to subdue cultural opposition and take her place as man's equal in society'.[25] Thus Fuller advocates what, some years later, Peirce would call the 'Sensible Heart', and what Le Guin uses as a dominant metaphor, duality in unity, the yin and the yang, the connection between the rational and the irrational. The private actions of the soul and its public actions must connect and the consequences of such acts on the community must be taken into account.

Balancing and mediating the tension between these dualities was one of the primary occupations of Fuller's life. The example I want to look at here is her account of a summer trip to the Great Lakes with a close friend, Sarah Clarke. Like *Walden, Summer on the Lakes* is both personal and public, and Emersonian thought in action – a pragmatic experiment of such thoughts. Von Mehren, in *Minerva and the Muse: A Life of Margaret Fuller,* argues that the 'major theme' of *Summer* was 'the dislocation and disjointedness that western settlement had forced on the lives of the newcomers and the Native Americans alike'. Or, recast in the vocabulary of romantic/ pragmatic rhetoric: the mediation of the tensions between the civilized and the primitive, the settlers and the Native Americans, between rural and urban. This working out of tensions in dualities is also evident when the book is read as something of a proto-ecological treatise, in which Fuller 'mourns the despoiling of the land and the displacement of the Indians, the insensitivity of the newcomers to natural beauty and to human suffering, and the futility of the settlers' clinging to old identities and forms in the new environment'.[26] Perhaps as important, and again similar to *Walden,* is the theme of 'self-discovery and self-evaluation', another trade-mark of the American romantic. Thoreau retires to Walden Pond; Fuller undertakes a physical journey to what was then the frontier. Both experiences are described in deeply personal and subjective voices. As Fuller says:

> I have not been particularly anxious to give the geography of the scene, inasmuch as it seemed to me no route, nor series of stations, but a garden interspersed with cottages, groves and flowery lawns, through which a stately river ran. I had no guide-book, kept no diary, do not know how many miles we traveled each day; nor how many in all. What I got from

the journey was the poetic impression of the country at large; it is all I have aimed to communicate.[27]

The high value placed on internal discovery that earmarks American romanticism is evident here, yet this internal search for self is exercised in community. There are two women, Fuller and Clarke, travelling together, and there are the various communities they encountered, settlers and Native Americans. This internal discovery also creates a dialectic. As Fuller makes this journey of self-discovery, she is also continuing her ongoing life-experiment in trying to strike a balance or mediate the tensions between the dichotomies of her life – the public and the private, the Minerva and the Muse. The tensions between the civilized and the so-called primitive are examined: are the changes she sees truly signs of civilization – were the Native Americans truly uncivilized? The internal journey mirrors the physical, the latter a metaphor for the former.

Le Guin frequently uses such an interaction between interior and exterior travel into self. Shevek's parallel interior and exterior journeys, on Urras and Anarres, as a child and as an adult, are but one example. Ged's journey across Earthsea to seek out the shadow he set loose, the shadow he can only stop when he gives it his own name, is another. And like Ged and Shevek, Fuller's journey is not circular; it is a spiral. She cannot return to the exact place she began: she has been changed by her travels.

That this travel is no straight path, and has digressions and wanderings, evokes a romantic/pragmatic approach to life: life is contingent, change is a constant, and learning must also be active, in motion, changing. The structure of *Summer on the Lakes* further reflects its rhetorical nature, as it 'follows the tradition of portfolio and sketchbook writings that began at the turn of the nineteenth century and was largely an art form practiced by women'.[28] As with an artist's portfolio, there is the feeling that pages can be moved, inserted here and there. Clarke's drawings, giving a literal quality to the sketchbook idea, could be moved with relatively little disruption of the text. This 'meandering, fragmentary subjective book, almost a diary, [employs] the voice of a traveling companion, rather than a guide', thus allowing Fuller to 'invite the reader to join her in her spontaneous thoughts, her self-exploration, her moods and misgivings', and share and participate in her thoughts and impressions.[29] Fuller 'likens [these] impressions to baubles on a string: "I wished I had thread long enough to string on it all these beads that take my fancy.'"' Baubles can be restrung and rearranged. The 'necklace' – Fuller's 'collection of autobiographical sketches, social criticism, inspirational passages, Transcendental meditations, and stories of her travels', as well as the poems and stories of which she was reminded and thus included – is a contingent work of art.[30]

There is also a pragmatic quality to this art of Fuller's. She hoped to teach her readers about many subjects, including making them aware of new American writers and that there was a difference between American and British literature (thus echoing 'The American Scholar'), the tragedy of the Native Americans forced from their land, education and the 'place of women in the new frontier'.[31] Thus, she is asking: is there validity to her ideas and what she has to say and has learned? This knowledge is contingent on her travels and her interpretations, and is knowledge acquired in the context of communities – American romantic/pragmatic rhetoric at work. *Summer on the Lakes* is not only Fuller's recollection of her summer's journey, but an 'illumination' of 'both the public and private life of her time' – as is *Walden* of Thoreau's, as is *The Dispossessed* of Shevek's life and times, and *Always Coming Home* of Stone Telling's. All are an argument for lives of action which are connected and integral to their communities.[32] Fuller is, then, the 'primary female American romanticist'. Her personal experience, her 'personal story', is offered as proof of her argument. Furthermore, to refute the stereotype of the long-suffering poet, Fuller does not use her personal story, and neither does Thoreau, 'to support the sanctity of individual experience', but rather offers her personal life in its context 'as experienced by many individuals' – self in community.[33] One's identity must be discovered in the context of others.

Walt Whitman (1819–92), who completes my triad of Emersonian practitioners, also found his identity in such a context. Like his contemporaries, Thoreau and Fuller, Whitman's life and work are rhetorical and serve as an exemplar of American romantic/ pragmatic rhetoric, an exemplar that is somewhere between the first two. As Thoreau calls for a connection to the natural world, so does Whitman; as Fuller speaks to a people – American women, Americans in general – and seeks to connect men and women as equals, so does Whitman. As both Fuller and Thoreau attempt to connect to the public and the private, so does Whitman – but his connections are perhaps the most public and the most private. Whitman seeks to connect the soul, not only of a person, but also the soul of American democracy, to the body, and to one of the body's most private aspects, sexuality. Given the rubric of the 'poet of democracy', Whitman saw his poetry as a connector. Thus he wanted to give his poetry to the American people, to all of them, including the lowest common denominator of society. Whitman 'introduced freer, speechlike rhythms into the poetry of verse and replaced the themes of New England villages (Thoreau's villages) and sentimental love with songs about the occupations and sexuality'. Whitman celebrated in 'free verse, not merely "Mother Nature", but his own nature as representative of all humankind in its endless variety'.[34]

This equating of nature with humankind is Emersonian, and Whitman unquestionably deserves the same adjective. Emerson can be said to be, in a certain sense, Whitman's mentor, the man Whitman called 'Master' in the second edition of *Leaves of Grass*.[35] It was Emerson, after all, who wrote to Whitman after reading the 1855 edition of *Leaves,* to 'greet [him] at the beginning of a great career'.[36] It is Emerson whom Whitman credits for bringing him to a creative boil. First, Whitman learned to love himself, and then 'from Emerson and the transcendentalists [he learned] to see himself and every other human being as an emblem of God because all were parts of nature', grass serving as Whitman's 'principle emblem of God's love. It was God's calling card and attention getter.'[37] Grass grows in great prairie seas and in between and out of city pavement, 'among black folks as well as among white', and in city cemeteries, making the promise 'that all the dead were "alive and well somewhere"'. Everything and everyone, like the grass, goes 'onward and outward'.[38] Grass is further emblematic of Whitman's America in its singularity and its multiplicity: the single blades, the lawns and prairie seas, the interconnected roots, and the individual, the communities – villages, towns, cities – and the American people. Self and other are parts of a whole. And the commonality and ubiquity of grass are emblematic of American democracy and its mythic ideal of the common man. Thus Whitman makes America and its community of communities into poetry. It is the role of America's poet to celebrate this, to weave poetry into the democratic fabric: the grass is the 'handkerchief of the Lord' or 'the beautiful uncut hair of graves' or it grows on 'the breasts of young men' ('Song of Myself', lines 103, 110, 112).[39] As Whitman says in the Preface to *Leaves,* 'the United States themselves are essentially the greatest poem'.[40]

In order to write this 'greatest poem', the poet must be active and engaged, a lesson Whitman learned from Emerson, particularly from Emerson's 1842 lecture, 'The Poet'. According to Emerson, the poet was to be a 'citizen of the world'.[41] America is identified by Emerson as the poet's subject matter: 'our stumps and their politics, our fisheries, our Negroes and Indians, our boats and our repudiations, the wrath of rogues and the pusillanimity of honest men, the northern trade, the southern planting, the western clearing, Oregon and Texas'. At the time all these were still 'unsung' and overdue for poetic expression: 'America is a poem in our eyes, its ample geography dazzles the imagination, and it will not wait long for metres.'[42] Emerson said in 'The Poet' that he had looked 'in vain' for such a poet – then he read *Leaves of Grass* and saluted Whitman: America had found its poet.

Working thus in an Emersonian context, Whitman's poem 'Song of Myself' (considered by many critics to be his greatest) becomes a statement of American romantic/pragmatic rhetoric.[43] The poem begins with the poet and the reader and the land all in communion: 'I celebrate myself and sing myself/And what I assume you shall assume/For every atom belonging to me as good belongs to you' (lines 1–3). All is connected: 'My tongue, every atom of my blood form'd from this soil, this air ... Everything is part of the whole... all the men ever born are also my brothers, and the women my sisters and lovers' (lines 6, 94). The list of those who are part of these connections, who make up this community is long: the carpenter, the married and unmarried children, the pilot, the duck-shooter, the deacons and the spinning girl, the lunatic, slave and free, black, white and red, the opium-eater, the prostitute (in lines 266–324). Parallels of such cosmic inclusiveness and connection are also found in Le Guin's fiction. As Ged explains to Yarrow in *A Wizard of Earthsea*: 'My name and yours, and the true name of the sun, or of a spring of water, or an unborn child, all are syllables of the great word that is very slowly spoken by the shining of the stars.'[44] All are within and a part, all are in communion, in community. Self is in the other, and the 'whole notion of self and identity' becomes a 'process of understanding the other; a process of discovery of individual identity becomes, necessarily, a discovery of Whitman's democratic vistas as well, a recognition of and plan for achieving commonality and community possibility'.[45]

If community is a public matter, it is a private one as well, which for Whitman, in many poems, is a matter of sexuality. Whitman seeks to mediate the tensions between body and soul, public and private, and to go past them to integration: 'I am the poet of the Body and I am the poet of the Soul ... I am the part of the woman the same as the man' ('Song of Myself', lines 422, 425–26). The body and all its parts '[figure] into the celebration of life', a celebration prior to Whitman, in which poems, according to Loving in his biography, *Walt Whitman: The Song of Himself*, 'hastily transcended the flesh into the sentimental'.[46] For Whitman, the flesh is real, just as the earth is real, therefore humans are sensual and sexual beings. Whitman's use of the body, in both the literal and the metaphoric sense, was 'unprecedented'.[47] No one before him had seen that the private sexual lives of men and women were the stuff of poetry, as was the nation of which they were a part. For Whitman, the tensions between the spiritual and the earthly, the soul and the body, were mediated by sex, which partook of each, and brought both into a union.[48]

The poems in *Children of Adam* exemplify this notion. They are nothing if not erotic paeans to the physical love between a man and a woman, a love, as in 'Pent-up Aching Rivers', that is at once both personal and private, and at the same time, cosmic and of the universe. The poet sings of the phallus, of the 'song of procreation', the 'true song of the soul fitful at random/Renascent with grossest Nature or among animals/Of that, of them, and what goes with them my poems informing/Of the smell of apples and lemons, of the pairing of birds/Of the wet of the woods, of the lapping of waves'. The entire universe is permeated with this creative urge: two hawks in flight, two fishes in the sea, a man and a woman, and for all, sex is an 'act divine' (lines 14–18, 30–34, 56). According to Bradley and Blodgett in a footnote to the 1973 Norton Critical Edition, *Children of Adam* is a 'daring and original celebration of the drive of sex, not only the procreative instinct, but the whole appetite of creation'.[49] The human body, male and female, is not sordid, but sacred, as Whitman makes clear in 'I Sing the Body Electric', when he celebrates the female as a 'divine nimbus', and the male as 'the flush of the universe'. Whitman even makes a litany of human body parts, 'And all of these parts are not only the body, but the soul' (lines 53, 77, 163). We cannot separate body and soul; to do so is to lessen our humanity. As in Le Guin's fiction, there are layers of community here: from that of a man and a woman, to a people, a tribe, a nation, the universe.

When Shevek and Takver, in *The Dispossessed*, meet after four

years of separation, they must recreate and renew their partnership, a private commitment, through touch, through sex, through
union, through a re-engagement in and with the process of their
relationship. At the same time that this most private and intimate
of connections is made, they '[circle] about the center of infinite
pleasure, about each other's being, like planets circling blindly,
quietly in the flood of sunlight':[50] microcosm and macrocosm.
Consequently their partnership is a public statement of a private
commitment, as is any marriage.

Whitman's *Calamus* series attests to love's many permutations
and shapes and arrangements. The *Calamus* poems are a series long
associated with the homoerotic. There is, of course, academic
debate about Whitman's sexuality: was he a homosexual, as these
poems suggest? Since there is no doubt of the eroticism and
sensuality in *Children of Adam*, was he bisexual? Whitman's
devotion to the Union wounded in wartime Washington is well
known, as is the great love and affection he had for these soldiers.
Also documented are such intense friendships as the one Whitman
had with Peter Doyle, a Washington trolley conductor – does this
make the poet homosexual? Yet, it is also true that romantic non-
sexual same-sex friendships were more prevalent and accepted in
the nineteenth century than they are today. Whitman's sexuality,
however, is not my point here; rather I want to suggest that in the
Calamus poems there is an argument for love, sexual or otherwise,
which crosses boundaries – for love as a force is a major tenet in
American romantic/pragmatic rhetoric. In these poems the poet
speaks of his 'burning desire for a lifelong lover who is male'.[51] In
these poems the poet 'rejoices in comrades' and will 'tell the secret
of [his] night and days/To celebrate the need of comrades' ('In
Paths Untrodden', lines 7, 17–18). It is this love that will make the
'continent indissoluble' – with such love, democracy, the Union,
can be saved. The poet dreams of a mythic utopia, a 'new city of
Friends', in which is shared the 'quality of robust love' – a love
which nothing exceeds ('I Dream'd in a Dream', lines 2–3).

Thus love, for Whitman, is not constrained by boundaries,
sexual, class, political, or otherwise. Love creates and sustains community, and love creates a contingent knowledge based on this
community: it is through Whitman's all-encompassing love that he
can sing of the country, himself, a song in which he asks the reader
to join. Love connects self and other and at the same time, it creates
self and other. Love is the force that mediates such dualities – and

love is a force that binds the continent together, a force that creates a utopia. So for Whitman to write of the sensual and the sexual in both heterosexual and homosexual imagery is to call another duality into question – is love just love, is it always a unifier and not sometimes a divider?

Le Guin recognizes love, in its many different shapes, as a mediating and binding force in her fiction. Shevek and Takver are a monogamous partnership; the people of O form a group-marriage of at least four people; the Gethenians enter kemmer and one month are female, the next male, and may couple with a partner who was the previous month also of a different gender. As Le Guin is pushing past the traditional duality of human sexuality, male and female, so does Whitman, as when he speaks of 'an avowed, empowered, unabashed development of sex'.[52]

Love and sexuality, for both Fuller and Thoreau, were a force that created tensions and dualities and, at least, for Fuller, a unity. Fuller writes frankly of being attracted to both men and women. For ten years, beginning in the early 1830s, Fuller's relationship with Anna Barker 'served as [her] most cherished romantic love'. Von Mehren goes on to further describe this relationship as of an idealized and imaginative nature, as was common in the nineteenth century, and that 'during her adolescent years Fuller's expressions of affection to her men and women friends were not remarkably different'.[53] She wanted, it seemed, to believe that her attraction to Baker and Sturgis (another close woman friend) transcended sexuality, and was of a pure and disinterested nature. As she wrote in her journal: 'It is so true that a woman may be in love with a woman, and a man with a man. It is so pleasant to be sure of it because undoubtedly it is the same love we shall feel when we are angels'.[54] Was Fuller a bisexual as the term is understood in the late twentieth century? Perhaps. That she had feelings as intense for James Nathan and later, for her husband, Ossoli, speak of her attraction to men. Of her husband, she wrote to her mother that 'In him I have found a home and one that interferes with no tie.'[55] And if one is at home in one's soul, there is the possibility of wholeness, a wholeness brought by love.

Thoreau is another story. Scholars have come to some 'astoundingly different conclusions as to [his] sexuality': asexual, 'somewhat heterosexual', androgynous, 'and in recent years ... homosexual'.[56] Walter Harding, in a 1991 essay 'Thoreau's Sexuality', explores the idea of Thoreau as a very repressed and tortured homosexual, who was extremely uncomfortable with sexual issues and matters. Harding bases his argument on Thoreau's journals, which seem to indicate an awareness that 'his were not the usual reactions of a man to the opposite sex', 'a deep longing for love and companionship' with women, and appear to reveal some degree of attraction towards men. Harding believes that Thoreau's sexual energies were redirected into his deep and passionate love of nature so much so that '[his] love life was centered on nature', a love evident in his writing – and that if this had not been so, his prose would not have approached the level of genius that it did. [57] And yet Thoreau also writes in his journals of his love for a woman, 'in 1839–40, when he was quite smitten with … Ellen Sewall', a woman to whom Thoreau made an epistolary proposal, which was rejected.[58]

It is not my point to suggest that one's sexuality necessarily shapes one's rhetoric and philosophy, but rather that Whitman, Fuller and Thoreau, as they attempted to enact Emerson's vision, attempted to mediate the tensions between their bodies and their souls, between their minds and their hearts, the accepted and the unacceptable – and that love was a force, a motivation and an enabler in such mediation. Thus, these three can be said to embody, literally, romantic/pragmatic rhetoric.

Le Guin also calls for love to be a force, to mediate duality – and to move past duality, to create unity. The ambisexual Gethenians, who can be either male or female, and are neither for most of the time, ask the reader to question the validity of accepted human dualities of masculinity and femininity. Is the masculine necessarily aggressive, dominating, strong, linear? Is the feminine necessarily passive, submissive, weak, circular? Are not these characteristics human as opposed to being gender-restricted? If we go past these dualities do we not find a whole being? A whole being that, as D. H. Lawrence says in his essay 'Whitman', is 'sensually throbbing, spiritually quivering, mentally, ideally speaking … It is perfect and whole.'[59]

As Roskelly and Ronald present it, American romanticism, particularly that of Emerson, Thoreau, Fuller and Whitman, is a philosophic predecessor of pragmatism, its progenitor as it were. When put into action, as Emerson advocated and Fuller, Thoreau and Whitman actually attempted, romanticism becomes rhetorical. Romanticism becomes, when coupled with pragmatism, the impetus that makes pragmatism more than just a philosophy, rather a way of making meaning, a way of knowing the world: 'To see romantic/pragmatic rhetoric as one concept requires a leap of faith, especially given the common (and current) assumptions associated with each part of this term.'[60] To understand this coupling, and how it works in Le Guin's own rhetoric, American pragmatism by itself, as Peirce expressed it, needs some examination.[61] I turn again to West's cogent explanation and definition of American pragmatism in *The American Evasion of Philosophy* and to Roskelly's working definitions from lectures and discussions in a UNC Greensboro graduate class.[62]

According to West, there are three fundamental claims of Peirce's pragmatism:

> first, that the most reasonable way of arriving at warranted and valid beliefs is by means of scientific method; second, that scientific method is a self-correcting social and communal process promoted by smoothly functioning habits, i.e. beliefs, upset by uncertain expectations, and whose sole end is 'settlement of opinion'; and third, that this scientific quest for truth is inextricably linked, though in no way reducible, to the ultimate good of furthering 'the development of concrete reasonableness,' i.e. evolutionary love.[63]

At first glance, this may seem oddly like Cartesian thinking: especially the belief in the scientific method. But West argues that Peirce saw Cartesian thinking as having a fatal error: it begins with doubt. For Peirce, and even more so for later romantic/pragmatic rhetoricians, the place to begin in the acquisition of knowledge is with the possibility of belief. The scientific method, as West notes, is 'self-correcting', and thus, as Roskelly points out, it is fallible. The scientific method is also 'communal' – the knowledge it operates with and within and produces is a result of a communal, social process, based on the 'settlement of opinion'. Knowledge, therefore, is community-based, contingent on what is known and can be known at a given time, and is the result of the consensus of a particular community. This is the truth as we know it – we anthropologists, we sociologists, we English professors – at this time, contingent on what we already know and are capable of learning. This 'centrality of contingency', as West puts, is key to American pragmatism. What we know, how we know and what we do as a result of this knowledge must be and is 'revisable'. Havzhiva, the title character in Le Guin's 'A Man of the People', in *Four Ways to*

Forgiveness, learns that what he has known to be true is only valid for where he grew up. What Havzhiva accepts as truth must be revisable and is contingent on the other knowledge he learns in the Ekumenical Schools, with students from the known human universe. In the *Earthsea* novella 'Dragonfly', the prohibition against women entering the Great House on Roke to learn magic is shown to be a custom, and not an eternal truth. The doors once closed must be opened.

The revisability of truth, of knowledge, hinges on another tenet of American pragmatic thought: truth, to be accepted as such, must be tried out, experimented with, put into action. According to Roskelly, one of pragmatism's primary questions is: 'what difference does it make?' What are the consequences of what we believe and what we do with those beliefs?[64] As Thoreau, Fuller and Whitman demonstrated, our actions must be embodied in our beliefs, and our actions must be a reflection of our beliefs. Our theories, to have validity, have to be put into practice. Then, according to West, we can determine 'the best available, yet revisable theories of reality'.[65]

How we decide is based on our beliefs and our resulting truths. Le Guin puts this idea of testing truth through practice into her fiction. Again, the story 'A Man of the People' offers an example. The character Havzhiva tests out and tries the truth of human freedom he learned in the Ekumenical Schools on Yeowe, a former slave colony. Can the Yeowans be free? Is the idea of human freedom transcendent? Is it integral to being human? On a more personal and private level, when Sov, in the story 'Coming of Age on Karhide', comes of age, he/she tests out the new knowledge of his/her body. Sov, an ambisexual Gethenian, is, until his/her fourteenth year, sexually latent, a neuter. With maturity comes new knowledge, of sex, of desire, of maleness and femaleness, that can only be experienced to be learned. Sov must learn a new body because the old one no longer fits – and he/she learns a new truth as to who and what he/she is.

This considering and reconsidering of the truth, testing and retesting, based on a community's consensus, makes pragmatism 'profoundly democratic'. More than one voice must be heard, more than one opinion must be examined. This multiplicity of thought and idea becomes a key to two other key tenets of American pragmatism: mediation and love. Peirce saw pragmatism as a way to mediate the tensions between dichotomies – to seek the third way, as opposed to either/or binary thinking. Cartesian thinking elevates the empirical, logical, linear choice as the way to truth and knowledge. Knowledge is traditionally seen as operating through action and reaction, practice and theory, or as Peirce describes them, chance and logic – first and second principles that make systems of thought and knowledge work. Peirce maintains that for good systems to work, 'the thirdness of ideas must be uncovered and explored'.[66] Knowledge is never fully formed without a third, love – the mediation between the first two. This third way is not necessarily a synthesis; rather it can be a consequence or a 'taking off from' the other two. To look at knowledge this way allows for a way to mediate tensions between such 'bipolar opposites' as love and hate, emotion and dispassionate inquiry, logic and emotion, self and community, private and public.[67] The third grows out of the interaction of the two. Rather than the rational and irrational, intellect and emotion in opposition, there is the third, the 'Sensible Heart', Peirce's emblem for pragmatic thought. 'Pragmatism can be seen as a working out of third principles'.[68]

Love itself, or *agape,* according to Peirce, allows us to listen, to talk, to exchange ideas, to mediate. According to Peirce, in his essay 'Evolutionary Love', growth comes only out of love, in an 'evolutionary philosophy ... from the ardent impulse to fulfill another's highest impulse'.[69] To progress, to go forward, Peirce claims, the individual must have sympathy or love for his or her neighbour, and seek the neighbour's betterment. Peirce saw around him, in nineteenth-century America, a Gospel of Greed, not the Christian Gospel of Love: 'every individual striving for himself, with all his might and trampling his neighbors underfoot'. 'Agapism, evolutionary love' – or the 'Sensible Heart', which seeks to mediate the needs of the individual as opposed to the needs of the other – allows us to go forward, to move on.[70] But this heart, unlike Cartesian thinking in which the rational is paramount, is more akin to how humans really operate. Peirce says: 'In regard to the greatest affairs of life, the wise man follows his heart and does not trust his head. Common sense witnesses unequivocally that the heart is more than the head, it is in fact everything in our highest concerns.'[71]

Le Guin sees and makes this connection of head and heart, with the heart of 'highest concern', in her fictional universe as well. Love is a primary force; it is the creator of community: through family, through neighbours, through education. Love is what brings change to each of the protagonists in *Four Ways to Forgiveness:*

for the old woman, Yoss, it is the compassion to reach across and through a man's history of betrayal and greed to the man himself; for Solly and Teyeo, love connects an alien woman, an offworlder, to a man whose own country has made him an alien; for Havzhiva and Rakam, love brings knowledge, local and universal, and for both, a realization that head and heart must be together. Love is a force; 'love is', as Takver says in *The Dispossessed*, 'the true condition of human life'.[72] Thoreau, Whitman, Fuller, Emerson or Peirce would have agreed with her.

It is not Peirce, however, whom West credits as being the 'greatest of American pragmatists'. The thinker who reached its 'highest level of sophisticated articulation', who achieved American pragmatism's true 'coming-of-age', is John Dewey. He saw philosophy as a form of 'cultural critical action that focuses on the ways and means by which human beings have, do, and can overcome obstacles, dispose of predicaments, and settle problematic situations'.[73] Dewey's concerns with the 'relation of the individual thinker to [a] community of thought' makes it clear he sees truth arising from a community context and consensus, always contingent. Any theory of how the world works must be 'based on practice based on theory' (or praxis, as Paulo Freire would say).[74] Dewey's pragmatism saw the universe as a work in progress in which truth, based on experience and practice, undergirded by theory, had to matter – it had to be tested by action, and it had to work.

Dewey's experiential-based progressive theory of education is pure American pragmatism. There must be, Dewey argues in *Experience and Education,* 'an intimate and necessary relation between actual experience and education'. What the student learns must come from an 'acquaintance with a changing world', through experience in the world. The student's personal experience, in and out of the classroom, is a source of learning. This is not to say that it is only important to learn contemporary knowledge, but that the 'knowledge of the past' is a means, and not an end. This is Dewey's principle of the 'continuity of experience … [which] means that every experience both takes up something from those which have gone before and modifies in some way the quality of those which come after'.[75] The student's individuality is to be given full expression, even as he or she functions in a learning environment with others, a learning environment that draws from the past and looks to the future.

Here, clearly, is American romantic/pragmatic rhetoric and philosophy implemented. The tension between self and other, between individual and community, is recognized and mediated. Personal knowledge, personal experience – the knowledge of self is valued and given free expression. It is with the individual that Dewey asks instruction to begin, 'with experience the learners already have, [with] subjects drawn from ordinary life-experiences'. These experiences, according to Dewey, 'provide the starting point for further learning'.[76] In effect, a learning spiral, or a helix, is created, as past experiences connect to the present and to the future, as information and ideas are obtained and integrated. That this experientially based education of the individual acknowledges the value of past learning, of others' learning, and draws from such connections, makes it in effect a mediation of self and other, community and individual.

The whole idea of education based on experience, on 'ordinary life-experiences', expresses the pragmatic question of what difference does it make – does this knowledge matter? Does it work in the world? Its truth becomes a matter, then, of action. The contingency West mentions as being central seems obvious here: one individual's life-experiences will invariably be different from another's. No subject's instruction can be assumed to be exactly the same from one person to another, from one class to another. What is taught becomes contingent on the students and what they already know. Such contingency sets up the mediation of another dichotomy between what is expected to be taught and learned, and what is actually taught and learned. Theory and practice must be constantly mediated as circumstances dictate; praxis must be practised. An example of this experiential education can be found in Le Guin's 'Forgiveness Day', in *Four Ways to Forgiveness*. Solly and Teyeo, who come from very different cultures, discover that to know each other, to understand each other, is to experience the other's life, beliefs and ways of knowing. That Le Guin so frequently uses as her narrators anthropologist/observers – who are teachers, as I have suggested earlier – further supports the idea of experiential education. Genly Ai in *The Left Hand of Darkness*, Pandora in *Always Coming Home* Serenity in 'Solitude' and others are telling the readers what they have learned and experienced from living in an alien culture. They are providing field data, as they were experienced: the truth of what was learned, contingent on the observer, and his or her relationship to and in the observed

community. That these data are given as a story – objective information presented subjectively – further attests to the value of
experiential education. To tell a story is to teach it, and it is to make
meaning out of the experiences on which the story is based. In
summary, pragmatism offers a mediated way of perceiving: with
both doubt and belief as part of the process of thinking, with
experience as the test for the truth of generalization, with truth
contingent on consensus and community, and with love as a force
that mediates, connects and creates.

American Romantic/Pragmatic Rhetoric and Philosophy: Contemporary

Obviously, Le Guin, a spiritual heir of Emerson, Thoreau, Fuller,
Whitman, Peirce and Dewey, is not working in isolation. She is part
of a greater community of like-thinkers – Cornel West, Paulo
Freire, Robert Coles, Mike Rose, Ann Berthoff and Karen LeFevre –
and like Le Guin, they are calling for a paradigm shift from the
primacy of Cartesian thinking. What Vico[77] called for in the
eighteenth century, Le Guin and these others call for now. They ask
that value be given to the subjective, the personal, the private and
the small, the feminine and to narrative. A look at the ideas of these
others makes Le Guin's contemporary rhetorical and philosophical
context evident.

Cornel West and Robert Coles operate, both as teachers and
philosophers of teaching, and as cultural critics, within the public
arena. While only Coles speaks specifically about what occurs in a
classroom, both he and West speak of how our culture works: how
our social customs and mores determine how we interact as a
people. Paulo Freire and Mike Rose, on the other hand, are
primarily concerned with issues of literacy at the classroom level:
how students learn how to read and write, and how they become
effective readers and writers. These above mentioned distinctions
are somewhat arbitrary, as these four educators, and others of like
mind – Berthoff and LeFevre – are all teachers, philosophers and
cultural critics. They are all concerned with the classroom as a place
of human activity and with how the attitudes and beliefs of the
classroom and the greater culture interact and overlap, and become
ways of knowing and making meaning.

Public Rhetoric

Cornel West, who has written so eloquently on Emerson, Peirce and Dewey, is equally eloquent in his own right as an American romantic/pragmatist. Robert Boynton in *The Atlantic Monthly* describes West as one of an 'impressive group of writers and thinkers' who have 'revived and revitalized' the role of the public intellectual. This role, by association, is one of mediation. The intellectual today is all too commonly characterized by the ivory tower, with a 'public' that 'barely extends beyond the campus walls'. His or her language and studies are considered abstract, esoteric, highly abstruse – and not connected to the man or woman in the street or to the issues making headlines and being debated in government. To be a public figure one would have to forsake the protection of a university, with its time and space and support for intellectual activity.[78]

Not so with West, Boynton argues, who, with Toni Morrison, Shelby Steele, Henry Louis Gates, Jr., and bell hooks, have brought back the public intellectual: writers and thinkers, 'informed by a strong moral impulse, who [address] a general, educated audience about the most important issues of the day'. 'They are bringing moral imagination and critical intelligence to bear on the defining American matter of race – and reaching beyond race to voice what one calls "the commonality of American concern".'[79] The very term 'public intellectual' is pragmatic, as it is a mediation between public and private, and it is praxis: theory and practice in action.

West sees this active 'Man Thinking' as the best role for the intellectual, a 'critical organic catalyst'. In *Keeping Faith: Philosophy and Race in America,* West argues, like Thoreau, that the intellectual should be 'grounded outside the academy, in progressive political organizations and cultural institutes as the most likely agents of social change in America'. It is the vocation of an 'engaged progressive intellectual to fuse the best of the life of the mind from within the academy with the best of the organized forces for greater democracy outside the academy'.[80] The pragmatist, then, is to use the tensions between the academy and the public to create a Peircean third force, that of constructive, progressive social change. He or she must operate with what West calls the 'public square – the common good that undergirds our national and global destinies', or, in other words, the community, be it local, regional, national or global, in which we live our lives, connected to one another.[81]

West is calling for a conversion of America, for a revitalization, rejuvenation and expansion of its democratic institutions to include such excluded groups as the poor, people of colour, lesbians and gays, and women. He acknowledges that this will create, and has created, tensions in society, and he offers, as did Peirce, an ethic of love, that 'must be at the center of a politics of conversion'. West offers, as example, Toni Morrison's novel *Beloved* as presenting on a 'number of levels' this ethic of love that will give a downtrodden people a 'sense of agency', and a sense that they are lovable.[82]

West, then, advocates a philosophy and rhetoric of action that are rooted in community and fuelled and motivated by love. As an American romantic/pragmatic rhetorician and philosopher, he decries a society in which 'Market calculations and cost-benefit analyses hold sway in almost every sphere' – a society in which Cartesian thinking holds that a man or woman can be measured quantitatively and therefore his or her quality determined. Through the mediations of dichotomies, public and private, community and individual, self and other, West sees the public square – the common good – as the place in which solutions and answers can found. As West does this, so too does Le Guin. Her fiction, her stories – of possible utopias, of human love, of the mediation of dichotomies – advocate a philosophy and rhetoric of action. She, too, operates in the public square.

It is in this same square, with the same fuel and motivation, that Robert Coles, educator, philosopher, medical doctor – and American romantic/pragmatic rhetorician – is found. Like all the romantic/ pragmatic rhetoricians I am considering, Coles calls for 'The Sensible Heart', a way of thinking that incorporates the rational and the irrational, the linear and the circular, the scientific and the humanistic. He argues, for example, that the education of medical students should include novels and poems. While this education must also, 'of course, require a mastery of biological factuality', the students 'also need ... to ask what is the meaning of the life [they] constantly try to protect, and how ought that life to be lived'.[83] Such questions are no less important for composition students, or any students for that matter. These are the questions that Le Guin asks in her fiction. Asking such questions and exploring the answers creates connections, between students, between the classroom and the outside, between schools and neighbourhoods, between people.

We need such a pedagogy, with such questions, Coles argues, because contemporary Americans have lives 'dominated by the natural sciences. Every time we flick a light switch, get into a car, or receive penicillin, we silently acknowledge the influence of engineers, scientists, and chemists on our everyday assumptions'. This, according to Coles, is a mixed blessing: 'We have at our fingertips the energy of the atom; we have dozens of notions why people do things as they do; but many of us have forgotten to ask what we really believe in, what we ought to *be* in contrast to *do*'.[84] The humanities, Coles says in true pragmatic fashion, 'begin for a scientist when he or she starts asking what a particular fact or discovery will mean for those who want to comprehend the obligations, the responsibilities a given society presents'[85] – what difference an idea makes when it is put into action. And, in true romantic fashion, the humanities 'demand that we heed the individual – each person worthy of respect and no person unworthy of careful, patient regard'.[86]

Coles calls for this heeding of the individual, this coupling of the humanities and the sciences, this asking of who and what we are – thought and action – in the education of our children. I want to examine, as a particular example of Coles's American romantic/pragmatic rhetoric, his vision of the classroom, of American education, as expressed in an address at the UNCG Bryan Business School Auditorium, on 6 April 1995.[87] Coles argued that the classroom in which our children are raised and educated provides an illustration of 'what it is that matters in American life'. And so also does Le Guin argue in *The Dispossessed*, when she contrasts the Anarresti education based on community, co-operation and individual initiative with that of the Urrasti, one based on male privilege and quantification. In Anarresti learning centers, courses were organized on 'student demand or on the teacher's initiative, or by students and teachers together'.[88] The Urrasti students Shevek teaches at Ieu Eun University are shocked by Shevek's approach to grading: 'They wanted him to set the problems, to ask the right questions; they did not want to think about questions, but to write down the answers they had learned. And some of them objected strongly to his giving everyone the same mark.'[89] They were *all* boys, who had not learnt (and few probably ever would learn) that 'work is done for the work's sake [or that] it is the lasting pleasure of life'.[90] The Anarresti, in sharp contrast, are taught that the arts and the crafts are the same: 'No distinction is drawn between [the two]; art was not considered as having a place in life, but as being a basic technique of life'.[91]

According to Coles, what America values is not so much the individual child but, like Shevek's Urrasti students, test achievement. It has equated intellect with numbers, and in doing so, has ceded moral and educational authority to the tests and the test-makers. The tests 'come as if they were made on Sinai'. If Hawthorne were writing today, Coles says, the scarlet letter would be a grade, not Puritan shorthand for adultery. To treat students as if test scores could sum them up creates an automatic tension in the classroom. To do so, Coles argues, ignores what Emerson told us in 'The American Scholar': 'Character is higher than intellect. Thinking is the function. Living is the functionary. A great soul must be strong to live, as well as strong to think'. The express purpose of Harvard, Coles reminds us, was, originally, to train young men for the ministry, 'to instill character in them'. A university should provide a moral education for young people, and '[hand on] a sense of purpose'. It matters how we are with each other; it makes a difference if we 'mind our manners'. Coles is seeking then to mediate the inherent tension in any classroom between intellect and heart, between the cognitive and the affective, and between truth and doubt – and by implication the lives we lead outside the classroom.

As was the case with Dewey, Coles's resolution is to conceive of the classroom as a community: a singular one of teachers and students, yet connected to a greater community, be it the neighbourhood, the city or the country, and ultimately, humanity. To do so, to see the classroom as community, as an arena of service, makes the classroom a place where one can learn how to live the active moral life. As Emerson calls the scholars into essential action, Coles calls them into a living classroom that exists as a community within a neighbourhood.

He is not calling for the heart to supplant the head. He is not asking that we give up the benefits and improvements in human life brought by scientific advance. Coles calls for 'intellectual standards, defiantly, insistently'. Let the text be at the centre; let it 'nourish intellectual life'. Coles is calling for a pedagogy that creates community and acknowledges the affective as it teaches the cognitive. This is Le Guin's pedagogy, in which there is no distinction between the art and the craft, between the process and the product. A course is taught as a result of connection and responsibility, and it is initiated by students seeking to learn, teachers seeking to teach, or both. There is no distinction made between one learner or another. This pedagogy calls for service, for 'the moral connection and responsibility'. Both Le Guin and Coles ask for good teachers who are 'willing to reach out to students in a moral way, that mixes heart and head'.[92] 'Learning *is* [as Roskelly and Ronald paraphrase Emerson] an action and choice that people must cultivate and seek out.'[93]

Redefined Literacy

Mike Rose is another educator in the American romantic/pragmatic rhetorical vein, and this is particularly evident in *Lives on the Boundary*, his account of 'the struggles and achievements of America's educationally underprepared'. Like Coles, Rose is an heir of Dewey's progressive educational theories, based on experience, on doing. Again like Coles, Rose tests his theories in the classroom and in his own life, as he was a product of the 'educationally underprepared'. Rose's book itself, as he describes it, exemplifies the pragmatic notion of connection and community, and the idea that a narrative of self and self-discovery is and can be, as Roskelly and Ronald describe such a narrative, a 'most powerful persuasive tool', as 'experience is always at once connected and unique; one person's life confronts and connects to another's'.[94] For Rose, *Lives on the Boundary* is just such a narrative:

> I started this book as an account of my journey from the high school vocational track up through the lattice work of the American university. At first I tried brief sketches: a description of the storefront commerce that surrounded my house in South Los Angeles, a reminiscence about language, lessons in grammar school and the teachers I had in Voc. Ed, some thoughts on my first disorienting year in college. But, as I wrote, the landscapes and inhabitants of the sketches began to intersect with other places, other people: schools I had worked in, children and adults I had taught. It seemed fruitful to articulate, to probe and carefully render the overlay of my scholastic past and my working present. The sketches grew into a book that, of necessity, mixed genres. Autobiography, case study, commentary – it was all of a piece.[95]

Or, as Vico says in *On Study Methods for our Time*, knowledge is 'all of a piece', an integrated whole. And as Coles notes, the cognitive and the affective, the sciences and the humanities – and here, for Rose, experiential social learning, formal study and so forth – all are ways humans come to know. For too long, as both Coles and Rose argue, America has accepted the 'cult of efficiency', or the idea that American education should be run on the principles of business and scientific management, principles which quantify and measure educational gains as a product. Pedagogical effectiveness, Rose says, has been equated with cost-effectiveness, and we have attempted to 'determine [it] with scientific accuracy'.[96] Educational success is a matter of yes, high scores, no, low scores. American pragmatism and Rose (and Peirce) would, of course, argue for triadic thinking: perhaps there is another way to determine whether children are learning than by passing or failing a test.

Education, Rose argues, is 'one culture embracing another', and this embrace, together with the cultural heritage received in it, is 'not from some pristine conduit, but exchanged through the heat of human relations' – precisely as Le Guin's teacher-protagonists educate and are educated. Education is an 'encouraging, communal embrace – at its best, an invitation, an opening'.[97] The classroom, then, for Rose, is community, a community engaged in connection, engaged in active thinking and participation. This connection, and sometimes this clash, while sometimes painful, as Rose admits, is 'generative'. Rose's classroom becomes a working out of the tensions between cultures, between students and teachers, between authority and powerlessness, between knowledge and attempts to determine whether knowledge has been acquired. It is in this 'generative' mediation of tension that, for Rose, education occurs. He calls for a new pedagogy to meet the needs of America's 'extraordinary social experiment: the attempt to provide education for all members of a vast pluralistic democracy'. Such a new pedagogy must include a 'philosophy of language that affirms the diverse sources of linguistic competence' as it 'deepens our understandings of the ways class and culture blind us to the logic of error'. Such a new pedagogy must have 'a revised store of images of educational excellence, ever closer to egalitarian ideals', images that recognize and mirror the 'plural, messy human reality' of education in America. Such a pedagogy, Rose insists, will 'move us closer to an understanding of the rich mix of speech and ritual and story that is America'.[98] Language, story and imagination, community, connection – these become the basis of Rose's pedagogy, a pedagogy that reflects and puts into practice American romantic/pragmatic rhetoric. And this is the basis of Le Guin's own expression of American romantic/pragmatic rhetoric, her rhetoric of myth.

Rose is a disciple of Brazilian educator Paulo Freire, as are Roskelly and Ronald, Peter Elbow and Ann Berthoff, to name a few influential rhetoricians and composition theorists – all of whom are teachers. Freire is one of the most influential of these contemporary romantic/pragmatic rhetoricians because he uses this rhetoric and its philosophy as a teacher of language and literacy for systemic and cultural change. Freire's concept of praxis – thought, followed by reflection on that thought and the resulting action – could be said to be a tenet of pragmatism. To use praxis and to use inquiry, Freire insists, is to be truly human: 'Knowledge emerges only through invention and re-inventing, through restless, impatient, continuing hopeful inquiry, men pursue in the world, with the world, and with each other'. Freire calls for education as action, in action, through problem-solving, which 'strives for emergence of consciousness and critical intervention in reality';[99] 'One has knowledge to the extent that one reacts by participating in a practice that is social.'[100]

Given this, Freire's approach to literacy education with Brazilian *campesinos* and African peasants, his pedagogy, can be said to be a working definition of American romantic/pragmatic rhetoric. Where the teaching of the students begins is contingent on what they already know and who they are in their community. They are taught in what Freire calls 'culture circles', and it is from the students' culture that the words they learn are generated. A lesson begins with a codification, or 'the representation of typical situations of the group' – a photograph of a fishing boat, a farm tool, a piece of factory machinery: 'The codifications represent familiar local situations – which, however, open perspectives for the analysis of regional and national problems.' From the codifications come 'generative words' – net, deck, sail, ax, assembly line, boat, factory – which are used to begin building vocabulary.[101] Adult literacy, for Freire, is 'a political and knowing act committed in the process of learning to read and write the word and "to read" and "to write" reality'.[102]

Freire, as Ann Berthoff points out in her Foreword to *Literacy: Reading the Word and the World,* rejects either/or thinking, and seeks the mediation of tensions inherent in dichotomies:

> Instead of education as extension – a reaching out to students with valuable ideas we want to share – there must be a dialogue, a dialectical exchange in which ideas take

shape and change as the learners in the Culture Circle think about their thinking and interpret their interpretations. The dichotomy of 'the affective' and 'the cognitive,' so important in American educational theory, plays no part in Freire's pedagogy. He sees thinking and feeling, along with action, as aspects of all that we do in making sense of the world.[103]

Three chapters of the book itself are in dialogue form, as Freire engages in dialectic with Donaldo Macedo (who was at the University of Massachusetts at Amherst at the time) on literacy issues in Guinea-Bissau and the United States, and on Freire's critical pedagogy of literacy. This demonstrates, as Karen LeFevre insists in *Invention as a Social Act*, that rhetorical invention – 'the process of actively creating as well as finding what comes to be known and said' – is dialectical and interactive. With Freire and Macedo, there are two men – but, as LeFevre points out, invention can occur through a dialectic and interaction with self, with past knowledge, an invented audience, with social institutions.[104] As Freire exemplifies in his culture circles and his own writing, knowledge is a part of the social process, in the context of the community, and is therefore contingent on each element in the process.

That knowledge is a part of social process, and is discovered through dialectic and dialogue, is a key element of Le Guin's fictional rhetoric. Two examples among many can be found in Hideo, the protagonist of 'Another Story or A Fisherman of the Inland Sea', and in Hadri, the protagonist of 'Unchosen Love' (the former story I will discuss further and in a somewhat different context in Chapter Five). Hideo comes to know who he is and what is important in his life almost exclusively through dialogue: with himself, his parents, his teachers and his lover, and through the actions taken as a result of these dialogues – truth must be tested, after all. As Hideo comes to know, so does the reader, who is also engaged in Hideo's dialectical dialogue. So it is with Hadri, who also comes to know who he is and what he needs in similar dialectics. He asks himself how Suord (Hadri's lover) can love *him* so much – 'a person Hadri himself was used to considering quite ordinary'.[105] Hadri asks An'nad, he asks Duun, he asks himself; and, as did Hideo, Hadri learns – through dialectic, and then through the actions taken in consequence. Like Hideo, and other Le Guin characters, Hadri learns to navigate the tensions between wanting love and being overwhelmed by it – where self and other overlap and mingle. In this story Le Guin asks the reader to learn that love itself is a mediation between self and other, and that the different shapes of love are different ways to mediate. Hideo falls in love with Isidri, a woman; Hadri, with Suord, a man.

Hideo's and Hadri's learning is also experientially based: both must try out different ways of living to find his own way. This idea of pedagogy as experientially based is key to Freire. Like Dewey and Rose, Freire insists that pedagogy be experientially based in the world of those who are learning how to read and write. Learning becomes again contingent and contextual:

> For this reason I have always insisted that words used in organizing a literacy program come from what I call the "word universe" of people who are learning, expressing their actual language, their anxieties, fears, demands, and dreams. Words should be laden with the meaning of the people's existential experience, and not of the teacher's experience. Surveying the word universe thus gives us the people's words, pregnant with the world, words from the people's reading of the world.[106]

Reading the world becomes a way, as Rose says, for the students to reclaim and tell and write their own stories. Narrative, as again Freire argues by example, when he tells the story of how he learned to read and write as a young boy growing up in Recife, Brazil, is a way of knowing, of making meaning – as valid as any empirical method. That he sees literacy as a political act, that education is undeniably political and interpretative, makes it clear that it is also rhetorical, and that what and how we choose to learn are also rhetorical.

To be taught and to teach in a certain way is to be persuaded and to persuade – of how the world works, of how knowledge is made and discovered, of what is of value and worth and what is not. To teach through story and the construction of story, as do Rose, Coles, Freire and Le Guin, is to argue that narrative, the intuitive and the imaginative are of value and are sources of knowledge and meaning. To insist that truth be examined and tested is to argue that truth is contingent and subject to change. To establish a classroom as a community is to argue that we learn socially and not in isolation. To reinterpret and reimagine myth and to use feminist theory and Native American beliefs as part of these reinter-pretations and reimaginations, as Le Guin does in her fiction, is to argue that myth is a way of knowing and making meaning. While the original truths still have validity, they are subject to new contexts and new communities. It is the greater community – one of the heart, one in which storytelling and language and myth are ways of constructing knowledge – which I argue Le Guin is presenting in her fiction, that I want to examine now, in the context of American romantic/pragmatic rhetoric and philosophy. Le Guin is not only a chronological contemporary of Rose, West, Berthoff, LeFevre and Freire, she is also their spiritual contemporary, as she is a spiritual descendant of Vico, Emerson, Whitman, Thoreau, Fuller, Peirce and Dewey.

Notes

1. Robert Coles, address, Associated Campus Ministries, Bryan School of Business Auditorium, UNC Greensboro, Greensboro, North Carolina, 6 April 1995. Also *The Call of Stories: Teaching and the Moral Imagination* (Boston: Houghton Mifflin, 1989).

2. Karen Sinclair, 'Solitary Being: The Hero as Anthropologist', cited in Donna R. White, *Dancing with Dragons: Ursula K. Le Guin and the Critics* (Columbia, SC: Camden House, 1999), p. 61.

3. Hephzibah Roskelly and Eleanor Kutz, *An Unquiet Pedagogy: Transforming Practice in the English Classroom* (Portsmouth, NH: Boynton/Cook, 1991), pp. 13, 14.

4. Coles, *The Call to Stories*, pp. 128, 129.

5. Hephzibah Roskelly and Kate Ronald, *Reason to Believe: Romanticism, Pragmatism, and the Teaching of Writing* (Albany: State University of New York Press, 1998), p. 3.

6. Le Guin sets much of her work in a fictional universe, that of the Hainish. Hain, in this universe, is the hearth world of humanity, the original world on which humankind evolved over a million years ago. After inventing space travel, the Hainish roamed the galaxy, establishing human colonies on hundreds of worlds. Some of these colonies, such as the ones on Winter (Gethen) and Terra, are experiments. After a long period of colonization, for reasons not explained, the Hainish withdraw and leave the colonies to develop on their own. After many millennia, so many that most colonies have forgotten their origins, the Hainish set out to rediscover the colonies they abandoned. Le Guin's novels and stories primarily take place in the time of rediscovery and afterwards, when the Ekumen, an interstellar alliance of human-settled worlds, is formed.

7. Cornel West, *The American Evasion of Philosophy: A Genealogy of Pragmatism* (Madison: University of Wisconsin Press, 1989), pp. 9, 10.

8. Roskelly and Ronald, *Reason to Believe*, p. 56.

9. West, *American Evasion of Philosophy*, p. 10.

10. I take note of William James (1842–1910) here, as he, along with Peirce and 'other leading New England intellectuals first described the principles of pragmatism at a meeting of the famous Metaphysical Club, in 1867'. As Peirce, in *How to Make Our Ideas Clear* (1872), 'established the philosophical principles that would require belief to be sustained through action and that would allow action to lead to belief', so James does in *Pragmatism* (1907) (Roskelly and Ronald, *Reason to Believe*, p. 83). This is the pragmatic method that James defines as 'the attitude of looking away from first things, principles, categories … and looking forward to last things, fruits, consequences' (in ibid., p. 85). West, in *The American Evasion of Philosophy*, describes James as the 'exemplary Emersonian embodiment of intellectual power, provocation, and personality', but, unlike Peirce, 'James moves the focus … away from the community and back to the individual person' (p. 54). Peirce 'applies Emersonian themes of contingency and revisability to the scientific method, James extends them to our personal and moral lives' (p. 53). West cites other divergences between James and Peirce and places the two of them as being 'between' Emerson and Dewey. I have chosen to focus on Peirce and subsequently Dewey as I feel Le Guin is more in the educator line of American romantic/pragmatic rhetoricians. Le Guin does, however, give credit to James (and Dostoyevsky) for the inspiration for 'The Ones Who Walk Away from Omelas'.

11. Ralph Waldo Emerson, 'The American Scholar', in *Selected Essays*, ed. Larzer Ziff (New York: Penguin, 1982), pp. 88–89.

12. Ibid., pp. 91, 93.

13. Ibid., p. 95.

14. Roskelly and Ronald, *Reason to Believe*, p. 57.

15. Emerson, 'The American Scholar', in *Selected Essays*, p.105.

16. Emerson, 'Nature', in *Selected Essays*, p. 52.

17. Ibid., p. 60.

18. Roskelly and Ronald, *Reason to Believe*, p. 59.

19. Ibid., p. 60.

20. Ibid., p. 60.

21. Ibid., pp. 61, 62.

22. This concept of the universe as both macrocosm and microcosm is also a very Eastern perception. It is no accident, I think, that Le Guin bases much of her own beliefs and philosophy in Taoism.

23. The *Dial*, the journal of the Transcendentalists, was originally published from 1840 to 1844. It was started by the Hedge's Club, a Cambridge discussion circle, including Emerson and other like-minded people, founded in imitation of German literary circles: 'a few friends meet together, converse on various topics relating to literature, Art & Life, read essays and tales which we have composed' (Joan Von Mehren,

Minerva and the Muse: A Life of Margaret Fuller (Amherst: University of Massachusetts Press, 1994), p. 57). The *Dial* was to be a 'platform for [the club's] progressive ideas. Since the club members were looked upon as no more than a band of heretics, the religious magazines were closed to them. The respectable, tedious *North American Review* was out of the question; it represented just what they were clamoring against.' After considering some New York and Philadelphia ladies' magazines and *Boston Quarterly Review*, 'the members decided a separate publication was the only solution' (p. 120). The journal went through several incarnations and moves, until its final ten years, 1920–29, a time in which it 'had an unparalleled influence on the development of art, literature, criticism in the United States and abroad' (T. A. Davis, 'The *Dial*', University of Texas, Austin, http://www.cwrl.utexas.edu/~slatin/20c_poetry/projects/relatproject/dial.html, accessed 21 July 1999).

24. Susan Belasco Smith, 'Introduction', in Margaret Fuller, *Summer on the Lakes, in 1843* (Urbana: University of Illinois Press, 1991), p. vii.

25. Joan Von Mehren, *Minerva and the Muse*, pp. 1–2.

26. Ibid, pp. 178–79,

27. Smith, 'Introduction', in Fuller, *Summer on the Lakes*, p. xiv.

28. Margaret Fuller, *Summer on the Lakes, in 1843* (1844; Urbana: University of Illinois Press, 1991), pp. 41–42.

29. Von Mehren, *Minerva and the Muse*, p. 178.

30. Smith, 'Introduction', in Fuller, *Summer on the Lakes*, p. xiv.

31. Ibid., pp. xv–xvi.

32. Von Mehren, *Minerva and the Muse*, p. 351.

33. Roskelly and Ronald, *Reason to Believe*, pp. 65–66, 67.

34. Jerome Loving, *Walt Whitman: The Song of Himself* (Berkeley: University of California Press, 1999), p. xi.

35. Ibid., p. 395.

36. Emerson, cited in ibid., p. 189.

37. Loving, *Walt Whitman*, pp. 23, 192.

38. Ibid., pp. 192–93.

39. All quotations of Whitman's poetry are taken from the 1973 Norton Critical Edition of *Leaves of Grass*, edited by Sculley Bradley and Harold W. Blodgett. This edition is described as having 'authoritative texts, prefaces, [commentary by] Whitman on His Art, [and] criticism'.

40. Whitman, cited in Loving, *Walt Whitman*, p. 182.

41. Emerson, cited in Loving, *Walt Whitman*, p. 103.

42. Emerson, cited in ibid., p. 182.

43. It is worth noting here that through Whitman's many revisions and subsequent different editions of *Leaves of Grass* he was again exemplifying American romantic/pragmatic rhetoric. His knowledge, as expressed in his poetry, was contingent to certain times and places in his life. As these changed, as what he knew of the world changed, so did his poetry.

44. Ursula K. Le Guin, *A Wizard of Earthsea* (New York: Bantam Books, 1968), p. 164.

45. Roskelly and Ronald, *Reason to Believe*, p. 68.

46. Loving, *Walt Whitman*, p. 227.

47. Ibid., p. 185.

48. Whitman was, of course, accused of obscenity and indecency; this was the century of Comstock, after all. Thoreau, while he thought *Leaves of Grass* was of greater value than 'the sermons so-called that have been preached in this land', also said Whitman 'does not celebrate love at all. It is as if the beast spoke' (cited in Loving, *Walt Whitman*, p. 226). Of course, this reaction may have had something to do with Thoreau's own ambivalent feelings about his body and sexuality, which I shall discuss briefly later in the chapter.

49. Sculley Bradley and Harold W. Blodgett, footnotes, in Walt Whitman, *Leaves of Grass*, eds. Sculley Bradley and Harold W. Blodgett (New York: W. W. Norton, 1973), p. 91.

50. Ursula K. Le Guin, *The Dispossessed* (New York: Harper & Row, 1974), p. 280.

51. Loving, *Walt Whitman*, p. 252.

52. Whitman to Emerson, letter, August 1856, in Whitman, *Leaves of Grass*, p. 739. Whitman also used this letter as the preface in the 1856 edition of *Leaves of Grass*.

53. Von Mehren, *Minerva and the Muse*, pp. 51–52.

54. Fuller, cited in ibid., p. 163.

55. Fuller, cited in ibid., p. 314.

56. Walter Harding, 'Thoreau's Sexuality', *Journal of Homosexuality*, 21 (3), 1991, p. 23.

57. Harding, 'Thoreau's Sexuality', pp. 24–25, 27, 40–41.

58. Betty Koed, "Frequently Asked Questions: Did Thoreau Ever Write about His First Love …" in Elizabeth Witherell, ed., *The Writings of Henry D. Thoreau*, University of California, Santa Barbara Library, 5 February 1999, http://library.ucsb.edu/depts/thoreau/thoreau.html (accessed 23 July 1999).

59. D. H. Lawrence, 'Whitman', in Whitman, *Leaves of Grass*, p. 850.

60. Roskelly and Ronald, *Reason to Believe*, p. 31.

61. That I have used the coupled term to refer to people and writings that pre-date Peirce may, at first, seem to be academic juggling. But the point I am trying to make, as Roskelly and Ronald do in *Reason to Believe*, is that history does not move forward in a neat, linear fashion. There is overlap, redundancy, repetition. Ideas and philosophies grow and change shape as they grow; they do not emerge, full grown, from a thinker's head.

62. Dr Hephzibah Roskelly and her graduate students explored American romantic/pragmatic rhetoric and philosophy in a UNC Greensboro graduate class in spring 1995.

63. West, *American Evasion*, p. 43.

64. Hephzibah Roskelly, course lecture, McIver Building, English Department, UNC Greensboro, 27 March 1995.

65. West, *American Evasion*, p. 51.

66. Hephzibah Roskelly, 'Journal from Hepsie: Notes on Peirce', teaching journal, ts. UNC Greensboro, spring 1995.

67. Roskelly, course lecture.

68. Roskelly, teaching journal.

69. C. S. Peirce, 'Evolutionary Love', in Nathan Houser and Christian Kloesel, eds, *The Essential Peirce: Selected Philosophical Writing* (Bloomington: University of Indiana Press, 1992), p. 354.

70. Ibid., p. 357.

71. Peirce, cited in Roskelly, teaching journal.

72. Le Guin, *The Dispossessed*, p. 53.

73. West, *American Evasion*, p. 86.

74. Roskelly, course lecture.

75. John Dewey, *Experience and Education* (New York: Macmillan, 1938), pp. 7, 6, 11, 26–27.

76. Ibid., pp. 86–87, 88.

77. Giambattista Vico (1668–1744) was professor of rhetoric at the University of Naples from 1699 to 1741. In his own time, he was considered a 'reactionary because of his opposition to Descartes', but today he is seen as a 'major force in the development of a culturally based epistemology' and highly influential in the growth and development of rhetoric. Vico's main criticism of Descartes was that he felt Descartes focused too 'narrowly on mathematics and science as the only legitimate sources of knowledge' – treating other branches of human inquiry, such as law, history and the arts, as inconsequential. In *On Study Methods of our Time* and *The New Science*, Vico argues that 'rhetoric provides a superior philosophy of knowledge, for all knowledge, even the scientific, is based on the value of language'. Descartes, Vico says, did not realize the value of knowledge. 'Without language, Vico says, the human knower is lost. Language reveals the process of reason, passion, and imagination, as well as the social conventions and historical circumstances that shape our concerns' (Patricia Bizzell and Bruce Herzberg, 'Giambattista Vico', in Bizzell and Herzberg, eds, *The Rhetorical Tradition: Readings from Classical Times to the Present* (Boston: Bedford Books, 1990), pp. 711–12). Knowledge, for Vico, should be studied as integrated, and both the Cartesian method and 'eloquence' (rhetoric) should be used.

78. Robert Boynton, 'The New Intellectuals', *The Atlantic Monthly*, March 1995, p. 53.

79. Ibid.

80. Cornel West, *Keeping Faith: Philosophy and Race in America* (New York: Routledge, 1993), pp. 102–03.

81. Cornel West, *Race Matters* (New York: Vintage Books, 1994), pp. 11–12.

82. Ibid., pp. 29–30.

83. Robert Coles, *Times of Surrender: Selected Essays* (Iowa City: University of Iowa Press, 1988), p. 59.

84. Ibid., p. 263.

85. Ibid., p. 264.

86. Ibid., p. 266.

87. Coles, address, UNC Greensboro.

88. Le Guin, *The Dispossessed*, p. 111.

89. Ibid., pp. 112–13.

90. Ibid., p. 132.

91. Ibid., p. 137.

92. Coles, address.

93. Roskelly and Ronald, *Reason to Believe*, p. 79.

94. Ibid., p. 63.

95. Mike Rose, *Lives on the Boundary* (New York: Penguin, 1989), p. 8.

96. Ibid., p. 208.

97. Ibid., p. 225.

98. Ibid., p. 238.

99. Paulo Freire, *Pedagogy of the Oppressed* (New York: Continuum, 1986), pp. 58, 67.

100. Paulo Freire and Donaldo Macedo, *Literacy: Reading the Word and the World* (South Hadley, MA: Bergin & Garvey, 1987), p. 69.

101. Paulo Freire, 'Education and *Conscientizcao*', in Eugene R. Kintgen, Barry M. Kroll and Mike Rose, eds, *Perspectives on Literacy* (Carbondale: Southern Illinois University Press, 1988), p. 406.

102. Freire and Macedo, *Literacy*, p. 66.

103. Ann E. Berthoff, Foreword, in Freire and Macedo, *Literacy*, p. xvi.

104. Karen Burke LeFevre, *Invention as a Social Act* (Carbondale: Southern Illinois University Press, 1987), pp. 33–34.

105. Ursula K. Le Guin, 'Unchosen Love', *Amazing Stories*, 69 (2) Fall 1994, p. 15.

106. Freire and Macedo, *Literacy*, p. 35.

CHAPTER FIVE
Communities of the Heart[1]

To place Le Guin's rhetorical use of myth in its broader context of American romantic/pragmatic rhetoric, I will first look at her fiction, particularly her science fiction, as a whole. As do most authors, Le Guin uses recurrent metaphors, symbols and mythic patterns, which, when considered as inherent in her entire opus, become rhetorical. Next, I am going to focus on selected recent stories to show Le Guin's rhetoric as progressive and evolutionary, much as her understanding of feminism is. In these more recent stories I feel the reader can see more clearly where Le Guin is now as an American 'romantic/pragmatic rhetorician' and whence she has come.

The idea of community and connection is an idea central to romantic rhetoric and pragmatism. The idea of community and connection is also a central metaphor in Le Guin's fiction. Coupled with community, as James Bittner says in *Approaches to the Fiction of Ursula K. Le Guin*, is storytelling's value 'for acquiring and forming perception and vision'.[2] Le Guin ties these two metaphors together in her Hainish universe and its history, in which the majority of her science fiction is placed. According to Bittner, Le Guin's Hainish history is 'dialectical, an interplay between teleological[3] and etiological[4] myths' – specifically the creation of the Ekumen, the all-encompassing interstellar human community, and that its creation is an end of human history.[5] The stories themselves have as their 'historical backdrop' various times in this Hainish history and each serves either to advance humankind's progression towards a greater unity in community or to provide a point or points of beginning of this community: the Ekumen, the Hearth of Man, the Human Household.

The Dispossessed and *The Left Hand of Darkness*, looked at together, are good examples of Bittner's dialectic between the teleological and the œtiological and the metaphor of community. Shevek's double grail quest, for the general temporal formula and for the end of his people's exile and their reconciliation with their mother world, becomes one of the points of origin for the Ekumen. The ansible, the device that is made as a result of his formula, allows for instantaneous interstellar communication – thus creating community, as the Terran ambassador explains to Shevek:

> And decisions could be made, and agreements reached, and information shared. I could talk to diplomats on Chiffewar, you could talk to physicists on Hain, it wouldn't take ideas a generation to get from world to world ... Do you know, Shevek, I think your simple matter might change the lives of all the billions of people in the nine Known Worlds? ... It would make a league of worlds possible. A federation. We have been held apart by the years, the decades between leaving and arriving, between question and response. It's as if you had invented human speech! We can talk – at last we can talk together.[6]

The greater community is thus born, and in *The Left Hand of Darkness*, we see its fruition, as Genly Ai, its Envoy, has come to the planet Gethen (Winter) to persuade its people to join, for 'Material profit. Increase of knowledge. The augmentation of the complexity and intensity of the field of intelligent life. The enrichment of harmony and the greater glory of God. Curiosity. Adventure. Delight.' As Genly tells the doubtful king of Karhide, the Ekumen is not a kingdom, but a 'co-ordinator, a clearing house for trade and knowledge' – a 'network', an extended community. We are 'all men', Genly tells the king, we are all connected: 'All the worlds of men were settled eons ago, from one world Hain ... we're all sons of the same Hearth'.[7] But Genly's Ekumen is not the small 'league of worlds' the Terran ambassador tells Shevek his ansible will make possible – it has grown into 'Three thousand nations on eighty-three worlds', a greater and more inclusive community.

Le Guin's choice of Ekumen as the name for her interstellar community is in itself rhetorical – like her use of feminism and Native American traditions in *Always Coming Home*. By using these ways of knowing in the creation of a future utopia, the implicit argument becomes that utopia is possible: it has been done, it is already here. The word *ecumenical* is from the Greek *oikoumenē*, 'the inhabited world'. *Oikoumenē* is from *okein*, to inhabit, and *oikos*, house. The word generally means 'worldwide or general in extent, influence or application', and more familiarly, 'of, relating to, or representing the whole or body of churches'. For Le Guin, in these words there is the further association of her father Alfred Kroeber's scientific hypothesis 'that the ecumenical culture of the Eurasian landmass spread out from Mesopotamia, "that first hearth of all higher civilization"'.[8] The connotation here for the interstellar Ekumen is again a universal community, yet one that has the intimacy of family, a house, with a warm fire cosily burning in the hearth. One draws near for light and heat, and by implication, human communion. And again, with Kroeber's anthropological hypothesis, the idea that it has already happened, and it could happen again. The need and desire for community may even be inherent in humanity. That *ecumenical* is also associated with churches adds another quality to Le Guin's rhetorical Hainish mythos: spirituality. Human union, and the impulse to it, is mystical, and operating at the level of the soul. That Le Guin's Hainish mythos should have a spiritual component creates another link to American romantic/pragmatic rhetoric. It was part of the Transcendentalist creed to live by inspiration, and to try to live 'in spiritual harmony with laws of nature'.[9] Spirituality was and is a connector, and thus it is inherent in community. Community can be said to be an archetype of the collective unconscious – it certainly is one for Le Guin, as it appears again and again in her fiction.

The creation of this Ekumen is not, however, without tension between community and individual, public and private, large and small. Le Guin examines these tensions as they are mediated in the stories, on both personal and public scales. In *The Dispossessed*, the personal scale is that of Shevek's life as he seeks to mediate his needs as a physicist for a supportive scientific community and for personal growth, with the demands of his own community, Anarresti society, a society that privileges community over individual. On a public scale, Shevek is unquestionably a public figure and his quest is played out in public and in part is public, as he seeks to reconcile two planetary societies, Anarres and Urras, and reconnect his people to the universe. In *The Left Hand of Darkness*, the personal scale is the relationship between Genly Ai, the Envoy of the Ekumen, and Estraven, the one-time prime minister of Karhide. On one level, the novel's story is of these two humans creating community and connection, as they resolve the inherent tensions between them: being alien to each other, gender differences, cultural differences. The public scale here is that of the people and culture of Gethen and of the Ekumen itself. The tensions here are between the choices the Gethenians must make. Should

they remain isolated, an isolation which means a disavowal of the
rest of humanity, or should they join the Ekumen and the rest of
humanity, knowing that to do so will also isolate them as their
sexuality is unique in the Ekumen?

Community becomes more than metaphor in *The Dispossessed,
The Left Hand of Darkness,* and in the other Hainish novels and
stories. Community is a master trope, one which encompasses such
dichotomies as public and private, community and individual, past
and present, and their rhetorical mediations. Robert Coles insists
such dichotomies and tensions are inherent in community, and the
resolution is to see communities as existing in connected layers,
community within community, each affecting the other, as Le Guin
does in her Hainish stories.[10] Such dichotomies, however, also
seem to be part of the definition of what is inherent in making a
community. As Roskelly and Ronald argue, for American romanticism, 'self from the beginning was created both socially and
individually'.[11] The trope of community in Le Guin's Hainish cycle,
as a master trope, includes story as metaphor, as a way of knowing,
and myth as a particular way of knowing. As Bittner points out,
story becomes a 'metalanguage that can carry meaning across
linguistic and cultural barriers, and presumably across biological
and psychological ones as well'.[12] Story, in *The Dispossessed,* merges
'the etiological and teleological impulses' and creates a 'synthesis in
the dialectic of beginnings and endings'.[13] This is done through the
telling of the story of Shevek's life, through alternating chapters on
Anarres and Urras, set in the past and the present, which merge
into an ongoing present, a story that continues past the novel, at
the end. Shevek's release of the necessary equations to develop the
ansible will transform all humankind. And his own return to
Anarres, in the face of opposition, with Kethoe, the Hainishman,
will transform his own people, the Anarresti, as he himself has
been and will continue to be transformed. Shevek's story operates
on multiple levels: the objective search for the theory, the public
search for reconciliation and the end of exile, and the personal,
subjective search for mediation between his life and the life of his
community. And on each level, Shevek acquires a certain truth, a
part of the whole. Thus it is in the making of Shevek's story, and its
telling, that meaning is made, as Mike Rose makes meaning through
story in *Lives on the Boundary.* Both Shevek's story and Rose's
multiple stories of students and classrooms serve as ways of knowing and understanding human experience, and as a way of

teaching. For Shevek, for Rose, as West asserts in *The American Evasion of Philosophy*, there is 'some kind of inseparable link between thought and action, theory and practice'.[14] To tell a story, to listen to and participate in story, link both knowing and meaning.

In *The Left Hand of Darkness*, story as a way of knowing, as a way to community and connection, is more overt. The entire novel is presented as a report to the Ekumen by the Ekuemen's Envoy to Gethen, Genly Ai, a report that he is making as a story. But the story being told is not just Genly's:

> The story is not all mine, nor told by me alone. Indeed, I am not sure whose story it is; you can judge better. But it is all one, and if at moments the facts seem to alter with an altered voice, why then you can choose the fact you like best; yet none of them are false, and it is all one story.[15]

The story is also Estraven's and it is his voice we hear, again in dialectical alternating chapters, as Le Guin is saying, as she did in *The Dispossessed*, truth is possible, but, as Peirce insists, contingent, based on the context and perspective of the knower, and what is known at the time. Interwoven between Genly and Estraven are more voices: myths and hearth-tales, and scientific reports – again more perspectives and contexts for truth, still more dialectic. These stories range from the objective and formal, to the personal and subjective – all presented as valid ways of knowing. Both *The Left Hand of Darkness* and *The Dispossessed* are multiple stories, stories within stories, that make one story – as the Hainish novels and stories make one great story. Shevek's life and work become part of this great story, of history, a part of an ongoing social narrative as his physics is part of what is known – contingent on the community consensus of truth. Thus Gveter, in "The Shobies' Story", can lecture his crewmates on 'the rebirth of Cetian physics since the revision of Shevekian temporalism'.[16]

Dialectic as part of the story's structure becomes rhetorical in many of the Hainish stories, and not just through alternating chapters and changes in narrators. The narrator or main character often (in addition to being a teacher and/or anthropologist) has insider/outsider status, and he or she is often juxtaposed against aliens of one kind or another. Shevek, Genly Ai, Estraven, even Ged in *Earthsea* and Stone Telling in *Always Coming Home*, are all, to some degree, outsiders or aliens in their own cultures, and travel to other cultures, where they are even more alien. Their difference –

whether in their home culture or outside it – creates Le Guin's utopian dialectic. This creation is often literal. As these characters attempt to understand their outsider position at home and observe and reflect on the alien culture they encounter, they engage in conversation and rumination. They ask questions, they consider; their dialogues are dialectical. Conversation becomes then a rhetorical element, as the preferred is set against the non-preferred and presented to the reader through these characters. The community trope is present as choice, as each character has to choose to which community he or she will ultimately belong.

This master trope of community is also in the *Earthsea* cycle and in *Always Coming Home*. As in the two Hainish novels, the trope includes the dichotomies and their mediations, and story as metaphor for knowledge and making meaning. In *Earthsea*, as it is a fantasy, Le Guin is more overt about evoking the ambience of a story being told, a tale being passed on: '[Ged's] life is told in the *Deed of Ged* and in many songs, but this is a tale of the time before his fame, before the songs were made.'[17] The tetralogy becomes the story of Ged's life as wizard, dragonlord and Archmage, and it is the history of Earthsea. The magic of Earthsea itself is one of words: the Art-Magic of Names is to know the name of everything – every person, creature and object in the world in the True Speech – and so meaning itself, life itself, is constructed in language, in an ongoing narrative. Story becomes the connecting metaphor for the community trope: narrative is what holds the trope together – 'Everything is held together with stories.'[18] Or as Fr Thomas McSweeney argues when he cites Daniel Taylor's *The Healing Power of Stories*: '… you and I *are* stories … we are the product of all the stories we have heard and lived: "They have shaped how you see yourself, the world, and your place in it".'[19] And as, according to Walter Fisher, we are *Homo narrans*, with all 'forms of human communication … seen fundamentally as stories',[20] then human community is made by story.

Story not only makes community in the *Earthsea* cycle, it renews it as well. Stories, as they create and define community, provide a way of connection, through instruction. According to Robert Coles in *The Call of Stories*, this is through the 'immediacy that a story can possess, as it connects so persuasively with human experience'.[21] This connection teaches the reader about both self and other and how both are part of the same human community, and thus it renews and makes community. Ged's great deed – which is told in

Earthsea as an epic, a defining story of Earthsea culture – is the restoration of community to the world of Earthsea when he regains the missing half of the lost ring of Erreth-Akbe in *The Tomb of Atuan.* This ring is one of the greatest treasures of Earthsea and until it is found and restored no king can rule all the isles and there can be no unity or real peace. When the missing half of the ring is found and the ring made whole, the Lost Rune, the 'Bond-Rune', the Sign of Dominion, the Sign of Peace, is reassembled. In *The Farthest Shore,* the final element of unity is the king himself. And it is Ged who prepares the young prince to take the long-empty throne. The fourth book, *Tehanu,* provides the needed balance and mediation between the needs of the community and those of the individual. His magic spent, Ged returns to his home island, where after years of public deeds and adventures, he, with Tenar, attends to his private and personal life. He creates a family, with her and Therru, the burnt child Tenar has taken in. The knowledge – his magic – which Ged used on the national scale, is gone. Now what he needs to know and what he learns are local, private and familiar – and both are valid in Ged's life for making meaning.

Community becomes something that can be either small or great or neither. It can be something internal, as Ged's bond with Tenar is the internal one of the heart. Indeed, in the end, in the Hainish stories, for Shevek and for Genly, and here in the *Earthsea* cycle, for Ged, it is the personal community from which the strength is drawn and used for everything else. For Shevek there is first his father, then his boyhood friends, his teachers, and later his partner, Takver, and his adult friends, all of whom make him human, connected, and give his knowledge context. For Genly there is the friendship with Estraven that literally saves his life and at the same time allows him to finally connect to the people of Gethen and bring them into the Ekumen. Community begets community.

Always Coming Home, as a fictional ethnography, can also be read as multiple stories that create the story of a people – their time, their place, their culture. As our knowledge of the Kesh is gained through many different stories collected by the ethnographer Pandora, the Kesh community becomes a product of the process of story. But this knowledge is contingent – on whom Pandora talks to, what data she collects, and what she is told and observes. It is also contingent on the perspectives of the many different storytellers – and how the reader assembles this knowledge and makes meaning out of it. That way, what is told becomes a mediation: between the personal and the public, between the knower and the known. Story mediates between the subjective and the objective: as a personal art form, it is subjective. As ethnographic data, it is a repository of objective facts and observations. Thus the master trope of community both creates and is created by story: the Kesh are their stories and myths, their history. These stories, this history, shape them as a people, and at the same time shape the reader's knowledge and understanding. The reader, in effect, enters the Kesh community, as both observer and participant, for she is asked to assemble the data and the stories in order to make meaning – to mediate between herself, the text, the fiction, and reality. The subjective nature of this making of meaning, as it is a matter of human interpretation, suggests that it is inherently fallible – fallibility being a primary tenet of American pragmatic thought. The reader's interpretation, her sense of what is true – all is contingent and subject to revision. That it is based on her 'theory of the world' that she brings to the text underscores this. Such knowledge can never be truly complete and must remain fallible and imperfect.

That myth is a certain type of story evident in the Hainish novels and short stories, the *Earthsea cycle* and *Always Coming Home*, calls attention to its value in Le Guin's master trope of community and as an element of American romantic/pragmatic rhetoric. Myth, which is passed as story, is part of story as metaphor. As such it is used for the construction of knowledge and meaning. Again the multiple uses of myth are worth noting. Le Guin uses the forms and content of the traditional myths of the Hero and the Quest and utopia. Through her subversion and inversion, she makes them rhetorical. Through her reinterpretation and reimagination, the stories become different. The hero has a new image, the quest a new grail, utopia a new location. But there is more going on with myth than the reimagination. Myth, more than story, becomes part of the master trope of community in that myth is a maker of community, as community, in turn, makes and defines myth.

The creation myths collected by the Ekumenical observers in *The Left Hand of Darkness* are a part of how the people of Gethen define themselves. The entire Hainish history, with humankind originating on Hain and then spreading out to more than a hundred worlds, is myth. The Colonization and the Withdrawal, and the rediscovery that sent the Hainish out again to find out what had happened to their colonies after many millennia, comprise so old a story that it can only be myth. The factual truth is lost in time, even as the mythical truth of what the Hainish did persists. In effect, Le Guin is creating a mythos in which to create her community. In the *Earthsea* cycle, stories handed down of the Creation, of heroes and long-ago quests are also myth. In *Always Coming Home*, we, the contemporary readers, are the mythic past – the time of exploitation and despoliation, the time of excess in whose ruins the Kesh now live. And their own myths – those of the Native American tribes from whom they seem to have descended – become parallel and a part of this past. In all these stories, myth creates, defines and sustains the community itself, and therefore becomes an argument for community that is made by the community through its myths.

Le Guin's later work clearly demonstrates the master trope of community and American romantic/pragmatic rhetoric, especially in two recent science fiction story collections, *Four Ways to Forgiveness* and *A Fisherman of the Inland Sea*, as well as the novella *Old Music and the Slave Women*. The four novellas in *Forgiveness* are Hainish stories, connected by setting and time, taking place on the planets Yeowe and Werel, immediately after the War of Liberation on Yeowe. *Old Music and the Slave Women* takes place sometime after events in *Forgiveness*. The stories in *Fisherman* are both Hainish and non-Hainish, such as the comic 'First Contact with the Gorgonids', the fable 'The Rock that Changed Things' and 'Newton's Sleep', the latter two being examined here. It is my argument here that these stories, much more obviously and explicitly, identify Le Guin's rhetoric as being American romantic/pragmatic rhetoric. These later stories are not only expressions of this rhetoric, but arguments for Le Guin's vision of a truly human community. Once again myth is rhetorical, and thus impetus and force for the way of knowing and making meaning that this rhetoric advocates.

A Fisherman of the Inland Sea

The myth of utopia, that human society can reach an ideal, is the operating theme in 'Newton's Sleep'. To reach this ideal, as in *The Dispossessed* and *Always Coming Home*, the creation of community is given paramount importance. The SPES (Special Earth Satellite) Society has placed in orbit an artificial habitat, designed to house a society which will avoid the mistakes made on Earth. According to D. H. Maston, 'the father of Spes', 'the ideal of the Society is that the concept of nationality meant nothing, while the concept of community meant everything'.[22] The Earth is a wreck, and the only hope for humanity is, according to Ike, the story's protagonist, the Special Earth Satellite: 'We risked everything for Spes – because we're future-oriented. These are the people who chose to leave the past behind, to start fresh. To form a true human community and to do it right, to do it right for once!'[23]

Obviously, the future and the present can't exist without the past. What we know, as Dewey points out in his theory of experiential-based education, is a continuum of past and present experiences – with the past informing and shaping the present, and the present informing and shaping what comes next.[24] Knowledge is connected and must be studied and acquired as a whole, not in discrete units, separated, as Ike would have it here, by time and place. The inhabitants of SPES find that, for them to move on, they must accept their connection to the community they were attempting to deny. The people left behind on Earth – old family members, blacks, other nationalities, the old – literally began to haunt SPES, appearing and disappearing. Yet they must be accepted, the connection validated and reaffirmed, the idea of community reinterpreted. As Susan, Ike's wife, says: 'How did we, how could we have thought we could just leave? Who did we think we are? All of it is, is we brought ourselves with us … The horses and the whales and the old women and the sick babies. They're just us, we're them, they're here.'[25] The part cannot exist without the whole, one makes the other, and there can be no true self without recognition of the other. Subjective knowledge – here ghosts, dreams and hallucinations – is as valid as the rational science that built the satellite, the kind of rationality with which Ike attempts to deny the subjective reality. For Ike, they merge when he at last sees and hears and accepts a personal subjective ghost, his mother – and thus restores community, past and present, in his own life.

Gaining knowledge of what is real comes when Ike sees and hears his mother when he rationally knows she isn't on SPES. Yet her voice is still present in his life and to hear it and listen to it is to accept that what she knows has validity. Knowledge, what is true, changes when the perspective of the knower changes. It is contingent, then, on who is the knower and how they have come to know, as Peirce suggested.[26]

Le Guin also examines this idea in 'The Rock that Changed Things'. In addition, she explores the idea Vico explained in the eighteenth century, that knowledge is an integrated whole and should be studied as such. In the story, which Le Guin presents as a fable, the nur have been enslaved by the obls for generations. 'The heart of an obl town is its college and the pride of every college is its terrace,' and one of the primary occupations of the slaves is to maintain the intricate pebble patterns of these terraces, which are 'set in elaborate mosaics and patterns in gravel. So long as the rocks are arranged in order of shape and size and the patterns are kept clear and tidy, the obls have peace of mind and think deeply.'[27] The obls are Cartesian thinkers: linear, orderly, empirical and rational. To seek knowledge only in this way, as Vico points out, is to ignore the human soul. We 'must resist the fragmentation of human knowledge'.[28]

This static and orderly existence is changed when one nur, Bu, sees these intricate designs from a perspective other than that of the master. The obls' patterns are 'shape-and-size arrangement(s)', and Bu, when she picks up a stone to be used in a test pattern, is 'struck by a quality of the stone she had never noticed before: the color'. When she places the stone in the true pattern, in the college terraces, she sees a pattern of colour that she had never realized was there before. The obls only interpret knowledge through shape and size – ignoring, not seeing, the knowledge available through colour, knowledge perceived by a slave. Bu brings her nur perspective to this stone text. Through her interaction with it, her awareness of the stone's colour, meaning is created. The neat, orderly and mathematical Cartesian knowledge of the obls has ignored the knowledge of the nurs, which is obtained by Bu in a flash of subjective intuition. She recognizes the colour patterns as valid: 'the patterns of the colors ... they aren't accidental. Not meaningless. All the time, we have been putting them here in patterns – not just ones the obls design and we execute, but other patterns – nur patterns – with new meanings ...'[29]

These colour patterns, or stories in stone, have always been there in the college terraces, but could not be seen until there was a shift in perspective, a change in awareness – until there was a reinterpretation of the story. Or in other words, a paradigm shift. The nurs, as slaves, have been left out of the story. Their inclusion in the story generates new meaning: 'wild designs of curves and colors, amazing phrases, unimagined significances, a wonderful newness of meaning and beauty'. Yet, as new as the colour patterns seem to be, they are old, they have always been there, despite their being considered obsolete by the obls. As the Canon explains to Bu:

> all verbal color-significance is long obsolete. Of mere anti-
> quarian interest to old fuddy-duddies such as myself, ha.
> Hue-words don't even occur in the most archaic patterns ...
> The hue of the blue-green – such as that stone you seem to
> be wearing as an ornament – might, in its adjectival form
> within a pattern, have indicated a quality of untrammeled
> volition. As a noun, the color would have functioned to
> signify, how shall I put it? – an absence of coercion; a lack of
> control; a condition of self-determination ...[30]

Or, more simply, the colour of Bu's stone means freedom. And once
freedom can be named and defined, it is real and desirable, and this
knowledge changes things. The obl community, in its exclusion and
non-seeing of the nur, is incomplete and not truly connected to the
whole. The community's totally linear thinking cuts it off from
what can be known through personal experience, subjectivity,
intuition, through story. It is no wonder that the Canon is totally
unprepared when the nur use their knowledge to take action, to
become free, and rocks come smashing through his window.

In 'The Shobies' Story' and 'Dancing to Ganam', the pragmatic
idea that knowledge is community-based, community-created and
contingent is given attention. The Shobies, a spaceship crew, named
after their ship, are to be the first humans to test out churten theory
– or faster-than-light travel, which Le Guin calls 'transilience'. To
be able to go faster than light will, as Dalzul explains in 'Dancing',
make the Ekumen 'the household of humankind truly one house,
one place'.[31]

To prepare for the experiment, the Shobies first must form a
functioning group or community, and begin by spending a month
together on their 'isyeye: the period of time and area of space in
which a group forms if it is going to form'.[32] When they actually
test out churten theory, the Shobies discover that the only way
they can successfully travel is as a group, and the only way they can
learn this new knowledge and make use of it is collaboratively and
co-operatively. When they can't, there is madness and distortion
and multiple, unconnected narratives of their space flight. It is only
when they connect their narratives and tell their stories together
that they escape the madness: 'There was a ship called the *Shoby* ...
on a test flight, trying out the churten, with a crew of ten ...' Story
thus makes meaning and provides coherence.

'Dancing to Ganam' is the story of the second experimental churten flight. Dalzul, the commander of the second crew, explains to them that the *Shoby*'s crew discovered 'that individual experiences of transilience can be made coherent only by a concerted effort. An effort to synchronize – to entrain.' To achieve transilience, Dalzul argues, is to recognize that it is a 'function of the rhythm that makes being' and 'access to that rhythm ... allows the individual to participate in eternity and ubiquity'.[33] This again suggests something of the spiritual and mystical nature of Le Guin's vision of community. For the Ekumen to progress, to evolve, this part of the human psyche has to be tapped. (The Force has to be with them, the life energy of all living things that binds us and the cosmos together in *Star Wars*, which is a retelling and re-envisioning of the monomyth.)

To feel this life energy, Dalzul tells his crew of four (of whom one travelled on the *Shoby*), is to entrain. To demonstrate, they sing: they create a chorus, a harmony. They will dance to Ganam, the target planet for this flight, because, as Shan, the former *Shoby* crewmember, points out, 'dancing is people being music'. Learning is both an individual and a social process, as LeFevre argues in *Invention as a Social Act*.[34] A chorus or a dance troupe is both individual-and-group and individual-in-group. It is in the creation of the group – the entrainment, if you will – that the tension is mediated, and the third, the knowledge, is made, in true Peircean fashion.

Story as a way of knowing and making meaning is the controlling metaphor in Le Guin's title story, 'Another Story or A Fisherman of the Inland Sea'. Hideo, the first-person narrator, begins as Genly Ai does in *The Left Hand of Darkness*, by submitting a report as a story, 'this having been the tradition for some time', and thus both the subjective and the objective are given value. Story, he says, 'is our only boat for sailing on the river of time, but in the great rapids and the winding shallows, no boat is safe'. This is his personal and therefore subjective account of his life, and thus it is local knowledge. Yet, local means his group-marriage, his culture on the planet O, and the knowledge he learns in the Ekumenical Schools on Hain – knowledge that becomes public and at least somewhat objective at the same time. The knowledge remains local and community-based, yet the community changes size and parameters: family, home, region, planet, solar system, Ekumen – all of which are interconnected, as Hideo's story illustrates. The idea of knowledge being local and therefore subject to community consensus and context is explored by example by Clifford Geertz in *Local Knowledge: Further Essays in Interpretative Anthropology*. One particular example is the societal place of intersexed individuals, those born with both male and female physical characteristics present. In one culture this fact leads to these people being regarded as cursed, and in another as merely peculiar, and in yet another, as blessed, thereby illustrating that what is known and believed to be true is local.[35]

Through the master trope of community, 'Fisherman' explores the idea of knowledge being local and that locality functions on more than one level. Of course, the group-marriage is a local community, and on O, 'the dispersed village, an association of farms, rather than the society or state, is the basic social unit'. The group-marriage is local knowledge itself, as this institution is peculiar to O in the story. Marriage, as it is both individual and social, becomes a way to investigate the tension between both – especially here in that four people are marrying. Another way of seeing knowledge as local is when it is connected to time, when time is seen as creating locality. Hideo leaves O for the Ekumenical Schools on Hain, a journey which is the equivalent of four years for those left behind. On Hain Hideo becomes a student of churten and faster-than-light travel. He does not return home for eighteen years – to a home that, of course, has been changed and yet hasn't changed. The land remains a constant, yet his family have aged, married and borne children. Later, through a churten experiment, Hideo is displaced in time and returns home *before* his time on Hain and his eighteen years there, a time in which he learned all knowledge is local and connected, a part of the whole. That he left and learned churten theory is what enabled him to return to the past, to the love that is the centre of his life, Isidri. Past and future merge into present, and the thread that makes the whole is the story – Hideo's own knowledge, that is his attempt to understand. The contingency of his knowledge – and that it is based on consensus and context – seems evident. What he knows is, in part, a matter of where and when he lives, and what is known then.

Another key element of American pragmatism expressed in Le Guin's fiction is love. As Peirce argues, love is an evolutionary force, a way of knowing and making meaning in and of itself.[36] Hideo's story is a love story – both his and his mother's. Hideo's mother, Isako, is from Terra and came to O as a Mobile of the Ekumen. She resigned her position when she fell in love with Hideo's father, but that was just the beginning of the complications of love: when she married Hideo's father, she also married two other people.[37] For Isako, the idea of marrying a woman was alien. Yet love was there. For Isako, an outsider, to enter a group-marriage on O, negotiation, persuasion and acceptance were required. When a community is made through marriage, it also requires a negotiation between self and other, between what is known and what is unknown.

It is for love that Hideo returns to O as it is for love that he leaves it. When he leaves for school, he falls in love with what he learns, 'temporal physics and engineering'. This same love draws him on to Hain and the schools there, separating him from his family and from Isidri, his germane[38] sister, who has fallen in love with him, a love that too late he realizes he reciprocates. It is only by experimenting with the churten technology that Hideo is displaced in time eighteen years, back to his family on O. There he can finally accept what Isidri told him before he left: 'Love has a right to be spoken. And you have a right to know that somebody loves you. That somebody has loved you, could love you. We all need that. Maybe it's all we need.'[39] It is this love, as an ethic, as a way of life, that Cornel West argues will, if accepted, save us. Such an ethic is one of affirmation, as it attempts to give worth to what was considered unworthy. It is 'self-love and love of others', and it will make us more human.[40]

Four Ways to Forgiveness and *Old Music and the Slave Women*

It is in the four interconnected novellas of *Forgiveness* and the 'postscript' novella *Old Music*, all connected by character and place, that one can find a full expression of where Le Guin's romantic/pragmatic rhetoric – her master trope of community, her use of story as metaphor for knowledge and meaning, and myth as a way of knowing, valuing the personal and the subjective, triadic thinking – has led us. We find ourselves where there is potential for a truly human community, a utopia that will always be in process and is the grail of its people's ongoing quest. To call this community a utopia in process is to place the reader squarely *in* the process. In *Four Ways to Forgiveness*, the people of Yeowe, one of the two planets in the story, are recovering from a thirty-year War of Liberation. The people of Werel are adjusting to defeat by a people they have enslaved for millennia. The stories of the novellas, when read as one connected story, become one of exploring what it means to be human, especially in the sense that freedom is a defining characteristic of humanness, and an essential word in the human vocabulary, as it was in the story of the obls and the nur, 'The Rock that Changed Things', and as it continues to be in *Old Music*. The story is also a definition of this community as another quality of being human, as story itself becomes a way of being human, in the sense of having the freedom to make one's story, and to know one's story, one's history.

As in *The Dispossessed* and *The Left Hand of Darkness,* and in the Hainish stories in *Fisherman,* particularly the title story, there are layers of community at work. But it is in these later stories that the layers of community are more apparent and more rhetorical. Encompassing everything, the known human universe if you will, is, of course, the Ekumen, the Human Household, the Hearth of Humanity. It is, as mentioned earlier, the origin and establishment of this greater interstellar community as the mythos of this universe, with its ideal of including all humankind, that provides the connecting web and context for all these stories. Here, on the two worlds of *Forgiveness*, Yeowe and Werel, the seemingly alien representatives of the Ekumen to each world accept the slaves as human and as members of the greater human family. This accepting defines the slaves as human and worthy of freedom. As Yoss, the main character in 'Betrayal', the first novella, says, 'There isn't any question that we're descended from the people of Hain, all of us. Us and the Aliens, too.'[41] Solly, the Ekumenical Envoy to the Werelian nation of Gatay in the second novella, 'Forgiveness Day', is an example of this universality and diversity of humanity:

> Solly had been a space brat, a Mobile's child, living on this ship and that, this world and that; she'd travelled five hundred light-years by the time she was ten. At twenty-five she had been through a revolution on Alterra, learned *ajii* on Terra and farthinking from an old hilfer on Rokanan, breezed through the Schools on Hain, and survived an assignment as Observer in murderous, dying Kheakh, skipping another half-millennium at near-lightspeed in the process. She was young, but she'd been around.[42]

Much as Freire's culture circles' use of the native language instead of the colonizer's language is an affirmation of national identity, so the arrival of the Ekumen on Werel and Yeowe not only extends the definition of being human to the slaves, it makes them the equal of the Bosses. To do so calls into question the entire structure of society on Werel, the Bosses' world. For the Werelian slaves, this is an invitation. For the people of Yeowe, newly free and yet still divided after the War of Liberation, it is an affirmation. And for Yeowe, this affirmation by the greater human community through expanding the definition of human becomes a way to expand the definition even further, to include women as well.

Within this greater community, there are layers of community, the planets, nation-states and continents. The local community is the most important as this is where Le Guin's stories take place. It includes the village, the slave plantation, the family, the couple, the old woman living alone, the young Envoy and the guard she comes to love. Being human, and what one knows as a human, are thus both, universal and local. Freedom is both parochial and catholic. And to know this, to learn this, is again part of being human. In 'A Man of the People', when Havzhiva, the Hainish historian and later the Ekumenical Envoy to Yeowe, learns this, it is a revelation.

His first lesson comes when, as a young man on Hain, he encounters a female historian, who explains:

> There are two kinds of knowledge, local and universal. There are two kinds of time, local and historical ... People who lived on this earth, a hundred, a thousand, a hundred thousand years ago. Minds and souls of people from worlds a hundred light-years from this one, all of them with their own knowledge, their own history. The world is sacred ... The cosmos is sacred ... There is nothing that is not sacred ...You can choose the local sacredness or the great one. In the end they are the same.[43]

But this lesson, with its Emersonian echoes of the connection between the divine and the natural, is only Havzhiva's first. When he leaves his home village or pueblo and travels first to the Hainish school for historians in Kathhad, and then to the Ekumenical Schools on Ve, he encounters people from not just other pueblos, but other worlds, who have other ways of knowing and other local knowledge. When he begins his own training to be a historian, this lesson is reaffirmed, as well as the lesson that he is creating the narrative of his life as he comes to know:

> Local knowledge is not partial knowledge [Havzhiva's teachers]
> said. There are different ways of knowing. Each has its own
> qualities, penalties, rewards. Historical knowledge and scien-
> tific knowledge are a way of knowing. Like local knowledge,
> they must be learned. The way they know in the Household
> isn't taught in the pueblos, but it wasn't hidden from you, by
> your people or by us. Everybody anywhere on Hain has
> access to all the information in the temple [information
> centre or library] ... The pueblos choose not to have any
> books. They prefer the live knowledge, spoken or passing on
> screens, passing from the breath to the breath, from living
> mind to living mind.[44]

Havzhiva learns that what he knows as a man of the pueblo, of
the people, is bizarre and strange, that the 'beliefs, practices, kin-
ship systems, technologies, art, intellectual organizing patterns of
the different pueblos were entirely different from each other, wildly
different, totally bizarre' – and therefore local for each pueblo. At the
same time, Havzhiva learns that 'such systems were to be met on
every Known World that contained human populations living in
small, stable groups with a technology adapted to their environment, a low, constant birth rate, and a political life based on
consent'.[45] Knowledge becomes, then, both local and universal, an
integrated whole, and altogether human. With such knowledge a
human community is built and maintained:

> What you select from, in order to tell your story, is nothing
> less than everything ... What you build your world from,
> your local, intelligible, rational, coherent world, is nothing
> less than everything. And so all selection is arbitrary. All
> knowledge is partial – infinitesimally partial. Reason is not
> thrown out into an ocean. What truth it brings in is a
> fragment, a glimpse, a scintillation of the whole truth. All
> human knowledge is local. Every life, each human life, is
> local, is arbitrary ...[46]

What Havzhiva has learned is pure pragmatism, with inquiry at its
core and its key question: *what difference does it make?* Such questioning would seem to work against the stability Le Guin is
advocating here. Yet, it is the freedom to ask questions she is truly
advocating, and such freedom can only come in a society in which
people are no longer hungry, poor, sick without care, or suffering
discrimination because they are different. It is also worth noting

here that such a stable society as Le Guin describes on Hain is parallel to that of the Kesh and the Anarresti – an alternative, preferred way of living that, she is arguing, is more human than the capitalistic and militaristic Cartesian-thinking Urrasti and the predecessors of the Kesh, the capitalistic, militaristic, environmentally damaging Cartesian-thinking us – a utopia, in other words.

It is from these different kinds of knowledge, local and universal, that the newly freed people of Yeowe are selecting what it means to be human and to live in human freedom. Havzhiva himself, as Envoy to Yeowe, represents this knowledge, as local and personal and available to all the Yeowe people. By their revolution, they have already chosen an alternative way of being opposed to that of the Werelian Bosses, 'the black-skinned races that conquered all the other peoples of the Great Continent, and finally all the world, those who call themselves the owners, [who] lived in the belief that there is only one way to be. They [believed] they [were] what a people should be, [did] as a people should do, and [knew] all the truth to be known.'[47] The Yeowans have rejected binary thinking – slave/master, black/white, superior/inferior – and have chosen the third, the alternative, individual freedom and choice and humanity. That the aliens, in the person of the Envoys, Havzhiva and Solly, recognize them as such is validation of their choice.

Rakam, the main character in the fourth novella, 'A Woman's Liberation', realizes this, when, at last free and finally getting the education she has always wanted, she encounters an alien, a woman from the Ekumen:

> I noticed a woman beside me in the crowd listening. Her skin was a curious orange-brown, like the rind of a pini, and the whites showed in the corners of her eyes ... It came upon me slowly what she was, that she had come here from a world unimaginably far. And the wonder of it was that for all her strange skin and eyes and hair and mind, she was human, as I was human: I had no doubt of that, I felt ... I wished to know her, to know what she knew.[48]

For Rakam, to be human means to know, to be educated, especially in history – and it is through history that she acquires a sense of who and what she is and where she is, what has happened to her, coming from the life of a kept pleasure woman on a slave plantation to that of a student. When she walks into the great Library of Voe Deo (the dominant nation on Werel), her freedom truly begins: 'So I began to read freely, to read any book I wanted in that library, every book in it if I could. That was my joy, that reading. That was the heart of my freedom.'[49] Humanity, for Rakam, is to be able to choose what to know. In effect, she has enacted what occurs in one of Freire's culture circles when the participants learn to read with their own world as text. They, like Rakam, choose what they will know.

Freedom, later, for Rakam also becomes a matter of gender and of love. She leaves Werel and goes to Yeowe, the world where there are no more slaves, where the slaves have chosen to be free. But freedom, and the establishment of a human community, is not a one-time and singular choice. The planet Yeowe may have driven the Bosses off after a thirty-year war, but every individual still must choose to be liberated, to be free, to not be a slave. Rakam learns that her freedom is constricted by being a woman in a culture where even owner-women 'formed a subclass or inferior caste' and were 'legally the property of a man'. Yeowe had chosen freedom, but not for each individual. It is again with the knowledge of an alternative, the Ekumen, in the person of Havzhiva, that the Yeowan women eventually win their own liberation – a liberation of their minds as well as their bodies. This freedom is also for the men – a freedom from the owner mentality that had enslaved their minds and the women's bodies and minds. When, at last, Rakam is able to choose to love Havzhiva, while before on the plantation she was a sex object for the owner's wife, she has become completely human, body and mind.

This choice of love as perhaps the greatest part of human freedom is presented not just to Rakam, but also, in 'Betrayal', to Yoss, an old village woman on Yeowe, who learns that to be human brings the choice to forgive and to love. In the desolate marshes where Yoss lives she meets Abberkam, the disgraced former chief of the World Party, who had betrayed his best friend. Abberkam lied and stole from his own people. Now, he is ill and abandoned, in body and spirit. Yoss is alone, her children having taken ship to Hain. All she has are her pets and her books of the other worlds, Hain, Chiffewar, O, Gethen and Terra. Yoss nurses Abberkam and eventually, as Abberkam comes to understand his actions and his betrayals, she comes to see past the stories of his actions to the man himself. As a result, they come together as a man and a woman, as two humans needing each other, needing community, needing love.

This same human choice is made by Solly, the Envoy to Gatay, and her guard, Teyeo, in 'Forgiveness Day'. A former Werelian solder in the war on Yeowe, Teyeo is a man of the veot warrior caste of Voe Deo, who finds himself in a changing world:

> It's strange. It's as if there hadn't been a war. As if we'd never been on Yeowe – the Colony, the Uprising, all of it. They don't talk about it. It didn't happen. We don't fight wars. This is a new age. They say that often on the net. The age of peace, brotherhood across the stars. So, are we brothers with Yeowe, now? Are we brothers with Gatay and Bambur and the Forty States? Are we brothers with our assets [slaves]? I don't know what they mean. I don't know where I fit in.[50]

It is from Solly, the child of the Ekumen, that Teyeo begins to learn, as Solly questions the basis of Teyeo's Voe Dean master/slave society. They have been kidnapped by political extremists and are being held captive together. Teyeo initially dismisses Solly as being 'too free'. He feels that she is flaunting the freedom her diplomatic status gives her in a culture in which women are property. Teyeo sees her as an 'aggressive, spoiled child with the sexuality of an adult'. But he finally comes to see her as a person who thinks and knows what he doesn't know. Solly questions the master/slave social order of which Teyeo has been an unquestioning product:

> You are the same species, race, people, exactly the same in every way, with a slight selection towards color. If you brought up an asset child as an owner it would *be* an owner in every respect, and vice versa. So you spend your lives keeping up this tremendous division that doesn't exist.[51]

Teyeo learns as well that the honour with which he fought his war, his loyalty, has been betrayed, that he and Solly have been betrayed by the government he fought to protect: 'it was all collusion among the powers of the world; that his loyalty to his country and service was wasted'.[52]

But Teyeo is not the only one to learn, to see that what he knows is local and contingent on class and skin colour, on the dominance of his community. Solly learns that Teyeo respected his enemies during the war: 'they fought better and harder and more intelligently and more bravely than we did'.[53] She learns that beyond Teyeo's stiff military decorum he is a man, a human being. For the two of them, first in prison and later, as husband and wife, their freedom is found in each other, in love.

Old Music and the Slave Women is the story of Esdan (who in Voe Deo was known by a nickname Esdardon Aya or 'Old Music') and the slave women at Yaramera,'the greatest estate in Voe Deo' and the 'Jewel of the East', during a civil war in Voe Deo which started as a slave uprising.[54] As this story is something of a sequel to Four Ways it becomes an argument for the continuity of experience, the connections made by and through story, and the power of an ongoing myth. Rakam, in 'A Woman's Liberation', ends her story in the Yeowan Year of Liberty 18, and it is a story she has told at the request of her beloved, Havzhiva, in hopes it will help others. Rakam's story, the account of her long personal struggle for freedom, begins in a slave compound on a plantation in Voe Deo, on Werel, and ends on Yeowe after the constitution has been amended to give women the same civil liberties as men. Before the Yeowan War of Liberation, Yeowe was only a green-blue (which is pretty close to the same colour of the rock that changed things – and a planet *is* a huge rock) star for the Voe Dean slaves. 'O, O, Ye-owe/Nobody never comes back' is the song of slaves, knowing that to be sent to Yeowe, to the slave world, meant probable death.

But there has been an uprising and a revolution, a civil war and freedom, and the song changes: 'Everybody going to go/O, O, Ye-o-we/Everybody's going to go.' Rakam's grandmother says, 'That slave world! They make freedom?'[55] Yes, and now the Voe Dean slaves know: at the end of the 'underground railroad' run by the Hame (a Voe Dean anti-slavery resistance group) there is Yeowe, a world without slavery. Furthermore those who won that freedom on the green-blue star are people like themselves. The Voe Dean armies *can* be defeated by the small and weak. The uprising on Yeowe began on the Nadami plantation and it was begun by a woman. The same story can be told here – and it will argue for the same things, for individual freedom, for solidarity of action, and that freedom must first be imagined before it can be obtained.

This story of freedom on Yeowe, which becomes the story in Voe Deo, is part of the greater story, the Hainish mythos: the Colonial Expansion, the Withdrawal, and then the return, seeking to create community, to exchange ideas, to share truth. The arrival of the Ekumen seemed, initially, to have the opposite effect on Werel. Paranoid and afraid of alien conquest, the Voe Deans rapidly developed a space technology, a technology that allowed them to settle Yeowe as a slave colony. If there had been no colony, there would not have been a War of Liberation, nor a Voe Dean defeat. There would not have been a star of freedom and stories of freedom for the Voe Dean slaves. And if there had been no Ekumenical observers, no aliens who were free, lived free – how long would either the Yeowan or the Voe Dean slave uprisings have been delayed? Story begets story, story feeds and sustains imagination, and from imagination there can be action. The subjective can become the objective. That Le Guin makes the masters dark-skinned is an argument for what we all have in common, regardless of skin colour. We are all capable of great cruelties and pain, of power and dominance – and we are capable of great kindnesses and comfort, of weakness and passivity. As romantic/pragmatic rhetoric suggests, there is both, resulting in a third way.

Dark and light, master and slave, is perhaps the dominant duality in this story that romantic/pragmatic rhetoric attempts to mediate. Esdan himself is an example of the mediation. Esdan is the chief intelligence officer for the Ekumenical embassy in the Voe Dean capital, but the embassy, in the third summer of the civil war, has been sealed off: no one comes or goes, no information comes in or goes out, except by ansible to Hain. Via the 'fieldnet', the whispering between slaves that passes information, he has learned that the Liberation Command want him to come and be seen with them, to prove that the Ekumen, regardless of government propaganda, has not taken sides.

When he attempts to meet the Liberation Command, Esdan is caught by the government forces in the Divide which separates the Free City and 'Jit City' (the half still controlled by the 'legitimate government'). They take him to Yaramera and, after torture and abuse, attempt to persuade him to support the government, to speak for the government to the rebels, warn them of the bibo, a devastating biological weapon. You are one of us, his captors tell him. 'I am not one of you. I am neither owner nor am owned. You must redefine yourselves to include me.'[56]

Esdan is also the embodiment of the emblem of romantic/pragmatic rhetoric. He is, as Rakam in 'A Woman's Liberation', describes him, 'a secret man, a man of secret power, but he always spoke truth, and I think he followed his own heart when he could'.[57] And he took action when he could – even at great risk. Trying to reach the Liberation Command was such an action – meant to be of practical help and yet a still romantic gesture for freedom. There are other dualities and juxtapositions in the story that are rhetorical as well. One more example would be the slave women themselves – weak, feminine, docile, submissive, seemingly almost polar opposites of the government troops, who are strong and armed, masculine, aggressive. Yet the women live; all the government soldiers die.

Perhaps the sharpest contrast between opposites in *Old Music* is in how the idea of utopia is presented. For the slaves, it is freedom: they see the green-blue star, the Free World. They know it exists, and they know it is hard to get there, which is, as Esdan tells the Ekumenical ambassador, always the trouble with utopias. But Yaramera, where these slave women live, is Le Guin's Omelas on a different scale: an estate, not a city; thousands of slaves ('perfectly trained, obedient, selfless, loyal'), not one child. Yaramera is and was beautiful: 'clean, orderly, industrious, peaceful. And the house on the hill above the river, a palace, three hundred rooms ...'[58] Esdan can admire the beauty of the gardens, but he knows they were built and maintained by slaves. Utopia, then, is also a matter of perspective: who is telling the story, to whom does the myth belong?

And now, as Esdan waits with the slave women after the government troops have been killed by a faction of the rebels, who in turn were killed by helicopters from the government-ruled east. There is no one but Esdan and the slave women; is utopia coming? Is the Liberation the 'ideal, the freedom of the enslaved – the myth – or has it become just another army, a political party, a great number of people and leaders and would-be leaders, ambitions and greeds clogging hopes and strength ...?' Esdan has, for years, worked and hoped that the ideal, the myth of utopia, of freedom, could become real. But here he is, 'caught in the insanity, the stupidity, the meaningless brutality of the event'.[59] And utopia is as ambiguous as it ever was – the soldiers of utopia are no less cruel, no less murderous.

What is utopia – only a myth, an ideal? A beautiful city with a rotten core? I think Le Guin's answer here is the same as it was in *Always Coming Home* and *The Dispossessed:* process, choosing again and again to value the small, the feminine, the irrational, the heart, as well as the big, the masculine, the rational, the head. They wait, Esdan and the slave women, to see where they will fit into the next part of the process, knowing, whatever future the coming army brings, that they have already begun the process themselves, here, now, in the ruins of the masters' utopia. The myth is a story, but it is a true story, and to tell it is to argue for its truths. Through acts of kindness, of comfort, of love, in the burial of a small child who was his grandmother's joy, they have made a human community, imperfect, but yet an effort to be truly and fully human. And the fact that they wait, and therefore become part of the process – Esdan (Old Music) and the slave women – is part of this very human and imperfect myth.

To be a true human community, then, is to be a utopia that is always becoming, and thus is always in process, always in mediation. To be a true human community is to understand that all knowledge is local, that what each person knows is of value and worth, and that what is true in one place is contingent on that place and the consensus of its people. Such knowledge is and must be fallible and subject to revision, and its making is an ongoing process. To be a true human community is also to know that knowledge is a universal, an integrated whole. To be a true human community is to be one in which individual humans are free to choose, to create their own stories, to believe their own myths. And, as Le Guin argues in these stories, with Yoss finding and loving Abberkam, with Rakam finding freedom in books and, later, with Havzhiva, with Havzhiva finding Rakam and learning to keep 'an acceptant spirit', and with Teyeo and Solly finding each other despite their differences, as with Esdan and the slave women, a true human community is one of the heart, in which each person's story is honoured. As Rakam writes in her book, her story of her life:

> I have told the story I was asked to tell. I have closed it, as so many stories close, with a joining of two people. What is one man's and one woman's love and desire, against the history of two worlds, the great revolutions of our lifetimes, the hope, the unending cruelty of our species? A little thing. But a key is a little thing, next to the door it opens. If you lose the key, the door may never be unlocked. It is in our bodies that we lose or begin our freedom, in our bodies that we accept or end our slavery. So I wrote this book for my friend, with whom I have lived and will die free.[60]

Le Guin's rhetoric of myth is more than just the taking of a classical myth, such as that of the Hero and the Quest, or a far older one, that of utopia, and inverting and subverting it, and thereby creating an argument for feminism or Native American practices and beliefs. By using myth rhetorically in science fiction and fantasy, Le Guin is arguing for a way of knowing and making meaning and discovering truth that is both very old and yet, surprisingly, still new. To argue that myth, story – and science fiction – are valid ways of discovering truth becomes an argument for the intuitive, the imaginative, the recursive, as well as the solely linear, the rational and the empirical. Yet, Le Guin and her fellow romantic/pragmatic rhetoricians are not offering an either/or choice. They reject binary thinking in favour of Peirce's triadic solution: the mediation of the tension between two dichotomies as a source of another solution. Le Guin is not a neo-Luddite, advocating the rejection of science or the scientific method, the dumping of the Apollonian in favor of the Dionysian. She writes in *The Dispossessed*, as just one example, of the elegance and beauty of mathematics, the beauty of the Number. The creation of community in *The Dispossessed* is through Shevek's general temporal formula, which allows the development of the ansible and thus instantaneous communication in the interstellar human community.

Through story, through language, she is asking us to reconsider, to reimagine, to look again, and to find words for that for which there are none yet. As Susan Wood, the editor of *Language of the Night*, says, Le Guin sees science fiction as 'a literature with both "the capacity to face an open universe" and the aesthetic and moral necessity to face that universe honestly'.[61] By reimagining myth, by revisioning it through the lens of feminism, we have a greater capacity to face this open universe, and to see it as it is – to see the people whom we have not seen before, the marginalized, the young, the old, gays and lesbians, women, and people of colour. These myths have always been theirs, but only now is that evident.

The understanding Le Guin is offering in her stories, her revisioned myths, is her vision of a community of the heart, and it is for the possibility of such a community, a utopia of the heart and mind, that she is arguing. She asks us to examine our culture, its technology and our use and misuse of it. By this examination, we should, as Pamela Sargent says in her essay 'Science Fiction, Historical Fiction, and Alternative History', 'wrestle with the dilemma a technological society presents ... to show possible future societies that are connected to the past and yet genuinely different from the past'.[62] Such societies Le Guin presents on Anarres, in the Na Valley of the Kesh, in the greater community of the Ekumen, the peaceful stable 'dispersed villages' of O, a planet on which there has been no war for five thousand years, and, yes, in the recovering, rebuilding and restructuring societies of Yeowe and Werel. These societies are placed in utopian dialectic with societies that resist change, are unconnected to their pasts and futures, societies that only see one kind of truth and knowledge.

But Le Guin's societies – societies that value individual worth, that call for human solidarity and co-operation – are in the future and light-years away in space. Or are they? After all, the vision behind these societies is not new. Robert Coles reminds us in his essay 'The Humanities and Human Dignity' that 'the humanities at their best give testimony to the continuing efforts to make moral, philosophical, and spiritual sense of the world – to evoke its complexity, its ironies, inconsistencies, contradictions, and ambiguities'.[63] And such an attempt to make sense of the world is not the exclusive purview of an academic elite, or even of an Envoy of the Ekumen. Yoss is an old village woman; Rakam is a freed slave; Teyeo is a soldier: 'The humanities do not belong to one kind of person; they are part of the lives of ordinary people who have their own ways of struggling for coherence, for a compelling faith, for social vision, for an ethical position, for a sense of historical perspective.'[64]

One might argue that Coles is privileging the humanities over science, but this is ignores the fact that Coles is a medical doctor. He and Le Guin seek to mediate the tensions between science and the humanities, to achieve a reconciliation, if you will, which values both ways of knowing. As James Bittner notes in *Approaches to the Fiction of Ursula K. Le Guin*:

> Le Guin has tried to fashion stories which, as they weave together the language of myth and science, as they make connections between fantasy-mindedness and scientific-mindedness, become themselves a new language in which myth and science can communicate with each other. That language becomes an elaborate tool in the search for harmony in life.[65]

Multiple ways of knowing, as Bittner points out, 'the relationships between different ways of knowledge or ways of knowing', are common in Le Guin's work. There is the 'what-knowledge, the product of advanced technology, based on rational scientific, and conscious thought', and there is 'who-knowledge ... from a story ... grounded in intuitive, subjective, artistic, and unconscious modes'. And it is the story itself 'that gives us, its readers, ways of seeing the connections between them: the story itself is the mediation between the two modes of knowing, the metalanguage that can synthesize seemingly irreconcilable opposites into complementary aspects of a whole'.[66]

It is for this whole, which we can know through language, through story, that Le Guin argues in her rhetoric of myth, the whole that will create her communities of the heart. Le Guin is calling for, as Clifford Geertz does in *Local Knowledge*, a 'reconfiguration of social thought', a reconfiguring in which 'analogies drawn from the humanities are coming to play the kind of role in sociological understanding that analogies drawn from the crafts and technology have long played in physical understanding'. Genre mixing or blurring, as Geertz defines it, occurs when social scientists (and physical scientists, with Stephen Jay Gould as an example) turn to a 'cases and interpretations' ideal of explanations which looks for the 'sort of thing' that 'connects chrysanthemums and swords'.[67] This is the same reconfiguring that allows the South Atlantic Modern Language Association to include in its November 1996 programme a panel on 'Science Fiction as Commentator on Society and Politics'.

Society can achieve order, stability and harmony and find answers and solutions not only from scientific truth and knowledge, and linear Cartesian thinking. Language creates order and meaning through story, through narrative. Narrative allows us to connect, to create 'bonds of analogy, possibility, probability, contingency, contiguity, memory, desire, fear and hope'.[68] Such connections, Le Guin argues, may be more real than the walls of the houses that surround us, the towns in which we live, the ground on which we stand. She makes this evident in 'Ether, OR', a story in her 1996 collection, *Unlocking the Air*. Ether, Oregon, is a restless town; it 'ranges, doesn't stay put'. You could go to bed facing the Pacific, and the next morning be facing the eastern desert. Its reality is in its people, its storytellers, and their stories of 'memory, desire, fear and hope', which interconnect, overlap, shift, merge. Narrative makes and sustains reality.

Le Guin describes this story collection as being not science fiction, but 'plain realism, or magical realism, or surrealism'. In 'Half Past Four', *Unlocking the Air*'s lead story, we meet Stephen, Ella, Ann, Todd and Marie. And we meet them again and again in an intriguing number of permutations and changing relationships: father and daughter, mother's boyfriend, lesbian lovers, gay lovers, friends, an unwed pregnant daughter, a son with Down's syndrome. Each permutation generates a different story, a different way of connecting. Connecting all is love, community, the love and community of lovers, of friends. Reality is approached 'frontally, confrontation-ally, in daylight, sometimes deviously, by a back road in the dark', but each story, each new permutation and relationship of the characters, is a human reality. This permutation of human relation-ships becomes literal in the story 'Coming of Age in Karhide', in which a young Gethenian ambisexual human, Sov, comes of age sexually and enters kemmer, thus acquiring a protean sexuality. For Sov, whether he/she is in kemmer as a male or a female, love is love. The 'walls between us, for a moment', are down, and we are together, 'in a celebration, a ceremony, an entertainment – a mutual affirmation of understanding, or of suffering, or of joy'.[69] We are together as human beings – as students, teachers, as readers, writers, thinkers – all Freire's 'children of God'.

This, in the end, is where Le Guin's rhetoric of myth, an express-ion of American romantic/pragmatic rhetoric, leads us, through language, through story and myth, to this connection of humanity. It is a rhetoric that argues for a true human community, one of the heart, in which a human life can be lived with worth, honour and value. It is a rhetoric that argues for multiple ways of knowing, of discovering the truth – and that, indeed, truth is possible. It is a rhetoric that calls for solutions that are neither black nor white, yes or no, A or B. This rhetoric calls for us to seek a third answer, C, the answer that mediates between A and B, the answer that comes in varying shades of grey. The Cartesian way of knowing is not invalidated; rather it becomes a part of knowing itself, a part of a whole that incorporates what too often has been called the other. Le Guin's rhetoric is an argument for being fully human: Apollonian and Dionysian, rational and irrational, body and soul, heart and mind. And to be fully human is to use language as story to make meaning. Myth tells the stories we have always told and will always tell, whether the intensely personal, yet universal story of the individual coming of age and embarking upon a quest for identity, or the public story of the quest for utopia, for true community, for full humanity. Myth, as it is an expression of the psyche, of universal human archetypes, permits us to gain understanding of our humanity on multiple levels, universal and local, public and private. Myth is persuasion of what we have always known about ourselves, about our lives and the world, the human community in which we live and create, the human community which creates us.

Notes

1. It is important to note here two works on community, one that examines community as an aspect of American culture, and the other that looks at community as an aspect of composition studies. The first work, an influential contemporary work on community in American culture, is *Habits of the Heart: Individualism and Commitment in American Life*, by Robert N. Bellah et al. (Berkeley: University of California Press, 1996). Bellah and his colleagues provide a cogent discussion of the sources of community in American culture and make a powerful argument for its importance. They also argue against the dangers of 'radical individualism', and sound a strong warning against further indulgence in such manifestations of individuality. Where we differ is Bellah's blaming of 'radical individualism' on Emerson and Thoreau. To me, as I have argued here, this is a misreading and misinterpretation of both Emerson and Thoreau.

The second work is *A Teaching Subject: Composition since 1966*, by Joseph Harris (Upper Saddle River, NJ: Prentice-Hall, 1997): 'This book traces how the teaching of college writing has been theorized and imagined since 1966.' Harris does so 'by closely looking at how five key words – *growth, voice, process, error,* and *community* – have figured in recent talk about writing and teaching'(p. ix). His primary concern is to look at and present composition as a 'teaching subject – as a loose set of practices, concerns, issues, and problems having to do with how writing gets taught'(p. x). In the chapter on community, Harris considers the centrality of the idea of community to the work of teachers and writing theorists, especially seeing us, as LeFevre does, writing not as 'isolated individuals, but as members of communities whose beliefs, concerns, and practices both instigate and constrain, at least in part, the sort of things we can say'(p. 98). He argues for an idea of community that doesn't strive for consensus, or a 'community of agreement, but a community of strangers, a public space where students can begin to form their own voices as writers and intellectuals'(p. 106). This space, or 'zone of contact', becomes a place to 'highlight and discuss differences', where students (and teachers)'will hold each other to account for their readings'(p. 110). He is arguing, I feel, for what West recommends, a public square in which we can work out our differences. And, as Le Guin presents in her Ekumen, a place in which differences are celebrated as a part of being human.

2. James W. Bittner, *Approaches to the Fiction of Ursula K. Le Guin* (Ann Arbor, MI: UMI Research Press, 1984), p. 4.

3. *Webster's Tenth Collegiate Dictionary* offers this definition of 'Teleology: 1 a: the study of evidences of design in nature b: a doctrine ... that ends are immanent in nature c: a doctrine explaining phenomena by final causes 2: the fact or character attributed to nature or natural processes of being directed toward an end or shaped by a purpose 3: the use of design or purpose as an explanation of natural phenomena' (p. 1211). Or as I

think Bittner is using the term in reference to Le Guin's Hainish history, teleology is the idea that there is an end to things, that the universe begins and will end, and that things have meaning or purpose and work towards an end.

4. An ætiological myth, in simple terms, is a creation myth or a myth of origins, how things began. *Webster's Tenth* puts it succinctly: '1: CAUSE, ORIGIN ... 2: a branch of knowledge concerned with causes ...'(399). The dictionary definition is primarily a medical one – the causes of a disease or a condition. Bittner here is using the word in its mythic sense: a creation story.

5. Bittner, *Approaches*, p. 87.

6. Ursula K. Le Guin, *The Dispossessed* (New York: Harper & Row, 1974), p. 300.

7. Le Guin, *The Left Hand of Darkness* (New York: Walher, 1969),p. 25, 26.

8. Kroeber, quoted in Bittner, *Approaches*, p. 105.

9. Brooks Atkinson, introduction, in Henry David Thoreau, *Walden and Other Writings* (New York: Random House, 1937), p. xvi.

10. Robert Coles, address, Associated Campus Ministries, Bryan School of Business Auditorium, UNC Greensboro, Greensboro, North Carolina, 6 April 1995.

11. Hephzibah Roskelly and Kate Ronald, *Reason to Believe: Romanticism, Pragmatism, and the Possibility of Teaching* (Albany: State University of New York Press, 1998), p. 39.

12. Bittner, *Approaches*, p. 114.

13. Ibid., p. 119.

14. Cornel West, *The American Evasion of Philosophy: A Genealogy of Pragmatism* (Madison: University of Wisconsin Press, 1989), p. 10.

15. Le Guin, *Left Hand*, p. 1.

16. Ursula K. Le Guin, 'The Shobies' Story', in *A Fisherman of the Inland Sea* (New York: HarperCollins, 1994), pp. 76–77.

17. Ursula K. Le Guin, *A Wizard of Earthsea* (New York: Bantam, 1968), p. 1.

18. Barry Lopez, quoted in Mary Lee Coe, 'The Irresistible Loop of Stories', *AWP Chronicle*, 28 (2) October/November 1995, p. 17.

19. Thomas McSweeney, 'Light One Candle', *Catholic News and Herald*, 25 October 1996, p. 15.

20. Walter Fisher, *Human Communication as Narration: Towards a Philosophy of Reason, Values, and Action* (Columbia, SC: University of South Caroline Press, 1989), p. xiii.

21. Robert Coles, *The Call of Stories: Teaching and the Moral Imagination* (Boston: Houghton Mifflin, 1989), p. 205.

22. Ursula K. Le Guin, 'Newton's Sleep', in *Fisherman*, p. 35.

23. Ibid., p. 32.

24. John Dewey, *Experience and Education* (New York: Macmillan, 1938), pp. 26–27.

25. Ursula K. Le Guin, 'Newton's Sleep', in *Fisherman*, p. 49.

26. Hephzibah Roskelly, course lecture, McIver Building, English Department, UNC Greensboro, 27 March 1995.

27. Ursula K. Le Guin, 'The Rock that Changed Things', in *Fisherman*, pp. 57–58.

28. Elio Gianturco, translator's introduction, in Giambattista Vico, *On the Study Methods of our Time* (Ithaca: Cornell University Press, 1990), p. xviii.

29. Ursula K. Le Guin, 'The Rock', in *Fisherman*, p. 62.

30. Ibid., p. 66.

31. Ursula K. Le Guin, 'Dancing to Ganam', in *Fisherman*, p. 112.

32. Le Guin, 'The Shobies' Story', in *Fisherman*, p. 75.

33. Ursula K. Le Guin, 'Dancing to Ganam', in *Fisherman*, pp. 115, 116.

34. Karen Burke LeFevre, *Invention as a Social Act* (Carbandale, IL: Souther Illinois University Press, 1987), p. 124.

35. Clifford Geertz, *Local Knowledge: Further Essays in Interpretative Anthropology* (New York: Basic Books, 1983), pp. 81–82.

36. C. S. Peirce, *The Essential Peirce*: Selected Philosophical Writings, eds Nathan Hauser and Christian Kloesel (Bloomington: University of Indiana Press, 1992), pp. 352, 354.

37. On O, the population is divided into 'two halves or moieties. A child is born into its mother's moiety, so that all ki'O (except the mountain folk of Ennik) belong to either the Morning People, whose time is from midnight to noon, or the Evening People, whose time is from noon to midnight ... One's identity as a Morning or Evening Person is as deeply and intimately part of one's self as one's gender, and has quite as much to do with one's sexual life ... A ki'O marriage, called a sedoretu, consists of a Morning woman and man and an Evening woman and man; the heterosexual pairs are called Morning and Evening according to the woman's moiety; the homosexual pairs are called Day – the two women – and Night – the two men' (Ursula K. Le Guin, 'Another Story or A Fisherman of the Inland Sea', in *Fisherman*, p. 151).
To explain the sexual relationships by further example, I turn to an uncollected story of Le Guin's, 'Unchosen Love', in the Fall 1994 issue of *Amazing Stories*. A man of O explains: 'When I marry ... I marry three people. I am a Morning man: I marry an Evening woman and an Evening man, with both of whom I have a sexual relationship, and a Morning woman, with whom I have no sexual relationship. Her sexual relationships are with the Evening man and the Evening woman ... Brothers and sisters of the four primary people can join the sedoretu, so that the number of people in the marriage sometimes gets to six or seven. The children are variously related as siblings, germanes, and cousins' (Ursula K. Le Guin, 'Unchosen Love', *Amazing Stories*, 69 (2) Fall 1994, p. 12).

38. If a person has attached him or herself to 'a brother or sister's marriage as an aunt or uncle ... they can have sex with either or both spouses of the other moiety ... Children of that relationship are called

cousins. The children of one mother are brothers or sisters to one another; the children of the Morning and the children of the Evening are germanes. Brothers, sisters, and first cousins may not marry, but germanes may' (Le Guin, 'A Fisherman of the Inland Sea', in *Fisherman*, pp. 152–53).

39. Le Guin, 'A Fisherman of the Inland Sea,' p. 161.
40. Cornel West, *Race Matters* (New York: Vintage Books, 1994), p. 29.
41. Ursula K. Le Guin, 'Betrayal', in *Four Ways*, p. 20.
42. Ursula K. Le Guin, 'Forgiveness Day", in *Four Ways*, p. 35.
43. Ursula K. Le Guin, 'A Man of the People', in *Four Ways*, p. 103.
44. Ibid., pp. 109–10.
45. Ibid., p. 109.
46. Ibid., p. 116.
47. Ursula K. Le Guin, 'A Woman's Liberation', in *Four Ways*, p. 174.
48. Ibid.
49. Ibid., p. 175.
50. Le Guin, 'Forgiveness Day', in *Four Ways*, p. 51.
51. Ibid., pp. 77–78.
52. Ibid., p. 84.
53. Ibid., p. 78.
54. Ursula K. Le Guin, *Old Music and the Slave Women*, in Robert Silverberg, ed., *Far Horizons: All New Tales from the Greatest Worlds of Science Fiction* (New York: Avon, 1999), p. 7.
55. Le Guin, 'A Woman's Liberation', in *Four Ways*, pp. 157, 159, 162.
56. Le Guin, *Old Music and the Slave Women*, in *Far Horizons*, p. 26.
57. Le Guin, 'A Woman's Liberation', in *Four Ways*, p. 183.
58. Le Guin, *Old Music and the Slave Women*, in *Far Horizons*, p. 12.
59. Ibid., p. 42.
60. Le Guin, 'A Woman's Liberation', p. 208.
61. Susan Wood, 'Introduction', in Ursula K. Le Guin, *Language of the Night: Essays on Science Fiction and Fantasy*, rev. edn (New York: HarperCollins, 1992), p. 191.
62. Pamela Sargent, 'Science Fiction, Historical Fiction, and Alternative History', *The Bulletin of the Science Fiction and Fantasy Writers of America*, 29 (3) Fall 1995, p. 6.
63. Robert Coles, 'The Humanities and Human Dignity', in *Selected Essays: Times of Surrender* (Iowa City: University of Iowa Press, 1988), p. 264.
64. Ibid., p. 266.
65. Bittner, *Approaches*, p. 83.
66. Ibid., p. 65.
67. Geertz, *Local Knowledge*, p. 19.
68. Le Guin, 'Some Thoughts on Narrative', in *Dancing at the Edge of the World: Thoughts on Words, Waves, Places* (New York: Wave Press 1989), p. 44.
69. Le Guin, 'The Stone Ax and the Muskoxen', in *Language of the Night*, p. 235.

Bibliography

Aldiss, Brian W. *Trillion Year Spree: The History of Science Fiction* (New York: Avon, 1986).

Alexander, Michael. Introduction, in *Beowulf*, trans. Michael Alexander (London: Penguin Books, 1973), pp. 9–49.

Algeo, John. 'Magic Names: Onomastics in the Fantasies of Ursula Le Guin', *Names: Journal of the American Name Society*, 30 (2) June 1982, pp. 59–67.

Antczak, Janice. *Science Fiction: The Mythos of a New Romance* (New York: Neal-Schuman, 1985).

Aristotle. *The Rhetoric and Poetics.*, trans. W. Rhys Roberts and Ingram Bywater (New York: Modern Library, 1984).

Asimov, Isaac. *Nightfall and Other Stories* (Garden City, NJ: Doubleday, 1969).

Atkinson, Brooks. Introduction, in Henry David Thoreau, *Walden and Other Writings* (New York: Random House, 1937), pp. ix–xxii.

Atwood, Margaret. *The Handmaid's Tale* (New York: Fawcett Crest, 1985).

Baker, Augusta, and Ellin Greene. *Storytelling: Art and Technique* (New York: Bowker, 1977).

Baker-Smith, Dominic. 'The Escape from the Cave: Thomas More and the Vision of Utopia', *Dutch Quarterly Review of Anglo-American Letters*, 15 (3) 1985, pp. 148–61.

Barr, Marleen S., ed., *Future Females: A Critical Anthology* (Bowling Green, OH: Bowling Green State University Popular Press, 1981).

—— *Lost in Space: Probing Feminist Science Fiction and Beyond* (Chapel Hill: University of North Carolina Press, 1993).

Belenky, Mary Field, Blythe McVicker Clinchy, Nancy Rule Goldberger and Jill Mattuck Tarule. *Women's Ways of Knowing: The Development of Self, Voice, and Mind* (New York: Basic Books, 1986).

Bellah, Robert, Richard Madsen, William M. Sullivan, Ann Swidler and Steven M. Tipton. *Habits of the Heart. Individualism and Commitment in American Life* (Berkeley: University of California Press, 1996).

Berthoff, Ann E. Foreword, in Paulo Freire and Donaldo Macedo, *Literacy: Reading the Word and the World* (South Hadley, MA: Bergin & Garvey, 1987), pp. xi–xxii.

—— *The Making of Meaning: Metaphors, Models, and Maxims for Writing Teachers* (Montclair, NJ: Boynton/Cook, 1981).

Bierhorst, John. *The Mythology of North America* (New York: William Morrow, 1985).

Bierlein, J. F. *Parallel Myths* (New York: Ballantine Books, 1994).

Bierman, Judah. 'Ambiguity in Utopia: *The Dispossessed*', *Science-Fiction Studies*, 2, 1975, pp. 249–55.

Bittner, James W. *Approaches to the Fiction of Ursula K. Le Guin* (Ann Arbor, MI: UMI Research Press, 1984).

Bizzell, Patricia, and Bruce Herzberg, eds. *The Rhetorical Tradition: Readings from Classical Times to the Present* (Boston: Bedford Books, 1990).

Bolle, Kees W. 'Myth: An Overview', in *The Encyclopedia of Religion* (New York: Macmillan, 1987).

Booth, Wayne. *The Rhetoric of Fiction*, 2nd edn (Chicago: University of Chicago Press, 1982).

Boynton, Robert S. 'The New Intellectuals', in *The Atlantic Monthly*, March 1995, pp. 53–70.

Brigg, Peter. 'The Archetype of the Journey', in Joseph Olander and Martin Greenberg, eds, *Ursula Le Guin* (New York: Taplinger, 1979), pp. 36–83.

Britton, James. *Language and Learning*, 2nd edn (Portsmouth, NH: Boynton/Cook, 1993).

—— *Prospect and Retrospect: Selected Essays of James Britton*, ed. Gordon M. Pradl (Montclair, NJ: Boynton/Cook, 1982).

Brown, Barbara. '*The Left Hand of Darkness*: Androgyny, Future, Present, and Past', *Extrapolation*, 21 (3), 1980, pp. 227–35.

Burke, Kenneth. *Language as Symbolic Action: Essays on Life, Literature, and Method* (Berkeley: University of California Press, 1966).

Campbell, Joseph. *The Hero with a Thousand Faces* (Princeton, NJ: Princeton University Press, 1968).

—— Editor's Introduction, in Carl Jung, *The Portable Jung*, ed. Joseph Campbell, trans. R. F. C. Hull (New York: Viking, 1971), pp. vii–xxxii.

—— *The Inner Reaches of Outer Space: Metaphor as Myth and Religion* (New York: A. van der Marck Edition, 1986).

—— *Transformations of Myth through Time* (New York: Harper & Row, 1990).

Campbell, Joseph with Bill Moyers. *The Power of Myth*, ed. Betty Sue Flowers (New York: Doubleday, 1988).

Cascardi, Anthony J. 'The Place of Language in Philosophy; Or the Uses of Rhetoric', *Philosophy and Rhetoric*, 16 (4), Fall 1983, pp. 217–27.

Cassirer, Ernst. 'Art', in Hazard Adams, ed., *Critical Theory since Plato* (New York: Harcourt Brace Jovanovich, 1971), pp. 994–1013.

—— *An Essay on Man: An Introduction to a Philosophy of Human Culture* (New Haven, CT: Yale University Press, 1944).

Childs, B. S. 'Eden', in George Arthur Buttrick, Thomas Samuel Kepler, John Knox, Herbert Gordon May, Samuel Terrier and Emory Stevens Burke, eds, *The Interpreter's Dictionary of the Bible* (4 vols, New York: Abingdon Press, 1962).

Chodorow, Nancy. *The Reproduction of Mothering: Psychoanalysis and the Sociology of Gender* (Berkeley: University of California Press, 1978).

Coe, Mary Lee. 'The Irresistible Loop of Story', *AWP Chronicle*, 28 (2) October/November 1995, pp. 17–18.

Coleridge, Samuel Taylor. Selections from *Biographia Literaria. Criticism: Major Statements*, eds, Charles Kaplan and William Anderson, 3rd edn (New York: St. Martin's Press, 1991), pp. 276–99.

Coles, Robert. Address. Associated Campus Ministries, UNC Greensboro. Greensboro, NC, 6 April 1995.

—— *The Call of Stories: Teaching and the Moral Imagination* (Boston: Houghton Mifflin, 1989).

—— *Times of Surrender: Selected Essays* (Iowa City: University of Iowa Press, 1988).

Cooper, James Fenimore. *The Last of the Mohicans: A Narrative of 1757* (Albany: State University of New York Press, 1983).

Covington, Coline. 'In Search of the Heroine', *Journal of Analytical Psychology*, 1989, pp. 243–54.

Crow, Charles L. 'Homecoming in the California Visionary Romance', *Western-American*, 24 (1) May 1989, pp. 1–19.

Cummins, Elizabeth. *Understanding Ursula K. Le Guin* (Columbia, SC: University of South Carolina Press, 1990).

Curtis, C. Michael. 'Introduction', in Curtis, ed., *American Stories II: Fiction from* The Atlantic Monthly (San Francisco: Chronicle Books, 1990), pp. ix–xiii.

Davis, T. A. 'The *Dial*', University of Texas, Austin, http://www.cwrl.utexas.edu/~slatin/20c_poetry/projects/relatproject/dial.html (accessed 21 July 1999).

Dewey, John. *Experience and Education* (New York: Macmillan, 1938).
—— *The Quest for Certainty: A Study of the Relation of Knowledge and Action* (New York: Macmillan, 1929).

Dickinson, Peter. 'Masks', *Horn Book*, 69 (2) March/April 1993, pp. 160–69.

Dirda, Michael. 'The Twilight of an Age of Magic', *Washington Post Book World*, 25 February 1990, pp. 1, 9.

Elbow, Peter. *Embracing Contraries: Explorations in Learning and Teaching* (New York: Oxford University Press, 1986).

Elliott, Robert C. *The Shape of Utopia: Studies in a Literary Genre* (Chicago: University of Chicago Press, 1970).

Emerson, Ralph Waldo. *Selected Essays*, ed. Larzer Ziff (New York: Penguin Books, 1982).

Ferns, Chris. 'Dreams of Freedom: Ideology and Narrative Structure in the Utopian Fictions of Marge Piercy and Ursula Le Guin', *English Studies in Canada*, 14 (4) December 1988, pp. 453–66.

Fisher, Walter. *Human Communication as Narration: Toward a Philosophy of Reason, Value, and Action* (Columbia, SC: University of South Carolina Press, 1989).

Fitting, Peter. 'The Turn from Utopia in Recent Feminist Fiction', in Libby Falk Jones and Sarah Webster Goodwin, eds, *Feminism, Utopia, and Narrative* (Knoxville: University of Tennessee Press, 1990). pp. 141–58.

Franko, Carol. 'Dialogic Narration and Ambivalent Utopian Hope in Lessing's *Shikasta* and Le Guin's *Always Coming Home*', *Journal of the Fantastic in the Arts*, 2 (3) 1990, pp. 23–33.

Freire, Paulo. 'Education and *Conscientizacao*', in Eugene R. Kintgen, Barry M. Kroll and Mike Rose, eds, *Perspectives on Literacy* (Carbondale: Southern Illinois University Press, 1988), pp. 403–09.
—— *Pedagogy of the Oppressed* (New York: Continuum, 1986).

Freire, Paulo and Donaldo Macedo. *Literacy: Reading the Word and the World* (South Hadley, MA: Bergin & Garvey, 1987).

Frye, Northrup. *The Secular Scripture: A Study of the Structure of Romance* (Cambridge, MA: Harvard University Press, 1976).

Fuller, Margaret. *Summer on the Lakes, in 1843*. Introd. Susan Belasco Smith (1844; Urbana: University of Illinois Press, 1991).

Gardner, Howard. *Frames of Mind: The Theory of Multiple Intelligences* (New York: Basic Books, 1983).

Garner, Michael. 'Fictionalizing the Disciplines: Literature and the Boundaries of Knowledge', in *College English* , 57 (3) March 1995, pp. 281–86.

Geertz, Clifford. *Local Knowledge: Further Essays in Interpretative Anthropology* (New York: Basic Books, 1983).

Gianturco, Elio. Translator's Introduction, in Giambattista Vico, *On the Study Methods of our Time* (Ithaca: Cornell University Press, 1990), pp. xxi–xlv.

Gill, Samuel D. *Native American Traditions: Sources and Interpretations* (Belmont, CA: Wadsworth, 1983).

Hamilton, Walter. Introduction to *Phaedrus*, in Plato, *Phaedrus*, trans. Walter Hamilton (London: Penguin Books, 1975), p. 50.

Harding, Walter. 'Thoreau's Sexuality', *Journal of Homosexuality*, 21 (3) 1991, pp. 23–45.

Harper, Mary Catherine. 'Spiraling around the Hinge: Working Solutions in *Always Coming Home*', in Barbara Howard Meldrum, ed., *Old West, New West: Centennial Essays* (Moscow, ID: University of Idaho Press, 1993), pp. 241–57.

Harris, Joseph. *A Teaching Subject: Composition since 1966* (Upper Saddle River, NJ: Prentice Hall, 1997).

Hauser, Gerard A. *Introduction to Rhetorical Theory* (Prospect Heights, IL: Waveland Press, 1986).

Haynes, Roslynn. 'Science, Myth and Utopia', in Kath Filmer and David Jasper, eds, *Twentieth-Century Fantasists: Essays on Culture, Society, and Belief in Twentieth-Century Mythopoeic Literature* (New York: St. Martin's Press, 1992), pp. 8–22.

Iser, Wolfgang. *The Act of Reading: A Theory of Aesthetic Response* (Baltimore: The Johns Hopkins University Press, 1978).

Jacobi, Jolande. *The Psychology of C. G. Jung*, rev. edn (New Haven, CT: Yale University Press, 1951).

Jacobs, Naomi. 'Beyond Stasis and Symmetry: Lessing, Le Guin, and the Remodeling of Utopia', *Extrapolation*, 29 (1) Spring 1980, pp. 34–45.

Jung, Carl. *Memories, Dreams, Reflections*, ed. Aniela Jaffi, trans. Richard and Clara Winston (New York: Pantheon Books, 1963).

—— *Psychology and Religion* (New Haven, CT: Yale University Press, 1938).

—— *Symbols of Transformation*, trans. R. F. C. Hull, 2nd edn (Princeton, NJ: Princeton University Press, 1956.

Jung, Carl, ed. *Man and His Symbols* (Garden City, NJ: Doubleday, 1964).

Kaplan, Charles, and William Anderson. 'Introduction to Sir Philip Sidney', in Charles Kaplan and William Anderson, eds, *Criticism: Major Statements*, 3rd edn (New York: St. Martin's Press, 1991), pp. 108–09.

Khanna, Lee Cullen. 'Women's Utopias: New Worlds, New Texts', in Libby Falk Jones and Sarah Webster Goodwin, eds, *Feminism, Utopia, and Narrative* (Knoxville, TN: University of Tennessee Press, 1990), pp. 130–40.

Koed, Betty. 'Frequently Asked Questions: Did Thoreau Ever Write about his First Love...', in Elizabeth Witherall, ed., *The Writings of Henry Thoreau* (University of California, Santa Barbara Library, 5 February 1999, http://www.library.ucsb.edu/depts/thoreau/thoreau.html, accessed 23 July 1999.)

Kroeber, Alfred L. *Handbook of the Indians of California* (New York: Dover Publications, 1976).

Kroeber, Theodora. *Ishi in Two Worlds: A Biography of the Last Wild Indian in North America* (Berkeley: University of California Press, 1976).

Langer, Susanne. *Philosophy in a New Key: A Study in the Symbolism of Reason, Rite, and Art*, 3rd edn (Cambridge, MA: Harvard University Press, 1957).

Leeming, David Adams. *The World of Myth* (New York: Oxford University Press, 1990).

LeFevre, Karen Burke. *Invention as a Social Act* (Carbondale, IL: Southern Illinois University Press, 1987).

Le Guin, Ursula K. *Always Coming Home* (New York: Harper & Row, 1985).

—— *Buffalo Gals & Other Animal Presences* (New York: Dutton, 1994).

—— 'Coming of Age in Karhide', in Greg Bear and Martin H. Greenberg, eds, *New Legends* (New York: Tor, 1995), pp. 89–105.

—— *Dancing at the Edge of the World: Thoughts on Words, Women, Places* (New York: Grove Press, 1989).

—— *The Dispossessed* (New York: Harper & Row, 1974).

—— *Dragonfly*, in Robert Silverberg, ed., *Legends: Short Novels by the Masters of Modern Fantasy* (New York: Tor, 1998), pp. 333–95.

—— *Earthsea Revisioned* (Cambridge, MA: Children's Literature New England, 1993).

—— *The Farthest Shore* (New York: Bantam Books, 1972).

—— *A Fisherman of the Inland Sea* (New York: HarperCollins, 1994).

—— *Four Ways to Forgiveness* (New York: HarperCollins, 1995).

—— *The Language of the Night: Essays on Fantasy and Science Fiction*, ed. Susan Wood, rev. edn (New York: HarperCollins, 1992).

—— *The Left Hand of Darkness* (New York: Walker, 1969).

—— *Old Music and the Slave Women*, in Robert Silverberg, ed., *Far Horizons: All New Tales from the Greatest Worlds of Science Fiction* (New York: Avon, 1999), pp. 5–52.

—— 'The Ones Who Walk Away from Omelas', in *The Wind's Twelve Quarters* (New York: Bantam Books, 1975), pp. 251–59.

—— 'Prophets and Mirrors: Science Fiction as a Way of Seeing', *Living Light: A Christian Education Review*, 7, Fall 1970, pp. 111–21.

—— *Tehanu: The Last Book of Earthsea* (New York: Bantam Books, 1990).

—— *The Tombs of Atuan* (New York: Bantam, 1971).

—— 'Unchosen Love', *Amazing Stories*, 69 (2) Fall 1994, pp. 11–26.

—— *Unlocking the Air and Other Stories* (New York: HarperCollins, 1996).

—— *A Wizard of Earthsea* (New York: Bantam, 1968).

Loving, Jerome. *Walt Whitman: The Song of Himself* (Berkeley: University of California Press, 1999).

Lowry, Shirley Park. *Familiar Mysteries: The Truth in Myth* (New York: Oxford University Press, 1982).

McSweeney, Thomas. 'Light One Candle', *Catholic News and Herald*, 25 October 1996, p. 15.

McWilliams, John. *The Last of the Mohicans: Civil Savagery and Savage Civility* (New York: Twayne, 1995).

May, Rollo. *The Cry of Myth* (New York: W. W. Norton, 1991).

Marx, Leo. *The Machine in the Garden: Technology and the Pastoral Ideal* (New York: Oxford University Press, 1964).

Merriam-Webster Collegiate Dictionary. 10th edn (Springfield, MA: Merriam-Webster, 1993).

Murphy, Patrick D. 'The High and Low Fantasies of Feminist (Re)Mythopoeia', *Mythlore*, 16 (2) Winter 1989, pp. 26–31.

The New Oxford Annotated Bible. New rev. standard version (New York: Oxford University Press, 1973).

Noel, Daniel C. 'Revisioning the Hero', in Christine Downing, ed., *Mirrors of the Self: Archetypal Images that Shape Your Life* (Los Angeles: Jeremy P. Tarcher, 1991), pp. 204–12.

Nussbaum, Martha. *The Fragility of Goodness: Luck and Ethics in Greek Tragedy and Philosophy* (Cambridge: Cambridge University Press, 1986).

O'Brien, Tim. *The Things They Carried* (Boston: Houghton Mifflin, 1990).

Ong, Walter. 'The Writer's Audience is Always a Fiction', *PMLA: Publication of the Modern Language Association of America*, 90, 1975, pp. 9–21.

Peirce, C. S. *The Essential Peirce: Selected Philosophical Writing*, eds. Nathan Houser and Christian Kloesel (Bloomington: University of Indiana Press, 1992).

Pfaelzer, Jean. 'Response: What Happened to History?', in Libby Falk Jones and Sarah Webster Goodwin, eds, *Feminism, Utopia, and Narrative* (Knoxville, TN: University of Tennessee Press, 1990), pp. 191–207.

Plato. *Phaedrus and Letters VII and VIII,* trans. Walter Hamilton (London: Penguin Books, 1975).

Pohl, Frederick, Martin Greenberg and Joseph Olander. 'Utopias and Dystopias', in Patricia Waricke, Martin Greenberg and Joseph Olander, eds, *Science Fiction: Contemporary Mythology. The SFWA-SRA Anthology* (New York: Harper & Row, 1978), pp. 393–400.

Pratt, Annis. 'The Female Hero', in Christine Downing, ed., *Mirrors of the Self: Archetypal Images that Shape Your Life* (Los Angeles: Jeremy P. Tarcher, 1991), pp. 213–18.

Rheingold, Howard. *They Have a Word for It* (Los Angeles: Jeremy P. Tarcher, 1988).

Richards, I. A. Selections from *The Philosophy of Rhetoric*, in Patricia Bizzell and Bruce Herzberg, eds, *The Rhetorical Tradition: Readings from Classical Times to the Present* (Boston: Bedford Books, 1990), pp. 975–88.

—— *How to Read a Page.* (1942; repr. Boston: Beacon Press, 1959).

Rose, Mike. *Lives on the Boundary* (New York: Penguin Books, 1989).

Rosenblatt, Louise. *The Reader, the Text, the Poem: The Transactional Theory of the Literary Work.* (Carbondale, IL: Southern Illinois University Press, 1978).

Roskelly, Hephzibah. 'Journal from Hepsie: Notes on Peirce', Teaching Journal, UNC Greensboro, 1995.

—— English 692 Course Lecture. English Dept., UNC Greensboro, Greensboro, 27 March 1995.

Roskelly, Hephzibah, and Eleanor Kutz. *An Unquiet Pedagogy: Transforming Practice in the English Classroom* (Portsmouth, NH: Boynton/Cook, 1991).

Roskelly, Hephzibah, and Kate Ronald. *Reason to Believe: Romanticism, Pragmatism, and the Possibility of Teaching* (Albany: State University of New York Press, 1998).

Russ, Joanna. 'Recent Feminist Utopias', in Marleen Barr, ed., *Future Females: A Critical Anthology* (Bowling Green, OH: Bowling Green State University Popular Press, 1981), pp. 71–85.

Sacks, Oliver. *Seeing Voices: A Journey into the World of the Deaf* (New York: HarperCollins, 1990).

Sanford, W. B. Foreword, in G. Karl Galinsky, *The Herakles Theme: The Adaptions of the Hero in Literature from Homer to the Twentieth*

Century (Totowa, NJ: Rowman & Littlefield, 1972), pp. ix–x.

Sapir, Edward. *Language: An Introduction to the Study of Speech* (New York: Harcourt, Brace, 1949).

Sargent, Pamela. 'Science Fiction, Historical Fiction and Alternative History', *The Bulletin of the Science Fiction and Fantasy Writers of America*, 29 (3) Fall 1995, pp. 3–7.

Saussure, Ferdinand de. *Course in General Linguistics*, trans. Wade Baskin, ed. Charles Bally and Albert Sechehaye (New York: Philosophical Library, 1959).

Schumacher, E. F. *Small is Beautiful: Economics as if People Mattered* (New York: Harper & Row, 1973).

Scollon, Ron. 'In Defense of Writing: The Contemporary Merger of Ethnography and Fiction', *Redneck Review of Literature*, 20, Spring 1991), pp. 35–7.

Segal, Robert A. *Joseph Campbell: An Introduction* (New York: Garland, 1987).

Selinger, Bernard. *Le Guin and Identity in Contemporary Fiction* (Ann Arbor, MI: UMI Research Press, 1988).

Sidney, Philip. 'An Apology for Poetry', in Charles Kaplan and William Anderson, eds, *Criticism: Major Statements* , 3rd edn (New York: St. Martin's Press, 1991), pp. 108–47.

Singer, June. *Boundaries of the Soul: The Practice of Jung's Psychology* (Garden City, NJ: Doubleday, 1972).

Slotkin, Richard. *Gunfighter Nation: The Myth of the Frontier In Twentieth-Century America* (New York: Atheneum, 1992).

——. *Regeneration through Violence: The Mythology of the American Frontier, 1600–1860* (Middletown, CT: Wesleyan University Press, 1973).

Smith, Susan Belasco. 'Introduction', in Margaret Fuller, ed., *Summer on the Lakes, in 1843* (Urbana: University of Illinois Press, 1991), pp. vii–xxii.

Steinberg, Erwin. 'Imaginative Literature in Composition Class-rooms?', *College English*, 57 (3) March 1995, pp. 266–81.

Stewart, Robert Scott. 'The Epistemological Function of Platonic Myth', *Philosophy and Rhetoric*, 22 (4) 1989, pp. 260–80.

Sullivan, Dennis C., and Larry L. Tifft. 'Possessed Sociology and Le Guin's *The Dispossessed:* From Exile to Anarchism', in Joe DeBolt and Barry N. Malzberg, eds, *Ursula K. Le Guin: Voyager to Inner Lands and Outer Space* (Port Washington: Kennikat Press, 1979), pp. 180–97.

Suvin, Darko. *Positions and Presuppositions in Science Fiction* (Kent,

OH: Kent State University Press, 1988).

Thompson, Raymond. 'Jungian Patterns in Ursula K. Le Guin's *The Farthest Shore*', in William Coyle, ed., *Aspects of Fantasy: Selected Essays from the Second International Conference on the Fantastic in Literature and Film* (Westport, CT: Greenwood Press, 1986), pp. 189–95.

Thoreau, Henry David. *Walden and Other Writings of Henry David Thoreau*, ed. Brooks Atkinson (New York: Modern Library, 1965).

Von Mehren, Joan. *Minerva and the Muse: A Life of Margaret Fuller* (Amherst: University of Massachusetts Press, 1994).

Vygotsky, Lev. *Thought and Language*, rev. edn, trans. and ed. Alex Kozulin (Cambridge, MA: MIT Press, 1986).

Walker, Steven F. *Jung and the Jungians on Myth* (New York: Garland, 1992).

West, Cornel. *The American Evasion of Philosophy: A Genealogy of Pragmatism* (Madison: University of Wisconsin Press, 1989).

——. *Keeping Faith: Philosophy and Race in America* (New York: Routledge, 1993).

——. *Race Matters* (New York: Vintage Books, 1994).

Weston, Jessie L. *From Ritual to Romance* (Garden City, NJ: Doubleday, 1957).

——. *The Quest of the Holy Grail* (reprint of 1913 edn; New York: Haskell House, 1973).

White, Donna R. *Dancing with Dragons: Ursula K. Le Guin and the Critics* (Columbia, SC: Camden House, 1999).

Whitman, Walt. *Leaves of Grass*, eds Sculley Bradley and Harold W. Blodgett (New York: W. W. Norton, 1973).

Wiemer, Annegret. 'Utopia and Science Fiction: A Contribution to their Generic Description', *Canadian Review of Comparative Literature*, 19, March/June 1992, pp. 171–200.

Witherell, Elizabeth, ed., *The Writings of Henry D. Thoreau*, University of California, Santa Barbara Library. 5 February 1999, http://library.ucsb.edu/depts/thoreau/thoreau.html.

Wolkstein, Diane. 'Twenty-Five Years of Storytelling: The Spirit of the Art', *Horn Book*, 68 (6) November/December 1992, pp. 702–08.

Wood, Susan. 'Introduction' in Ursula K. Le Guin, *The Language of The Night: Essays on Science Fiction and Fantasy*, rev. edn (New York: HarperCollins, 1992), pp. 189–91.

Woodward, Kenneth L. 'Gender & Religion', *Commonweal*, 123 (20) 22 November 1996, pp. 9–14.

Index of Works
by Ursula K. Le Guin

General Index

AEE-3073